Contemporary Plays from Iraq

Volume II

Translated and edited by
AMIR AL-AZRAKI *and* JEFF CASEY

methuen | drama
LONDON • NEW YORK • OXFORD • NEW DELHI • SYDNEY

METHUEN DRAMA
Bloomsbury Publishing Plc
50 Bedford Square, London, WC1B 3DP, UK
1385 Broadway, New York, NY 10018, USA
29 Earlsfort Terrace, Dublin 2, Ireland

BLOOMSBURY, METHUEN DRAMA and the Methuen Drama logo are trademarks of
Bloomsbury Publishing Plc

First published in Great Britain 2025

Copyright and General Introduction © Amir Al-Azraki and James Al-Shamma, 2025
Foreword © Marvin Carlson, 2025
A Cemetery © Ali Al-Abadi, 2025
Robots © Faten Al-Taee, 2025
Women of War © Jawad Al-Asadi, 2025
The Mug © Amir Al-Azraki, 2025
Azrael © Mithal Ghazi, 2025
Almas © Muhaned Al-Hadi, 2025
Sardanapalus © Khazal Al-Majidi, 2025
The Clock © Nahedh Al-Ramadhani, 2025
Curse of Chopin © Atyaf Rashid, 2025
Princes of Hell © Abdul Razaq Al-Rubai, 2025
Counterfeit © Ali Abdel-Nabi Al-Zaidi, 2025

The authors have asserted their right under the Copyright, Designs and Patents Act, 1988, to be identified as authors of this work.

Cover design by Matt Thame

All rights reserved. No part of this publication may be reproduced or transmitted in any form or by any means, electronic or mechanical, including photocopying, recording, or any information storage or retrieval system, without prior permission in writing from the publishers.

Bloomsbury Publishing Plc does not have any control over, or responsibility for, any third-party websites referred to or in this book. All internet addresses given in this book were correct at the time of going to press. The author and publisher regret any inconvenience caused if addresses have changed or sites have ceased to exist, but can accept no responsibility for any such changes.

No rights in incidental music or songs contained in the work are hereby granted and performance rights for any performance/presentation whatsoever must be obtained from the respective copyright owners.

All rights whatsoever in this play are strictly reserved and application for performance etc. should be made before rehearsals to Permissions Department, Bloomsbury Publishing Plc, 50 Bedford Square, London, WC1B 3DP, UK. No performance may be given unless a licence has been obtained. No rights in incidental music or songs contained in the Work are hereby granted and performance rights for any performance/presentation whatsoever must be obtained from the respective copyright owners.

A catalogue record for this book is available from the British Library.

A catalog record for this book is available from the Library of Congress.

ISBN: HB: 978-1-3504-6527-5
PB: 978-1-3504-6526-8
ePDF: 978-1-3504-6529-9
eBook: 978-1-3504-6528-2

Series: Methuen Drama Play Collections

Typeset by RefineCatch Limited, Bungay, Suffolk
Printed and bound in Great Britain

To find out more about our authors and books visit www.bloomsbury.com
and sign up for our newsletters.

Contemporary Plays from Iraq

Contents

Foreword by Marvin Carlson   vi
Biographies   ix
General Introduction by Amir Al-Azraki and James Al-Shamma   xii

Introduction to *A Cemetery*   1
A Cemetery by Ali Al-Abadi   3

Introduction to *Robots*   25
Robots by Faten Al-Taee   27

Introduction to *Women of War*   43
Women of War by Jawad Al-Asadi   45

Introduction to *The Mug*   79
The Mug by Amir Al-Azraki   81

Introduction to *Azrael*   87
Azrael by Mithal Ghazi   89

Introduction to *Almas*   105
Almas by Muhaned Al-Hadi   107

Introduction to *Sardanbāl*   131
Sardanapalus by Khazal Al-Majidi   133

Introduction to *The Clock*   155
The Clock by Nahedh Al-Ramadhani   157

Introduction to *The Curse of Chopin*   183
The Curse of Chopin by Atyaf Rashid   185

Introduction to *Princes of Hell*   199
Princes of Hell by Abdul Razaq Al-Rubai   201

Introduction to *Counterfeit*   215
Counterfeit by Ali Abdel-Nabi Al-Zaidi   217

Foreword

In 2017 the publication of Al-Azraki and Al-Shamma's *Contemporary Plays from Iraq* allowed English readers for the first time to gain some appreciation of the rich theatrical culture that has developed in contemporary Iraq despite the burden of a crushing authoritarian rule, a series of catastrophic wars, a military occupation and continuing civil unrest. The present collection provides further and even more current examples of the still struggling but engaged and vibrant Iraqi theatre, continuing to fulfill the drama's mission to bring hope and vision to its audiences.

The central event of modern Iraqi history, the US-led invasion of 2003 which ended the repressive dictatorship of Saddam Hussein and the following occupation and civil unrest, not surprisingly was reflected in different ways in each of the works in that first collection. The US-led occupation ended in 2011, but political instability continued. In these difficult times, the arts contributed significantly to developing stability in the society. The National Theatre, which reopened in Baghdad in 2009, has been particularly important in this undertaking. In 2021 it began an annual international festival of theatre, which has not only provided inspiration and opportunities for native artists but has also given the Iraqi theatregoers a more comprehensive vision of the international stage.

This welcome opening and stabilizing of Iraqi society is reflected in this second collection of contemporary dramatic works, which, although still clearly marked by the difficult years of the early twenty-first century, are much more varied in their dramatic concerns and approaches. A kind of bridge between the changing orientations of the two collections is provided by Dr. Al-Azraki's powerful monologue, *The Mug*. The final and most recent play in the first collection, by the same author, was the only one to move outside Iraq into the international exile community created by the Iraqis who fled their country during its recent troubled years.

Majeed, the protagonist of *The Mug*, like that of the earlier play and their creator, is an Iraqi exile in Canada, and his story ties him closely to his country's recent suffering. He was imprisoned and tortured under Saddam, lost his two sons in the US invasion, and escaped the ensuing upheavals by becoming a refugee in Canada. Even more than Al-Azraki's previous work, *The Mug* deeply examines the tensions of refugee life, moving into a major new phase of the modern Iraqi experience.

Princes of Hell, by Baghdadi poet and dramatist Abdul Al-Rubai, moves beyond the agonies of the Hussein years and the US invasion and occupation to the more random but deadly terrorism that has represented a continuing source of tension and instability. Almost every year in the past decade has seen a major café or car suicide bombing in Baghdad, with dozens of resulting deaths. Two of the plays in this collection are based on this particular form of terrorism. The first is by one of Baghdad's leading current dramatists, Al-Rubai, who was also represented by a work in the previous collection. Not surprisingly, most of the plays in these two collections take us into the experiences, thoughts and memories of the Iraqi victims of the violence and oppression of recent years. Here the dramatist offers us a fascinating different perspective into the complex mind and motives of a terrorist suicide bomber. This alternative perspective provides new evidence of the ability of theatre to open insights into multiple aspects of human conflicts, including those with which we would normally have little sympathy or understanding.

Al-Zaidi's satiric play, *Counterfeit*, makes a perfect companion piece to *Princes of Hell*. Its protagonist is the victim of the sort of café bombing being undertaken by the terrorist of Al-Rubai's play. To make the situation much more emotionally complex, the protagonist of *Counterfeit* lost his sexual organs in the explosion, which were replaced by those of the bomber who died in the blast. Here again the modern Iraqi theatre demonstrates powerfully drama's ability to explore the most complex, emotional and intimate human conflicts and tensions in powerful human and symbolic terms.

Although the horrors of war, despotism and occupation have been primarily depicted by Iraqi dramatists with the powerful tools of realism, some have seen this tempest of suffering in terms more reminiscent of surrealism or the theatre of the absurd. Al-Abadi's *A Cemetery* presents three symbolic gravediggers, who at first lament the decline of their profession as death, perhaps from overfeeding, is declining. Inevitably their half-ironic desire for the return of death's bounty is fulfilled.

Though the sufferings of war dominate this collection, as they did the earlier one, another major dramatic theme is pursued in three of the plays in this volume, the relationship between the sexes—a complex and eternally interesting concern in all theatre cultures, but with special power in traditionally paternalistic Arab society. Two of the dramas here presented powerfully blend the themes of war's horrors with the particular suffering of women. Al-Hadi's *Almas* presents the story of a Yazidi woman who is captured and raped by ISIS but then finds a subtler but also powerful attempt to suppress her when a presumably sympathetic film director seeks to tell her story in his own terms. Jawad Al-Asadi's *Women of War* also examines the continuing aftereffects of the upheavals in Iraq and Syria upon women survivors in the person of three refugees struggling to find sanctuary in an inhospitable Europe.

Both Faten Altaee's *Robots* and Mithal Ghazi's *'Azrā'īl* consider the restrictions imposed by rigid traditions and gender roles from a less realistic perspective. *Robots* enters the future, where a newly married couple's interaction with a human-like robot who reveals dangerous and even fatal preconceptions that only gradually become apparent to the characters. *'Azrā'īl* presents an even less realistic symbolic parable of gender relationships, showing a dying actress, to whom the Angel of Death appears as a symbolic representation of Man, who gradually comes to a new understanding of his relationship with Woman, in the person of the dying actress.

These two plays provide welcome evidence of current Iraqi playwriting taking up subjects not directly related to the wars and political upheavals that have so much dominated the recent history of this long-suffering nation. Further evidence is provided by Nahedh Al-Ramadhani's *The Clock*, which, despite its obvious political commentary, is basically a whimsical small-town farce, whose playful confusions and misunderstandings offer a kind of celebration of life that has long been understandably absent from the Iraqi theatre.

The majority of these plays, although on the whole more contemporary both in actual date of creation as well as in subject matter, are clearly closely related to those in the earlier volume, in which every selection reflected more or less directly upon Iraq's recent social and political upheavals. The remaining plays in this more recent collection, however, suggest an Iraqi theatre which is much more varied in tone and concerns, moving away from specific exploration of the agonies of recent Iraqi history to more general and often more abstract and symbolic considerations of the human condition. Khazal Al-Majidi's *Sardanapalus* opens another major area of dramatic exploration, delving into the enormously rich history of this ancient region. If anything, this broadening of scope and style has made this collection even more powerful and more relevant, an impressive representation of this productive national theatre.

Marvin Carlson,
Sidney E. Cohn Distinguished Professor of Theatre,
Comparative Literature and Middle Eastern Studies,
City University of New York

Biographies

Ali Abdel-Nabi Al-Zaidi was born in Nasiriyah in 1965 and graduated from the Teachers' Institute of that city in 1987. His plays have been performed on stages across Iraq and the Arab world and internationally, earning him numerous national and international awards. His play collections include *The Eighth Day of the Week* (*Thāmin Ayām al-'Usbu'*; 2000), *The Return of the Man Who Has Not Been Absent* (*'Awadat al-Rajul alladhi lam Yaghīb*; 2005), *A Show in Arabic* (*'Arḍ bil 'Arabi*; 2011), *The Divine Plays* (*Al-'Ilāhiyāt*; 2014), and *Plays of the Corrupt City* (*Nuṣūs al-Madīna al-Fāsida*; 2021).

Muhaned Al-Hadi is an actor, director, and playwright, originally from Baghdad but currently lives in France. He obtained his Diploma in Fine Arts from Baghdad in 1990. His plays include *Curfew* (*Haḍar Tijwāl*), *Hotspot* (*Qalb al-Ḥadath*), and *Camp* (*Kāmb*). He has received numerous awards, including best actor at the National Award for Young Actors in Baghdad in 1999, best production at the Carthage Theatre Days Armature in Tunisia in 2007, and best director at the Baghdad International Theatre Festival in 2013.

Jawad Al-Asadi, born in Karbala, Iraq in 1947, is a distinguished theatre director and playwright. He studied theatre at the Baghdad Academy of Fine Arts and graduated in 1972. He began his career in Baghdad, working alongside the renowned Modern Art Theatre Group for several years then went to Bulgaria and finished his PhD in 1983. Al-Assadi is widely recognized as a leading director and playwright in the Arab world and has been honored with the prestigious Prince Claus Award for his commitment to the freedom of cultural expression. Over the course of 25 years as an expatriate, residing in various Arab countries, he has written several plays that have been translated into English, Russian, and French. Among his notable works are *Baghdadi Bath* (*Ḥammām Baghdadi*), *Women of War* (*Nisā' al-Harb*), and *Forget Hamlet* (*Ensū Hamlet*).

Mithal Ghazi is an Iraqi playwright born in 1967 in Baghdad. He holds a PhD in literature and theatrical criticism from the University of Baghdad, College of Fine Arts. Among his plays are *What Doesn't Come* (*Malā Ya'tī*; 1990), *Abdullah bin Zubair* (2001), *Glut* (*al-Tukhma*; 2003), and *Blackout* (*'Ẓlām*; 2011). Some of his plays have been translated into German and Japanese. He has made contributions to television drama and has written numerous plays for children's theatre. He was awarded several accolades, including the Creativity Award from the Ministry of Culture in 2010 for his play *Waiting for Rain* (*Fi 'Itiẓāral-Maṭar*) and Sharjah Award for Arab Creativity in 2000.

Khazal Al-Majidi is playwright, poet, and scholar in religions and ancient civilizations. He worked in the Cinema and Theatre Department, radio, TV, Iraqi magazines, and newspapers in Iraq. He taught at Babel College of Philosophy and Theology in Baghdad, Derna University in Libya, Leiden University in the Netherlands. Author of 114 books translated into English, French, Spanish, Romanian, Persian, and Kurdish. His 60 books cover civilizations, religions, mythology, Orientalism, art, and literary history. His plays are published in two volumes and eight collections. Among his plays are

Hamlet without Hamlet (*Hamlet Bilā Hamlet*; 1992), *Ziusudra* (*Sīdrā*;1999), *Yellow Music* (*Musīqā Ṣafrā*; 2008), *The Descent of Ishtar's to Amiriya Shelter* (*Nizūl 'Ishtār 'lā Malja' al-'āmrīya*; 1994), and *Sardanapalus* (*Sardanbāl*; 2022)

Abdul Razaq Al-Rubai was born in Baghdad in 1961 and received his BA in Arabic Language from Baghdad University. He has served as an editor for many cultural and literary magazines, and he is a well-known poet whose verse has been anthologized in numerous volumes, including *A Tribute to Her Laughter* (*Fil Thanā' 'ala Ḍiḥkatihā*; Muscat, 2015), *Speicher's Birds* (*Ṭiyūr Speicher*; Baghdad, 2014), and *Nostalgia Diary* (*Yaumīyāt al-Ḥanīn*; Muscat, 2012). His plays include: *A Strange Bird on Our Roof* (*'Ala Saṭḥinā Ṭā'ir Gharīb*), published in Muscat in 2013; *Princes of Hell* (*'Umrā al-Jaḥīm*), produced in Auckland in 2007; and *Tramps Catching Stars* (*al-Ṣa'ālīk Yaṣṭādūn al-Nijūm*) and *Planets of the Personal System* (*Kawākib al-Majmū'a al-Shakhṣīya*), both produced in Cairo in 2004. He currently resides in Muscat, Sultanate of Oman, and works as a cultural advisor at Athir Media Foundation and the Vice President of the Board of Directors of the Omani Cultural Club.

Nahedh Al-Ramadhani, born in 1964, is a writer from Mosul but currently resides in Istanbul. He holds a Bachelor's degree in arts from the University of Mosul in 1987, and a Master's in education (Arabic Language) specializing in modern literature. His works include 14 plays, four novels, and numerous short stories. Some of his works have been translated into English, German, Italian, and Kurdish. He has received several awards for his theatrical works, including the Sharjah Award for Creativity for his play *Shahriar's Companion* (*Nadīm Shahrayār*) in 2002, the Theatre Association Award in the UAE for his play *Rehearsal for the Fall of Baghdad* (*Brova Suqūṭ Baghdad*) in 2004, and the Monodrama Competition Award in Fujairah in 2010 for his play *The Belly of the Whale* (*Jawf al-Ḥūt*).

Atyaf Rashid is an Iraqi writer born in Baghdad in 1969. She holds a Bachelor's degree in Theatre Arts from the College of Fine Arts. She is a lecturer of playwrighting at the Institute of Fine Arts in Al-Kadhimiya. Atyaf has published collections of plays such as *Transparent Blue Curtain* (*Sitāra Zarqā' Shafāfa*; 2015) and *Beauty Salon* (*Ṣālun Tajmīl*; 2018).

Faten Al-Taee is a writer from Babel and an Assistant Professor at the Department of Theatre Arts, University of Babylon. Among her plays are *Ash Color Bread* (*Khubz bilawn al-Ramād*), *Colonization* (*'Istīṭān*), and *Another Enemy* (*'Adu Ākhar*). She is an award-winning actress, having received accolades for her performances at several festivals. Among her research work are *Chaos Theory in Postmodern Theatre*, *Satire in Arab Theatre*, and *Intellectual Transformations and Their Impact on Women*.

Ali Al-Abadi is a playwright, director, and actor from Karbala and holds a Master's degree in Theatre Arts from the College of Fine Arts at the University of Baghdad. Among his plays are *The Black Suitcases (al-Ḥaqā'ib al-Sūd)*, *I Am Not Crazy (Anā Lastu Majnūn)*, and *Women's Bath* (*Ḥammam Niswān*). His plays have been presented in numerous countries, including Oman, Kuwait, Jordan, Libya, Belgium, Germany, Morocco, Algeria, and Tunisia. He has received numerous awards, including the best play at the International Cairo University Theater Forum in Egypt in 2021.

Amir Al-Azraki is a playwright, literary translator, Theatre of the Oppressed practitioner, and Associate Professor and Coordinator of the Studies in Islamic and Arab Cultures Program at Renison University College, University of Waterloo. Among his plays are: *Waiting for Gilgamesh: Scenes from Iraq*, *The Mug*, and *The Widow*. Al-Azraki is the translator of *Africanism: Blacks in the Medieval Arab Imaginary*, author of *The Discourse of War in Contemporary Theatre* (in Arabic), co-editor and co-translator of *Contemporary Plays from Iraq*, *"A Rehearsal for Revolution": An Approach to Theatre of the Oppressed* (in Arabic), and co-editor and co-translator of Arabic poetry in *Consequence*, *The Common*, *Poetry Foundation*, and *Talking Writing*.

Jeff Casey is Associate Professor of Theatre and Theatre Director at Norwich University. His scholarly articles have appeared in *Theatre Topics*, *Quarterly Review of Film and Video*, *Modern Drama*, and *Ecumenica*. He works extensively as a theatre director, producer, designer, dramaturge, and playwright. His directing credits include *Cabaret*, *Chicago*, *Kafka's The Trial*, *Voices from a People's History of the United States*, Harold Pinter's *Party Time* and *The New World Order*, and Neil Simon's *Rumors*.

General Introduction
Amir Al-Azraki and James Al-Shamma

Contemporary Plays from Iraq, Volume II, is an anthology of eleven plays by Iraqi playwrights, offering perspectives on Iraq and its diaspora in the years that followed the end of the American-led occupation, marked by the withdrawal of American combat troops in 2011. The previous volume consisted primarily of works written and produced under the occupation, which began with the invasion, which deposed Saddam Hussein, in 2003. It was the first anthology of Iraqi plays published in English. With this new volume, Amir Al-Azraki and co-translator Jeff Casey extend the mission of introducing Iraqi theatre to a global audience and expanding the discourse on related critical issues through dramatic works written, with a few exceptions, after 2011. Taken together, these volumes open a window onto Iraq's cultural and theatrical landscape during a time of profound change, during which its people faced unrelenting challenges.

The anthology incorporates diverse voices, male and female, established and emerging, by authors from various geographical areas in Iraq, written in-country and from the diaspora. As with the first volume, this book includes an introduction to each work provided by the playwright. These introductions illuminate the playwrights' motivations and the historical, political, and cultural context within which they shaped their plays.

In this introduction, we will provide an overview of contemporary theatre in Iraq. We are concerned primarily with theatre after the end of the occupation in 2011, but will discuss some plays and events that occurred prior to then as needed, to encompass all of the works and issues in this volume. Although a major shift took place at the end of the occupation, the crisis within which Iraq found itself was continuous in many ways, as were the host of issues that accompanied it. The remainder of this introduction will consist of two sections. In the first, we will discuss the major themes of, and issues addressed by, Iraqi theatre during this time period and, in the second, theatrical and dramatic styles. Within this discussion, we will provide brief plot summaries of the plays included in this anthology. Important works not included in this anthology will be mentioned as well for the sake of completeness, and for the purpose of illustration.

The plays included in this anthology explore many themes and issues, including terrorism, immigration, the status of women, corruption, protest movements, and 'madness'. Theatrical and dramatic styles utilized by Iraqi playwrights include some specific to the Iraqi context, post-2003, as have been defined by Iraqi critics: the Theatre of Biography, which dramatizes the lives of secular and religious figures; The Theatre of Husayn, which stages the death of the Shiʻa Imam Husayn and the Battle of Karbala; Theatre of the Event, which honors the victims of terrorist attacks; and the Theatre of Daily Incidents, which portrays the impact of terrorism, sectarianism, and political turmoil on the daily lives of ordinary citizens. Other styles and approaches are more broadly recognized; they include fantasy and surrealism, metatheatre, physical theatre, dark comedy, political satire, participatory theatre, adaptation and the incorporation of mythology.

The diverse playwrights assembled in this anthology employ a variety of dramaturgical approaches as they address a range of themes and topics that are of crucial importance to Iraq. The theatre of Iraq is, to a great extent, a political theatre, and contemporary playwrights are committed to engaging with the issues of the day and taking part in sociopolitical discourse. Our hope is that this second volume of *Contemporary Plays from Iraq* continues to expose their work to a wider audience.

Themes and issues

Following the withdrawal of American combat troops in 2011, Iraq's political scene has been characterized by chaos punctuated by catastrophe. The brutal onslaught of the Islamic State of Iraq and Syria (ISIS), between 2014 and 2017, inflicted widespread devastation – the Yazidi and Christian communities were amongst those decimated by the Islamist organization. Civil unrest erupted during the Tishreen (October) Revolution in 2019, with protesters demanding justice and reform. The followers of Shiʻa cleric Muqtada al-Sadr joined the dissent, as he broke away from parliament and the political establishment. Amidst this chaos, Al-Ḥashd al-Shaʻbī (the Popular Mobilization Units), a state-sponsored coalition of armed factions primarily comprised of Shiʻa Muslim groups but also including Sunni Muslim, Christian, and Yazidi factions, emerged as a key player in combating ISIS but engaged in many other arenas as well, and proved difficult for the government to control. Foreign interference, notably from Iran, added another layer of complexity. Furthermore, internal problems caused by partisanism, factionalism, regionalism, and tribalism fractured an already imperiled notion of Iraqi national identity and unity, pushing the nation toward a precarious future.

Terrorism is one of the main issues represented in Iraqi drama after 2003. Iraqi playwrights engage with terrorism from multiple perspectives, addressing its origins, processes, and impact. For example, Abdul Razaq Al-Rubai's *Umrāʾ al-Jaḥīm* (*Princes of Hell*, 2007), a play featured in this anthology, stands out as an early exploration of the insidious phenomenon of terrorist indoctrination in post-2003 Iraq. In it, Al-Rubai dramatizes a manipulative recruiter who sends a group of trainees on a series of suicidal missions. The play is written as a monologue for a single actor, using masks to depict the multiple characters.[1] The playwright dissects the mechanics of indoctrination, revealing the recruiter's arsenal of tactics: exploiting religious fervor to justify and glorify violence, vilifying perceived enemies, providing a false sense of belonging and purpose to vulnerable individuals, leveraging blackmail and shame to coerce compliance, and ultimately inciting recruits to sacrifice themselves in pursuit of a misplaced sense of righteousness.

The depiction of terror and its aftermath, as dispensed by ISIS, exists as a subgenre of Iraqi theatre. Muhaned Al-Hadi's *Almas* (2023) is included in this volume. The narrative of *Almas* parallels that of Iraqi-American writer Dunya Mikhail's novel *The Bird Tattoo*, which was published in Arabic and English and nominated for the International Prize for Arabic Fiction in 2021. Both writers recount the travails of a Yazidi woman, whose simple but happy life is shattered by the ISIS invasion; the protagonist witnesses genocide and her captors force her into sexual slavery. Another example is Awatif Naeem's *Sabāyā Baghdad* (*Captives of Baghdad*, 2019). The play depicts the harrowing experience of women and children affected by ISIS in Iraq. In

Shingāl (*Sinjar*, 2017), Abd Ali Gʻiyyid portrays events that occurred during the aftermath of ISIS's occupation of the Yazidi town. The play shows the crimes committed by ISIS against the inhabitants, such as the abduction of women, the killing of families, and the forced displacement of the population.

The Camp Speicher massacre is another event related to terror that was depicted in Iraqi drama. In 2014, ISIS fighters killed up to 1,700, mostly Shiʻa, Iraqi military recruits at a former US base, disposing of the bodies in mass graves. Abdul Kareem Al-Ameri's *Juʻbān* (*Ants*, 2015) and Naeem's *Halwasa Taḥt al-Naṣb* (*Hallucination under the Monument*, 2015) address the massacre. In *Juʻbān*, a son fights ISIS in Speicher as his family, back home, longs for his return. As they grapple with the uncertainty of his fate, his mother confronts the looming specter of death. His father, however, is incapacitated, compelled to defend his country but unable to take action, as he prepares for the inevitable confluence of love and mortality. In *Hallucination under the Monument*, a teacher helps a survivor of the Speicher massacre reclaim lost memories and uncover the harrowing truths of the massacre.

Iraqis were displaced, internally and externally, in vast numbers under occupation, and in the years that followed, as the result of terror, sectarian conflict, and other factors, enumerated above, that disrupted millions of lives. Unsurprisingly, Iraqi dramatists charted the immigrant's journey, with all of its perils, in plays such as Jawad Al-Asadi's *Nisāʼ al-Ḥarb* (*Women of War*, 2005), Saʻd Hdabi's *Abṣum Bʼism Allah* (*In the Name of God, I Sign*, 2016), and Haider Juma's *Basport* (*Passport*, 2013). *Women of War*, included herein, dramatizes the complex psychological experiences of three Arab women who seek refuge in Germany, having escaped their homeland with fake European passports. The characters come from different backgrounds and have endured profound trauma in their home country. However, their hopes are shattered when they are denied asylum. In *In the Name of God, I Sign*, Ayoub, an Iraqi immigrant, flees his homeland amidst political and social turmoil, embarking on a perilous journey with fellow Iraqis across the sea to Europe. Upon reaching a foreign shore, he is dismayed to discover he lacks travel documents, resulting in denial. Through flashbacks, he recounts his life, from his childhood to compulsory military service and the wars that drove him to migrate. Witnessing the endless queues of hopeful immigrants awaiting entry, he resolves to return home. In *Passport*, four Iraqi youths escape Iraq, only to arrive at a train station where, ironically, they die in an explosion. They emerge from the rubble to review their lives. Although from different social strata, they share a common motivation for leaving Iraq: it is the fear of death and destruction.

The one-person piece, *The Mug* (written in English, 2017), by Amir Al-Azraki, the editor of this anthology, situates an aging Iraqi actor near the end of his journey, as an immigrant who has settled in Canada. He has become a purveyor of a sort of horror pornography, making the rounds of universities, relating tales of his survival, when he was faced with the hardships of life in Iraq and the loss of two of his sons in the invasion. He reflects on the great roles he has played, uncertain of who he has become, alienated and embittered.

The status of women is another common theme in Iraqi plays. Playwrights depict the oppression of women and advocate for their rights. Plays by Naeem, Fatin al-Taee and Atyaf Rashid serve as examples. In *Anā Wajhī* (*I Am My Face*, 2020), Naeem depicts three contemporary Iraqi women who occupy diverse roles and endure hardship as they strive for authenticity amidst social and political complexity, in a world marked by chaos and violence.

Al-Taee's *Insālāt* (*Robots*, 2022) is included in this volume. On her wedding night, a bride interacts with her groom and a robot; as she strives to adhere to traditional roles, she becomes, in action, more and more akin to the robot. The evening ends in tragedy, with her husband facing allegations of murder. As seen in the wife's metamorphosis and the husband's indictment, Al-Taee interrogates the dehumanizing impact of societal oppression.

Rashid's *La'nat Shobān* (*The Curse of Chopin*, 2020), also included in this anthology, approaches women's issues through a romantic encounter. In this play, a music teacher's life takes a surprising turn when she gives private lessons to a male student who shares her passion for Chopin. As they bond over music, they reveal their inner doubts, dreams, and their growing love for one another. The play culminates in a dream-like dance which symbolizes their connection, but ends mysteriously, leaving the teacher and audience questioning the events of the evening. The play explores forbidden love and desire.

Corruption is addressed in numerous Iraqi plays, often in the genres of comedy and political satire, but sometimes in tragedy. Works such as Naeem's *Barlamān al-Nisā'* (*Women's Parliament*, 2013), Ali Hussein and Haider Muna'thar's *Jīb El-Malik, Jībah* (*Fetch the King, Fetch Him* 2008), Kadhim al-Nassar's *Sīnamā* (*Cinema*, 2017), and al-Maliki's *al-'Arabānā* (*The Cart*, 2013), are just a few examples.

Drawing inspiration from Aristophanes' *AssemblyWomen*, *Women's Parliament* serves as a satirical commentary on the state of governance. The plot revolves around women convening in parliament in the absence of their husbands, employing various tactics to prevent their attendance. The play culminates in the establishment of a women's parliament, directly challenging the authority of the male-led government.

Fetch the King, Fetch Him serves as a political satire, portraying the titular King as a modern-day prime minister, adept at making promises but primarily concerned with his own interests. In addition to satirizing the leader, the playwrights lampoon various facets of government, particularly inadequate measures taken to protect women's safety and rights, the squandering of billions on failed projects, and the self-serving hypocrisy of Parliament's empty promises.

In *Cinema*, al-Nassar portrays a journalist, a taxi driver, a poet, and a general disturbed in their graves due to overcrowding in the cemetery, prompting them to protest against the owner. The journalist suggests establishing a council to represent the deceased, leading to humorous debates on governance and showcasing bureaucratic dysfunction.

The Cart is set in a contemporary Iraq ravaged by war, economic turmoil, and political upheaval. Hanoun, a middle-aged man, ekes out a living selling vegetables. Driven to despair by the chaos around him, he attempts suicide but ultimately succumbs to alcohol poisoning. As Hanoun grapples with his disillusionment, his tragic demise intertwines with the story of Mohamed Bouaziz, the Tunisian catalyst for the Arab Spring. Together, they embody the desperation of poverty and the fight for reform against corruption.

Iraqi dramatists have represented political protest, as has occurred in their country in recent years. In Ali Al-Abadi's surrealist *Maqbara* (*A Cemetery*, 2021), included in this volume, three undertakers face a scarcity of corpses, a highly unlikely probability in contemporary Iraq; to solve their problem, they entertain ideas for alternative professions, from beggars to pimps. They attempt to awaken the dead to protest the lack of corpses, but fail.

Mother activism has become visible in Iraq in recent years, as mothers protest the deaths of their sons, sometimes at the hands of militias attached to political parties. In *Yā Rab! (Oh Lord!*, 2016), Ali Abdel-Nabi Al-Zaidi references mother activism as his protagonist appeals to an unheeding God to halt the violence that is causing the deaths of children in Iraq. She convinces even Moses, who intercedes on God's behalf, to leave Paradise and join her protest on earth. The play is daring in its content, crossing the line into what might be considered sacrilegious within conservative Iraqi society.

In ʿAlaa Qahtan's *25 Rīkhtar (25 Rectors*, 2021), the October 25th Revolution serves as a backdrop, and is likened to an earthquake that shook up the miserable reality of Iraq. A divorced music teacher battles denial and longing in an abandoned nightclub, consumed by nostalgia. His former lover, now a beacon of hope, tries to rescue him from his despair amidst police interrogation and street protests. Their defiance against corruption symbolizes the resilience of the human spirit against oppression, echoing Iraq's October 25th Revolution.

Against the backdrop of political oppression and devastating conflict, the theme of madness occurs in plays such as Bayat Marʿee's *al-Jān wal Majnūn (The Jinn and the Madman*, 2012), Khḍayyir Miri's *Ayām al-Junūn wal ʿAsal (Days of Madness and Honey)*, and Al-Asadi's *Taqāsīm ʿala al-Ḥayāt (Improvisations on Life*, adapted from Chekhov's novella *Ward No. 6*, 2018). In *The Jinn and the Madman*, Saeed seeks solace in the sanctuary of a cemetery. Tormented by the taunts of children calling him a 'madman', he retreats to a realm of imagination where his departed sister, Sadiyya, awaits. Amidst the silent gravestones, they weave dreams of a kingdom in which they can reign together, free from the ravages of war. In *Days of Madness and Honey* (2012), Miri tells the story of patients abandoned in a psychiatric hospital during the war in 1991, among them a patient who feigns madness to escape the war.

Theatrical and dramatic styles

One of the earliest forms of theatre to emerge after the 2003 invasion was Masraḥ al-Sirah (Biographical Theatre), which dramatizes the lives of secular, literary, and religious figures. Subjects have included mid-twentieth century Iraqi president Abdel Karim Qasim and Iraqi poet Mohammed Mahdi al-Jawahiri, as well as revered religious figures including Shiʿa Imams and intellectuals. Notable plays in this genre include Ali al-Jabiri's *Rāhib Bani Hashim (Monk of Banu Hashim*, 2013), Falah Shakir's *Alf Miḥna fi Miḥnatih (A Thousand Hardships in His Adversity*, 2004), and Sami Abdelhamid's *Wabidhāk Tantaṣur al-Ḥayāt (And Thereby Life Triumphs*, unknown year). *Monk of the Banu Hashim* celebrates the life and martyrdom of Imam Musa ibn Jaʿfar, the seventh Shiʿa Imam; *A Thousand Hardships in His Adversity* and *And Thereby Life Triumphs* pay homage to the life and martyrdom of Shiʿa cleric Muhammad Baqir al-Sadr, offering reflections on his enduring impact. Through these theatrical portrayals, audiences, especially observing Shiʿa audience members, are

General Introduction xvii

invited to explore and commemorate the influence of these historical figures on Iraqi society and beyond.

Alongside the traditional Taʿziyeh street rituals practiced during Ashura, the emergence of al-Masraḥ al-Husayni (The Theatre of Husayn) could be interpreted as a theatrical reaction to the oppression faced by Shiʿa under the Baʿth regime. This emergence is also attributed to the growing religious fervor following the regime's downfall in 2003, along with the impact of Iranian Husayni theatre. This type of theatre encompasses productions such as Abdul Rahaman al-Sharqawi's *al-Husayn Thāʾran* (*Husayn as Revolutionary*), and festivals like al-Taf First Theatre Festival in Najaf in 2012, which featured Abdul Razzaq Abdul Wahid's dramatic poem 'al-Ḥur al-Riyaḥī'.[2] Additionally, Husayni theatre festivals across various Iraqi provinces featured plays centered on the martyrdom of Imam Husayn and the Battle of Karbala. Theoretical discourse and scholarly writings about Husayni theatre have also begun to emerge, reflecting its growing significance within cultural and theatrical circles.

Masraḥ al-Ḥadath (Theatre of the Event) is a type of site-specific performance that emerged as a response to terrorism. Plays are performed at the location of tragic events, such as attacks on cultural and religious landmarks that resulted in fatalities. In *Ṣarkha fi Shārʿ al-Mutanabbi* (*A Cry in al-Mutanabbi Street*; unknown playwright and year), characters reflect on the 2007 car bomb explosion which took place on al-Mutanabbi Street, renowned for its booksellers. *Nāfidha ʿala Ẓilāl Ghāʾib* (*Window to Ghaʾib's Shadows*, 2007, which is Ali Hussein and Haidar Munathar's adaptation of Ghaʾib Ṭuʿmah Farman's novel *Ẓilāl ʿala al-Nāfidha* (*Shadows on the Window*), was staged on al-Mutanabbi Street as well; it portrays a renowned Iraqi author coming back to his hometown of Baghdad following years of exile, only to witness his people changed and streets overrun by violence. *Ajrās al-Najāt* (*Bells of Salvation*, 2010, which is Yousif Hashim's reworking of texts from Latifa Al-Dulaimi, Salman Dawood, Zahir Musa, Yousif Hashim, and Dunya Mikhail) and Ali Kareem's *Saʾukmil Ṣalātī* (*I Will Finish My Prayers*, 2010) both address the 2010 terrorist attack on al-Najat Church in Baghdad. These plays honor the memory of the victims of terror while collectively making a call for peace, and reaching the general public through site-specific performance.

Masraḥ al-Waqāiʿ (Theatre of Daily Incidents), a term coined by theatre critic Saad Aziz Abedalsahib, focuses on portraying the impact of issues such as terrorism, sectarianism, and political turmoil on the daily lives of ordinary citizens. In Muhaned al-Hadi's *Ḥaẓar Tijwāl* (*Curfew*, 2006), two homeless characters scramble to survive in Baghdad at the height of the sectarian conflict. The play documents the impact on their lives of issues such as terrorism, sectarianism, and the lack of basic services, including electricity and security. Kareem Sheghaidil's *Kharij al-Taghṭiya* (*Out of Coverage*, 2009), is an adaptation of Max Frisch's *The Fire Raisers*. In it, a stranger (the wrestler) arrives at the theatre and persuades the manager that he will depart once he has finished his meal. However, he stays until the arrival of another stranger (the garçon). Both the garçon and the wrestler manipulate others and kill the author, eventually seizing control of the theatre and setting it ablaze—a symbolic representation of the occupation and destruction of Iraq.

Iraqi playwrights often make use of fantasy and the surreal. *Maqbara*, discussed above, is a dark absurdist comedy invoking the dead to support gravediggers who protest the lack of corpses. In al-Hadi's *Qalb al-Ḥadath* (*Hotspot*, 2009), Iraqi bystanders killed in an explosion meet in the afterlife to learn that an important American died amongst them; they attempt to prove to one another their 'Iraqiness' while the actual American, a general, maneuvers against their country in the background. *Cinema*, also discussed above, offers a surreal depiction of characters convening in the afterlife to voice their grievances and form a cemetery council. In Kareem Sheghaidil's *Aḥlām Kārtūn* (*Cartoon Dreams*, 2014), included in the first volume of *Contemporary Plays from Iraq*, a diverse assembly of Iraqis – comprised of both men and women, spanning secular and religious persuasions – find themselves trapped in a dreamlike airport lounge, and then a dreamlike aircraft, as they endeavour to flee their homeland.

Physical theatre is also represented in Iraq after 2003. In *Ḥulum fi Baghdad* (*A Dream in Baghdad*, 2006), by Anas Abdul Samad, the protagonist, Adam, descends to earth with Eve. Adam exploits the vulnerability of an intellectual who has isolated himself and lost faith in culture; Adam asserts power over others and destroys items symbolic of that culture. Through physical theatre, Samad presents a vision of a once-secure country devastated by invasion, internal conflict, and terrorism. Critics characterize Anas Abdul Samad's *Naʿam Ghodo* (*Yes, Godot*, 2019) as meta-theatrical and post-dramatic, and see it more as a rejection than as an acceptance of *Waiting for Godot*. Through physical, mostly non-verbal performance, the actors respond to Beckett's text and clutter the stage with objects that include such things as boxes, plants, and live rabbits. At one point, they hurl eggs at a huge projection of Samuel Beckett's face. If one might identify a primary theme within this complex work, it might be exhaustion with waiting for the promised, improved future for Iraq, which has been repeatedly and indefinitely deferred.

The movement theatre of Tal'at al-Samawi and Muhammed Muayyad borders on dance theatre, inclusive of ritualistic choreography. In one scene of Muayyad's production of *Tathakar Ayuha al-Jasad* (*Remember, O Body!*, 2011), a group of young men and women in red attire circle a girl cradling a doll, their movements imbued with anguish. In another scene, the girl in white, with other mourners, grieves the corpse of a young man. Performers traverse a wooden bridge, with deliberate solemnity, in a later scene, evoking a sense of impending conflict, and themes of mortality, or emptiness, before eventually retreating beneath its structure. The work expressionistically references the challenges that have confronted Iraqis over the preceding decades.

Dark comedies such as *Taḥwīr* (*Counterfeit*, 2013) and *al-Sāʿa* (*The Clock*, 2010), along with political satire such as *Women's Parliament*, *Fetch the King, Fetch Him*, and *Cartoon Dreams* provide biting commentary on political issues while entertaining audiences with their sharp wit and satire. In Al-Zaidi's *Counterfeit*, included here, after surviving a café explosion, a husband undergoes a genital organ transplant, leading to tension with his wife and their religious neighbor. The playwright satirizes the sanctimonious response of the man's neighbors and acquaintances and thereby references religious superficiality in Iraqi public discourse. In Al-Ramadhani's *The Clock*, included in this volume, set in a quirky town, chaos erupts when the only public clock stops ticking and an out-of-step intellectual attempts to navigate the confusion. The playwright offers a critique of oppressive systems that adhere to a singular ideology and explores the role of the intelligentsia during crises.

The Clock, *Robots*, *A Cemetery*, and *Counterfeit* could arguably all be classified as works of absurdism. The European tradition of Theatre of the Absurd, a retrospective designation coined by Martin Esslin and applied to playwrights such as Samuel Beckett and Eugène Ionesco, was readily adopted by Arab playwrights and reimagined to pertain less to existentialist themes than the painful material realities of postcolonial Arab nations that at times brought to life Kafkaesque absurdities. Tawfiq Al-Hakim and ʿIsam Mahfuz both were pioneers of using absurdist premises to obliquely comment on the authoritarian politics of their day. Among the plays in this collection, *The Clock* exemplifies this tradition through the use of a broadly symbolic but comically absurd premise, not unlike Ionesco's *Rhinoceros* (1959).

A Cemetery, with its shambling group of gravediggers stuck in their own circular logic, has more in common with Mahfuz's *The Dictator* and Beckett's *Waiting for Godot*, where endless repetition and waiting define the dramaturgy. However, where Beckett's drama evades straightforward interpretation, *A Cemetery* (like other Arabic works of absurdism) is clearly aimed at immediate material concerns, namely the numerous cycles of violence that have engulfed Iraq in the past two decades. The play *Robots*, in style and manner, is more of an expressionist work, but one that uses a rather absurd, vaguely science fiction theme. *Counterfeit*, though it uses an absurd premise, is perhaps better understood as a broad satirical comedy that comments on religious sanctimony and men's insecurity about their masculinity. Both objects of satire may reveal a deeper insecurity for post-invasion Iraqis about the authenticity, quality, or 'genuineness' of anything in their country, be it material or human. It should be noted that the idea of blown-apart bodies being reassembled is also explored in Ahmed Saʿdawi's *Frankenstein in Baghdad*, the first Iraqi novel to win the International Prize for Arabic Fiction. Though the play has a smaller scope (a domestic setting) than the novel, which ranges across the city of Baghdad, both use the tragic phenomenon of Iraqi bodies dismembered by suicide bombs as a premise to inquire and critique the Iraqi 'body politic'.

Iraqi plays such as *Iʿzayza* and *Sajāda Ḥamrāʾ* (*Red Carpet*) offer audiences an immersive experience. In *Iʿzayza* (The Curse, created by the actors, 2015), directed by Basim al-Tayyib, audiences traverse ten rooms, each of which represents a facet of Iraqi society. As audience members pass through the rooms, they are invited to interact with actors who portray characters ancient and modern, to grieve Iraq's past and imagine a hopeful future. In *Red Carpet* (2015), playwright Jabbar Judi immerses the audience in a series of transformative scenes, incorporating film and live performance: for example, a politician's public facade falls away to reveal acts of violence in service of sectarianism; a fraudulent religious figure amplifies societal discord; public intellectuals are shown to be ineffectual.

Iraqi theatre frequently draws inspiration from Western classics such as plays by Shakespeare, Genet, and Lorca, adapting their works to reflect on contemporary issues in Iraqi society. Monadhil Daoud Albayati's *Romeo and Juliet fi Baghdad* (*Romeo and Juliet in Baghdad*, 2012), included in the first volume of *Contemporary Plays from Iraq*, employs Shakespeare to comment on the sectarian divide between Shiʿa and Sunni. In Judi's *Khiyāna* (*Betrayal*, 2016), the betrayals that various political entities have inflicted upon the Iraqi people politically, socially, and intellectually are juxtaposed against those in Shakespeare's tragedies and histories (*King Lear*, *Hamlet*, *Macbeth*,

Othello, *Richard III*, and *Julius Caesar*). Tahrir al-Asadi's *Nishāz* (*Dissonance*, 2012) consists of scenes from plays from the Western canon, including Shakespeare's *Hamlet* and *Macbeth*, as well as *Caligula*, by Albert Camus. In metatheatrical fashion, the actors try to persuade the director to present scenes about love and peace, but he refuses, as he deems them unrealistic. Instead, he instructs them to present grim scenes that demonstrate the violence and bleakness that prevail in the country, and which align with the audience's reality.

Naeem's two plays, *al-Ṣāmitāt* (*The Silent Women*, 2015, an adaptation of Genet's *The Maids*) and *Nisā' Lorca* (*Lorca's Women*, 2006), both build on Lorca's works. *Lorca's Women* depicts four daughters whose mother locks them away and forces them to mourn their father's death; the drama draws attention to the confinement of Iraqi women under occupation. In *Insu Hamlet* (*Forget Hamlet*, 2008), Jawad Al-Asadi reimagines the original play's dynamics, highlighting Claudius's blatant tyranny while portraying Hamlet as weak, indecisive, and unable to confront his father's murderer.

Several playwrights incorporate elements of Mesopotamian mythology and history to address modern-day political and social issues, as seen in the works of Khazal Al-Majidi and Rasha Fadhil. In *Sardanbāl* (2022), Al-Majidi depicts the tragic downfall of the last Assyrian king of the title, who fights for peace in a bellicose society. In Fadhil's *Ishtar fi Baghdad* (*Ishtar in Baghdad*, 2004), included in the first volume of *Contemporary Plays from Iraq*, the Mesopotamian goddess Ishtar descends to Baghdad during the invasion to rescue her people but is captured and tortured by American soldiers. Fadhil suggests that Iraqis are severed from their Mesopotamian heritage, leaving their country open to invasion.

Notes

1 See https://www.youtube.com/watch?v=Lqwg0CCw3tU
2 Al-Riyaḥī, serving as the general of the Umayyad army, was sent from Kufa, Iraq, with the mission to intercept Imam Husayn, who was in his way to Karbala.

Introduction to *A Cemetery*
Ali Al-Abadi

A Cemetery combines protest and satire, reflecting the grim reality of gratuitous death in Iraq. Iraq offers fertile ground to engage in dialogues about our culture through art to address topics that distinguish it from other countries. The rhythm of memory shifts progressively from tragedy to massacre to the bloody present, at times making one feel as though each Iraqi is nothing but a potential corpse. Given the upheavals the country has faced, epitomized by the phenomenon of gratuitous death, it became imperative for us to confront it, often through satire. *A Cemetery* belongs to the realm of theatre of the absurd, seeking to critically expose the crisis of existence in the Arab region through the politics of death, condemning it and the destruction that has befallen Arabs and Iraqis in particular.

A Cemetery

Ali Al-Abadi

Characters

Gravedigger 1
Gravedigger 2
Gravedigger 3

An empty graveyard with no one except three gravediggers. At first, the gravediggers are invisible, only their voices can be heard.

Gravedigger 1   Where are you?

Gravedigger 2   Where are you?

Gravedigger 3   Where are you?

Gravedigger 1   Are you there?

Gravedigger 2   Are you there?

Gravedigger 3   Are you there?

Gravedigger 1 (*appears*)   I'm here.

Gravedigger 2 (*appears*)   I'm here.

Gravedigger 3 (*appears*)   I'm here.

They stumble around the graveyard in confusion.

Gravedigger 1   What is this inexcusable absence? Where did you all go?

Gravedigger 2 (*scratching his nose*)   I'm trying to get rid of the creatures hiding in my nose.

Gravedigger 3   I went to shroud my mouth.

Gravedigger 2   There's no one here.

Gravedigger 3   Are you still here?

Gravedigger 1   You, me, and him - we are a wandering graveyard.

Gravedigger 2   Tell me, how do I get rid of this problem?

Gravedigger 3   What problem?

Gravedigger 2   The problem.

Gravedigger 1   I suggest we laugh a lot.

They laugh for a short while.

Gravedigger 1 (*asks* **Gravedigger 2**)   Is the problem solved?

Gravedigger 2   No.

Gravedigger 3   I suggest we cry.

They cry for a short while.

Gravedigger 1   Has the problem ended?

Gravedigger 2   No.

Gravedigger 3   So, what's the solution? We must find one.

Gravedigger 1   Let's think.

They contemplate.

Gravedigger 3   I have a suggestion.

Gravedigger 1   I don't suggest anything.

Gravedigger 2   What about my problem?

Gravedigger 3   Your problem?

Gravedigger 1   Do you have a problem?

Gravedigger 2   No.

Gravedigger 1   Then you don't have a problem.

Gravedigger 2   My problem.

Gravedigger 3   What's your problem?

Gravedigger 2   The creatures in my nose.

Gravedigger 1 *and* **Gravedigger 3** *are surprised and look at each other.*

Gravedigger 1   What about them?

Gravedigger 2   They bother me, and I must get rid of them.

Gravedigger 3   This is an easy problem, easily solved. Just do what I do.

They mimic **Gravedigger 1**, *who blows his nose, and* **Gravedigger 2** *and* **Gravedigger 3** *do the same.*

Gravedigger 1   How are you feeling now?

Gravedigger 2   I need time to see the results.

Gravedigger 3   I fear you may not succeed in the experiment.

Gravedigger 2 (*to* **Gravedigger 1**)   I fear you may be a bad teacher.

Gravedigger 1 (*surprised and agitated*)   Blame me . . . I tried my best to help you in your ordeal.

Gravedigger 2   What ordeal?

Gravedigger 3   Is there an ordeal?

Gravedigger 1   Damn you!

Gravedigger 3   What is this drought that has befallen us?

Gravedigger 1   There's nothing here except three fools.

Gravedigger 2   No one has entered the graveyard for a week. Has death stopped?

Gravedigger 3   Maybe he's busy with bigger things we can't understand.

Gravedigger 2 (*to* **Gravedigger 1**)   What's your take on these things?

Gravedigger 1   Maybe he's negotiating with several countries for investments?

Gravedigger 3   Today marks his seventh absence, and thus he has reached the final limit. We have to fire him; the seventh day is set aside for terminating the absentee.

Gravedigger 2   I object!

Gravedigger 1   Why?

Gravedigger 2   If we fire him, how will we find our daily bread?

Gravedigger 3   Indeed, I agree with you.

Gravedigger 1   We must look for another job.

Gravedigger 3   I wonder, what job is that?

Gravedigger 2   Begging.

Gravedigger 3   There are so many of them.

Gravedigger 2   Shoe polishing.

Gravedigger 3   Hahaha! I've been polishing my shoes for years, and the more I polish them, the dirtier they get. Hahaha!

Gravedigger 2   We must continue our work.

Gravedigger 1   And who will die?

Gravedigger 2   I'll volunteer.

Gravedigger 3   And who will bury you? It's just you and me.

Gravedigger 2   You both participated in burying me.

Gravedigger 1   I think it's a valid idea.

Gravedigger 3   Here comes the catastrophe.

Gravedigger 1 and 2 (*astonished*)   What catastrophe?

Gravedigger 3   What are we working for?

Gravedigger 1   For money.

Gravedigger 3   If this fool has died, we buried him, where will we get the money?

Gravedigger 2   So, it's a money matter.

Gravedigger 3 Yes.

Gravedigger 2 How naive I was.

Gravedigger 1 Why?

Gravedigger 2 I expected you both to mourn me.

Gravedigger 3 Why should we mourn you, you fool?

Gravedigger 2 Don't you see my death as a great loss of a national asset that cannot be replaced?

Gravedigger 3 Your presence is a great loss to us. We wanted to reward you with a loaf of bread, but you couldn't even earn that. What have you done to become a national asset?

Gravedigger 2 (*with regret*) All these (*pointing to the dead*) passed through my hands, both the good and the bad.

Gravedigger 1 That's your duty, and it doesn't prove anything.

Gravedigger 2 Damn you all!

Gravedigger 3 What's this dilemma we're in?

Gravedigger 1 We must find another way.

Gravedigger 2 We must find a job that will suit us.

Gravedigger 1 Let's think.

They contemplate for a moment.

Gravedigger 3 I got it.

Gravedigger 2 (*enthusiastically*) What is it?

Gravedigger 1 Tell us, what is it? Sacrifice is necessary.

Gravedigger 2 Why?

Gravedigger 1 I'm willing to sacrifice. Speak, what is the job?

Gravedigger 2 I'm in too.

Gravedigger 3 You agreed to sacrifice without knowing what the job is!

Gravedigger 1 What's the job?

Gravedigger 3 A pimp.

Gravedigger 2 What?

Gravedigger 3 One of us must work as a pimp.

Gravedigger 1 It's impossible.

Gravedigger 2 Absolutely not.

Gravedigger 3 Why not?

Gravedigger 1 I come from a respected family, and this would bring shame to me and them, the ones I've promised to uphold the honor of.

Gravedigger 2 What will I tell all these (*pointing to the dead*) after all this struggle in life?

Gravedigger 3 Why did you agree then?

Gravedigger 1 We must find another option.

Gravedigger 1 Let's look for another job.

Gravedigger 2 Yes, let's find another job.

Gravedigger 3 Pimping is the only job that will bring us enough money. Can we agree to draw lots?

Gravedigger 1 Let's give it a try.

Gravedigger 3 *writes the three names, closes them, and asks* **Gravedigger 1** *to draw a paper and read it.* **Gravedigger 1** *draws a paper, revealing the name of* **Gravedigger 3**.

Gravedigger 1 (*astonished*)   It's you, after all!

Gravedigger 3 I . . . (*interrupted by the other two*)

Gravedigger 1 and 2 (*applauding*)

Gravedigger 3 I've decided . . . (*interrupted*)

Gravedigger 1 and 2 (*applauding*)

Gravedigger 3 I . . . (*interrupted*)

Gravedigger 1 and 2 (*applauding*)   We're with you.

Gravedigger 3 (*trying to speak, interrupted by the other two*)

Gravedigger 1 and 2 (*applauding*)   We stand by you!

Gravedigger 3 (*nodding, then interrupted*)

Gravedigger 1 and 2 (*applauding*)   We will support you!

Gravedigger 3 I've decided that we should find another way to make a living.

Gravedigger 2 Didn't you say that your job is our salvation, a better chance to live?

Gravedigger 1 I believe your job will make us the happiest people in the world.

Gravedigger 3 Am I not optimistic?

Gravedigger 1 Hahaha! Was optimism ever your trait?

Gravedigger 2 (*sarcastically*) Were you happy before and now miserable?

Gravedigger 3 *acts the pimp character.*

Pimp I'm determined to implement several reforms to improve our lives and break this painful silence.

Gravedigger 1 and 2 (*shouting*) We stand by you!

Pimp I've decided to wake up all the dead who lie here.

Gravedigger 1 How?

Gravedigger 2 By all means, legitimate or otherwise.

Gravedigger 1 Why wake them up?

Gravedigger 2 Are we suffering from such a critical shortage of noise that we need to wake up the dead?

Gravedigger 1 Isn't the noise surrounding us enough?

Gravedigger 2 And what about their families?

Gravedigger 1 Yes, what about their families?

Pimp I am the pim . . . person in charge here.

Gravedigger 2 What's the point of waking them up?

Gravedigger 1 I'm very afraid.

Gravedigger 2 Why?

Gravedigger 1 They'll surely kill me once they find out I'm the one who buried them. What will I say to that body I buried without a head?

Gravedigger 2 Woe is me! What will I say to that body I buried without hands?

Gravedigger 1 What will I say to the youth that I buried with his mother's tears?

Gravedigger 2 What will I say to the dozens of corpses washed in blood?

Gravedigger 1 What will I say to the dozens of children I buried, some drowned, some burnt, and some diseased? No, no, can I bear all this pain?

Gravedigger 2 I'm very afraid of the children.

Gravedigger 1 What's the point of waking them up?

Gravedigger 2 Yes, what's the point of waking them up?

Pimp So they can protest with us.

Gravedigger 1 What would they protest about?

Pimp   The absence of death. It's been seven days, and we haven't seen a trace of death.

Gravedigger 1   And if they refuse?

Gravedigger 2   And if they disobey?

Pimp   I'll teach them a lesson they'll never forget.

Gravedigger 2   What if I refuse to participate with you?

Gravedigger 1   I don't like protesting, and I'm sure I won't participate.

Gravedigger 3 *becomes the* **Leader**.

Leader   I'll take revenge on you, feeding scandalous morsels about you to news media scavengers.

Gravedigger 1 (*astonished*)   What?

Gravedigger 2 (*also surprised*)   What?

Leader   Remember well, I have sacrificed and become a pimp . . . I mean, I'm responsible for this paradise whose abundant blessings you now enjoy.

Gravedigger 1   What if death comes because of our protest?

Gravedigger 2 (*sarcastically*)   Oh, God! We'll return to our work and save a lot of money.

Gravedigger 1   Be silent, you fool.

Gravedigger 2   Why?

Gravedigger 1 (*to* **Gravedigger 2**)   What if death takes you away? (*To* **Pimp**.) What if death takes you away?

Gravedigger 2   He's been searching for me for years and hasn't found me yet. What a fool he is!

Gravedigger 1   Be silent. If there's a fool among us, it's you, you imbecile.

Pimp (*shouting*)   Me and him won't meet.

Gravedigger 1   What if . . .

Pimp   And would he dare?

Gravedigger 1   I'm speaking within the realm of possibility.

Pimp   There's no possibility here, only certainty.

Gravedigger 2   I can't bear it.

Gravedigger 1   I can bear it.

Gravedigger 2   I'm certain.

Gravedigger 1 I'm not certain.

Pimp Enough of your nonsense!

Gravedigger 1 Enough.

Gravedigger 2 Nonsense.

Gravedigger 1 Enough.

Gravedigger 2 Nonsense.

Gravedigger 1 I can bear it.

Gravedigger 2 Enough.

Gravedigger 1 I'm not certain.

Gravedigger 2 Nonsense.

Pimp (*shouting*) Silence, you scoundrels!

Gravedigger 1 (*to* **Gravedigger 2**) Be silent.

Gravedigger 2 (*to* **Gravedigger 1**) Be silent.

Gravedigger 1 (*to* **Gravedigger 2**) Be silent.

Gravedigger 2 (*to* **Gravedigger 1**) Be silent.

Pimp Come on, move, and wake up all the dead here.

Gravedigger 2 (*sarcastically*) Why?

Gravedigger 1 (*nudges* **Gravedigger 2**)

Gravedigger 2 Right . . . so they can protest.

Gravedigger 1 Heard and obeyed.

Gravedigger 2 And what about those who don't want to wake up?

Pimp Get out of my sight, both of you.

They start moving to exit, taking two steps, but **Gravedigger 2** *returns.*

Gravedigger 2 What about those who have romantic dates?

Pimp Get out of my sight.

He quickly moves along with **Gravedigger 2**, *wandering through the cemetery, trying to wake up the dead.*

Gravedigger 1 This cemetery doesn't age.

Gravedigger 2 How old is it now?

Gravedigger 1 I don't know.

Gravedigger 2 It's become a storehouse of secrets created by powder kegs and the tongues of flames.

Gravedigger 1   Since my first day here, I've buried my life in it, past and future.

Gravedigger 2   Hahaha, I surpassed you; I left mine to die in the wilderness.

Gravedigger 1 (*to one of the dead*)   Wake up!

Gravedigger 2 (*to another dead*)   Haven't you had enough sleep?

Gravedigger 1   Come on, come on.

Gravedigger 2   Wake up! You and you and you, wake up!

Gravedigger 1 (*to the dead*)   The time is upon us.

Gravedigger 2   There isn't much time left for protesting.

Gravedigger 1   The time is upon us.

Gravedigger 2   Come on, come on.

Gravedigger 1   Wake up!

Gravedigger 2   Don't you hear?

Gravedigger 1 (*shouting*)   Wake up!

Gravedigger 2   Come on. Damn you.

Gravedigger 1   What do we do now? It seems they're quite stubborn.

Gravedigger 2   Let's go and inform him.

Gravedigger 1   Inform him about what?

Gravedigger 2   About their stubbornness.

Gravedigger 1   Whose stubbornness?

Gravedigger 2   The dead's.

Gravedigger 1   Which dead?

Gravedigger 2 (*pointing to the dead*)   These.

Gravedigger 1   Oh, I remember. What's wrong with them?

Gravedigger 2   They're too disobedient. They won't obey orders.

Gravedigger 1   I protest.

Gravedigger 2   About what?

Gravedigger 1 (*pointing to the dead*)   Against these.

Gravedigger 2   Why?

Gravedigger 1   Because they're too disobedient. Will you protest with me?

Gravedigger 2   We were supposed to protest with them, but they disappointed us.

Gravedigger 1   Why should we protest?

Gravedigger 2 We haven't seen any activity or movement from death for seven days.

Gravedigger 1 Hahaha, why should they protest? They've had their share of death.

Gravedigger 2 I haven't had my share yet.

Gravedigger 1 Neither have I.

Gravedigger 2 We need a solution.

Gravedigger 1 I'll go to him and inform him of their disobedience.

Gravedigger 2 Let's go.

They return to the **Pimp** *and greet him in a sarcastically antiquated manner.*

Gravedigger 1 Greetings to our esteemed master.

Gravedigger 2 Greetings to our revered master.

Pimp Have you agreed on a protest date?

Gravedigger 1 What protest?

Gravedigger 2 What are you talking about?

Gravedigger 1 What kind of protest is this?

Gravedigger 2 What does it look like?

Gravedigger 1 Will there be food?

Gravedigger 2 Will it be free?

Gravedigger 1 Is it available everywhere?

Gravedigger 2 Scattered like garbage?

Pimp Be quiet, you madmen. The blame is on me for sending you to the dead.

Gravedigger 1 (*sarcastically*) Yes, my lord, the blame is indeed on you for sending us.

Gravedigger 2 Seriously, why did you send us if you knew we were crazy?

Pimp What did you two do? Explain to me in excruciating detail.

Gravedigger 1 (*to* **Gravedigger 2**) You explain to him.

Gravedigger 2 (*to* **Gravedigger 1**) No, you explain to him.

Gravedigger 1 No, you.

Pimp Enough! One of you explain to me.

Gravedigger 1 In tedious detail.

Pimp Yes.

Gravedigger 2 Are there really any details?

Gravedigger 1 The only thing that is tedious is living through this situation.

Pimp (*losing patience*)   What do you have for me? Tell me! What about the dead? Will they protest with us? Have you informed them of the protest date?

Gravedigger 2   No.

Pimp (*surprised*)   Why not?

Gravedigger 2   Because they won't protest.

Gravedigger 1   What's the solution?

Gravedigger 2   There must be a solution.

Pimp   The solution is for me to go back to how I was. I protest.

Gravedigger 2   Protest against what?

The pimp returns to his **Gravedigger 3** *character.*

Gravedigger 3   I won't be a pimp anymore.

Gravedigger 2 (*sarcastically*)   A failed pimp.

Gravedigger 1   He couldn't even command the dead.

Gravedigger 3   We must find a solution. The drought of death surrounds us from every corner.

Gravedigger 1   I don't know what this land has done to deserve such a drought.

Gravedigger 2   It's afflicted with life.

Gravedigger 1   We need a solution.

Gravedigger 3   We need a solution.

Gravedigger 2   A solution for this mire.

Gravedigger 1   What do you think about praying for the drought to end?

Gravedigger 2   That's a nice idea.

All three nod in agreement and begin to pray. There is a moment of silence.

Gravedigger 3 (*to* **Gravedigger 1**)   What did you pray for?

Gravedigger 1   I didn't pray.

Gravedigger 3 (*to* **Gravedigger 2**)   What did you pray for?

Gravedigger 2   I didn't pray.

Gravedigger 1 (*to* **Gravedigger 3**)   What did you pray for?

Gravedigger 3   I've never prayed.

Gravedigger 3   What if . . .

Gravedigger 2   No, no, I disagree with that idea.

Gravedigger 3   I think . . .

Gravedigger 1 No, no, I don't agree with that.

Gravedigger 3 What do you think if . . .

Gravedigger 1 I reserve my opinion.

Gravedigger 2 I say . . .

Gravedigger 3 You don't say.

Gravedigger 2 From my side . . .

Gravedigger 1 and 3 (*to* **Gravedigger 2**) Be quiet.

Silence.

Gravedigger 1 I got it.

Gravedigger 3 Say, what is it?

Gravedigger 2 What are you waiting for? Why don't you speak?

Gravedigger 1 The lethargy of death can only be awakened by the call of a prophet.

Gravedigger 3 What?

Gravedigger 1 How?

Gravedigger 2 I don't know; there must be a way.

Gravedigger 3 And in your opinion, what's the way?

Gravedigger 1 One of us must become a prophet.

Gravedigger 2 Hahaha, thank goodness I lack the qualifications for that task.

Gravedigger 3 No, no, this is a monumental task. Let's think of another way.

Gravedigger 2 Yes, let's think of another way. Perhaps death will change his mind and return.

Gravedigger 3 (*to* **Gravedigger 2**) I agree with you.

Gravedigger 1 We have no other choice.

Gravedigger 3 Another death is necessary.

Gravedigger 2 Why should we rush? Let's wait; maybe he'll come back.

Gravedigger 3 Perhaps he's lost his way.

Gravedigger 2 Maybe he's busy with another task.

Gravedigger 3 Another task? What could that be?

Gravedigger 2 I don't know.

Gravedigger 1 I've decided.

Gravedigger 2 I really don't like decisions.

Gravedigger 3   What have you decided?

Gravedigger 1   One of us has to become a prophet to call upon the dead and the living to protest.

Gravedigger 2 and 3   How?

Gravedigger 1   By drawing lots.

Gravedigger 2   I doubt its fairness.

Gravedigger 3   Me too.

Gravedigger 1   We have no other choice.

Gravedigger 3   Isn't there another way?

Gravedigger 1   No.

Gravedigger 3   Then let's draw.

Gravedigger 1 *draws lots and asks* **Gravedigger 2** *to pick a paper and read it.* **Gravedigger 2** *picks a paper, and it shows* **Gravedigger 1***'s name.*

Gravedigger 2 (*looking at* **Gravedigger 1** *in amazement*)   It's you! Thank goodness.

Gravedigger 3   You've passed the danger.

Gravedigger 1 (*astonished*)   Me?

Gravedigger 3   Yes.

Gravedigger 2 (*joyfully*)   Yes, yes!

Gravedigger 1 (*nervously*)   What do you think?

Gravedigger 2   Yes.

Gravedigger 1   Let's redraw.

Gravedigger 3   Why should we redraw?

Gravedigger 2   Didn't I tell you that I doubted its fairness?

Gravedigger 3   Wasn't this your choice to resolve the crisis?

Gravedigger 2   (*sarcastically*)   Didn't you conduct the draw with your blessed hands?

Gravedigger 3   I disagree.

Gravedigger 2   Me too.

Gravedigger 1   If I must bear this heavy burden for both of you, then there's no harm in that.

Gravedigger 1 *changes his character into a prophet.*

Gravedigger 3 (*to* **Gravedigger 2**)   Is he here?

Gravedigger 2   I don't know.

Gravedigger 3 Will he come?

Gravedigger 2 I don't know . . . Will the famine end?

Gravedigger 3 I don't know.

Gravedigger 2 What if the prophet comes here and asks one of us about our name? What will you say to him?

Gravedigger 3 My name. I lost my name back in those years when smoke was the only language of life.

Gravedigger 2 I don't remember ever having a name.

Gravedigger 3 Hahaha, I'll tell him my name is inscribed on all these tombstones.

Gravedigger 2 Hahaha, I'll tell him my name is Cat Thief.

Gravedigger 3 What if he asks you about your wishes?

Gravedigger 2 (*surprised*)   What . . . What did you say? Repeat the question?

Gravedigger 3 What if he asks you about your wishes?

Gravedigger 2 No one has ever asked me anything like that before . . . What do you mean by wishes?

Gravedigger 3 Your wishes mean . . .

Gravedigger 2 Yes.

Gravedigger 3 They mean . . .

Gravedigger 2 Yes.

Gravedigger 3 I don't know.

Gravedigger 2 Hahaha, you're a fool. Why are you asking me, then?

Gravedigger 3 Hahaha, I've heard this question many times, but I don't know its meaning. Hahaha, maybe because I fail to understand its essence.

Gravedigger 2 Ah, ah, the prophet is here.

Gravedigger 3 The prophet is here?

Prophet How long has this famine lasted?

Gravedigger 3 A week.

Gravedigger 2 And three hours.

Gravedigger 3 And three minutes, until now.

Prophet We must find a way out of this predicament.

Gravedigger 3 What predicament are you referring to, O Prophet?

Gravedigger 2 A predicament!

Prophet   The predicament you're in—the famine.

Gravedigger 2   Is there hope for that?

Gravedigger 3   Hope? It died before the famine struck us.

Prophet   I mean there's hope in ending the famine.

Gravedigger 2   O Prophet, hope is dead.

Prophet   I mean there is hope to resolve this.

Gravedigger 2   What's the way to do that?

Prophet   We need to protest.

Gravedigger 3   We've tried that many times.

Gravedigger 2   We tried with all our might during the era of the pimp, who used to be in charge, but we failed.

Gravedigger 3   Let's look for another way to face this famine.

Gravedigger 2   Yes, I agree with you, my friend.

Prophet   I'm listening to your suggestions.

Gravedigger 2   I suggest that we don't suggest anything.

Gravedigger 3   I suggest the same.

Prophet   What are your suggestions?

Gravedigger 3   That we don't suggest anything.

Gravedigger 2   It's a terrible suggestion.

Prophet   I propose that you go to the dead so that they can protest with us.

Gravedigger 2   They are preoccupied with other matters.

Gravedigger 3   They declared disobedience a while ago.

Prophet   Go to them and tell them . . . The Prophet invites you to protest.

Gravedigger 3   Protest against what?

Prophet   Against death that has covered them up during times of war and endless smoke.

Gravedigger 3   What?

Gravedigger 2   What did you say, noble one?

Prophet   I suggest that you go to the dead and ask them to join us in supplicating to the Lord, to thank Him together for the blessing of famine.

Gravedigger 2   What will happen to me?

Gravedigger 3   What will happen to me, O Prophet?

Prophet We together, our fate will be one.

Gravedigger 3 How can that be?

Prophet Go to where I asked you.

Gravedigger 2 And what if they rebel again?

Gravedigger 3 What will we do then?

Prophet Go.

Gravedigger 2 *and* **Gravedigger 3** *wander through the graveyard and awaken the dead.*

Gravedigger 3 O inhabitants of the graveyard, hear what the Prophet says!

Gravedigger 2 The Prophet invites you to protest today.

Gravedigger 3 Against death that has taken you during times of gunpowder and endless smoke.

Gravedigger 2 He also invites you to join us in supplicating to the Lord, to thank Him together for the blessing of famine.

Gravediggers try to awaken the dead.

Gravedigger 2 Hey, don't you hear the call?

Gravedigger 3 Aren't you tired of sleeping?

Gravedigger 2 Hey, do you want to defy the Prophet?

Gravedigger 3 What's wrong with you? Why don't you get up?

Gravedigger 2 (*to one of the dead*) You, the one I buried one day without a head, how will you protest? Hahaha, come on, get up.

Gravedigger 3 (*to one of the dead*) Have you forgotten me? I didn't know you could be so ungrateful. Have you forgotten? I was the one who buried you after they found your body in the garbage with the marks of torture on your body. Have you forgotten?

Gravedigger 2 (*to one of the dead*) Hahaha, do you remember when I buried you without a tongue? During the funeral, I asked you for your name, and you didn't answer, so I wrote on your tombstone, "tongueless." Hahaha.

Gravedigger 3 (*to another dead person*) Have you forgotten me? It's so painful, this ingratitude.

Gravedigger 2 (*to another dead person*) Do you remember how they brought you here, looking like a piece of charcoal?

Gravedigger 3 (*to another dead person*) You, the losing warrior, your body was like a sieve. Worms and insects wander in it as they please.

Gravedigger 2 I wonder, what does the Prophet want from these remnants of people?

Gravedigger 3 I don't understand these diplomatic matters, my friend.

Gravedigger 2   Neither do I.

Gravedigger 3 (*fearfully*)   Could he be trying to turn the dead against us?

Gravedigger 2   I reject that.

Gravedigger 3   I protest.

Gravedigger 2   A firm refusal.

Gravedigger 3   A strong and eternal protest.

Gravedigger 2   I won't back down from my decision.

Gravedigger 3   Woe, woe to anyone who tries to make me change my mind.

Gravedigger 2   What are you protesting against?

Gravedigger 3   Against anything and nothing . . . And what are you refusing?

Gravedigger 2   Who?

Gravedigger 3   You.

Gravedigger 2   What's wrong with you?

Gravedigger 3 (*shouting*)   What are you refusing?

Gravedigger 2   Hahaha, a miserable gravedigger like me isn't able to refuse I assure you I refuse nothing.

Gravedigger 3   What do you think about waking the dead and burying them again without the Prophet's knowledge? That way, we could rid ourselves of the famine.

Gravedigger 2   And who will pay us for the burials?

Gravedigger 3   Good point. After we wake the dead, we'll seize all their wealth.

Gravedigger 2   You must also settle any debts they owe us.

Gravedigger 3   Are they indebted to us?

Gravedigger 2   No.

Gravedigger 3   Then why would they pay?

Gravedigger 2   Fool, it's just an excuse.

Followed by the dead, **Gravediggers 2** *and* **3** *go to the* **Prophet***.*

Gravedigger 2   O Prophet, we have come with the dead, following your orders.

Prophet   Blessings upon you. We must choose a day for the protest.

Gravedigger 3   With your permission, my lord, what do you think about tomorrow?

Gravedigger 2   I don't prefer tomorrow. We are not prepared yet. We need more time to complete the rest of the preparations for the protest, like the protest location, signs, and slogans, etc.

Gravedigger 3 The protest location! O Prophet, where will we protest?

Prophet Here.

Gravedigger 2 And why here?

Prophet No place can contain the hell of your dreams except this one.

Gravedigger 3 What about the slogans we will write on the signs? What should we write?

Gravedigger 2 Yes, O Prophet, what should we write?

Prophet Leave them blank, white.

Gravedigger 2 (*surprised*)   What?

Prophet Let them be a window to your hearts, bearing witness to your oppression.

Gravedigger 2 So, there is nothing left but to proceed with the protest now.

Gravedigger 3 (*to the dead*) Listen . . . Listen . . . What is all this noise and side conversations? Have you forgotten that you are in the presence of the Prophet? Please, maintain silence and listen to what the Prophet will say to you. (*To the Prophet.*) Please, proceed, O Prophet.

Prophet O pure and kind ones.

Gravediggers whisper to each other.

Gravedigger 2 I know many of them are so wicked it would leave your mouth agape.

Gravedigger 3 Among them are thieves.

Gravedigger 2 And highway robbers . . . I remember one night I was robbed by one of them, who was often drunk.

Prophet Death has made you absent from the world for many years.

Gravediggers continue to whisper to each other.

Gravedigger 2 Those were beautiful days.

Gravedigger 3 Days filled with prosperity.

Gravedigger 2 I fear they may never return.

Prophet Today, you have no choice but to declare your dissent to the world.

Gravediggers continue to whisper.

Gravedigger 3 Didn't I tell you there might be agitation against us?

Gravedigger 2 If there is any agitation, I will protest because I hate agitation.

Prophet And beseech the Lord to increase His blessing of the famine upon us.

Gravedigger 3 O Allah, we are afflicted with hardship, have mercy on us, O Allah.

Gravedigger 2 Remove the cursed cloud of famine from us, O Allah.

Gravedigger 3 Bless us with the grace of death, O Allah.

Prophet Come, let us protest together!

A gunshot. **Gravedigger 2** *and* **Gravedigger 3** *rush towards the* **Prophet** *to make sure he is OK.*

Gravedigger 3 The Prophet is dead.

Gravedigger 2 O Prophet, death has lodged a protest against you.

Introduction to *Robots*
Faten Al-Taee

Breaking the norms of Iraqi traditions, this play focuses on the customs of marriage and gender. In this marriage, the husband and wife have differing awarenesses of the traditions that shape their consciousness. While the husband seeks a path of non-conformity, the wife remains in the cycle of repeating the roles of mother, sister, and daughter and all the customs of the wedding night. She fears her mother, her father, the cat, and those relatives who stand behind the door. However, despite all this, the husband remains steadfast, afraid of nothing but his wife rehearsing social norms to please him.

Surprisingly, it is the wife who feels compelled to subjugate herself to the husband. She becomes a machine imitating cultural norms, evolving into an actual robot. The play depicts a normal day in the life of the couple, from eating together to the sound of the tea kettle, the game between the husband and the robot, then transitioning to the dark bedroom, the robot at the center, with the hymn of the child confirming the controlling routine that neither the husband nor the wife tries to break.

The wife is metaphorically no longer alive, and in the courtroom, the husband is found guilty of murdering his wife. The judge, limited in his thinking by cultural norms, is unable to see the case critically. As such, the play emphasizes that each individual should critically examine their culture and become agents who develop their own opinions and principles not dictated by customs and traditions.

Social issues occupy a significant space in my thinking as a playwright. I pay attention to my surrounding environment, to portray societal phenomena vividly through drama. The play depicts several issues and conflicts: the customs and traditions of the wedding night and marriage; the idea of women's eternal honor and their role as victims and sacrifices; the dysfunctional relationship between the husband and wife; the husband and his father about the inheritance; and, finally, the husband and the judge about the murder of his wife. The other core problematic issue is the individual's self-flagellation and self-conflict, exhibited in the wife who is adhering to the traditional role of her gender, accepted by her society but rejected by her husband. By representing societal issues, I explore and unveil a relationship between social and human ideas and their laws, all shaped through artistic frames. My aim is to create aesthetic and philosophical images of what society should be and what it can become.

Robots

Faten Al-Taee

Characters

Husband
Wife
Man
Judge
Robot

Scene One

A bedroom with a wide bed in the center. The wife, in a wedding dress, holding a white cloth in her hand,[1] stands in front of her husband. Music and women singing can be heard from a distance. The husband smiles and lifts her wedding veil. She tries to stop him and then runs away. He smiles and sits on the bed while she stands far away. He remains smiling on the bed. Minutes pass and the image freezes suddenly. The wife approaches him again, lifts the cloth from her face, and the husband stops smiling, moving closer to her. Then he starts smiling again foolishly.

Husband My mother told me to sacrifice a cat for her, so she fears meowing.[2]

Wife Sacrifice . . . and sacrifice . . .

Husband I sacrificed it, but I hid it.

Wife Sacrifice . . .

Husband Will you sacrifice something tonight?

Wife A white cloth!

Husband Above the pillow.

Wife Above the hand of death.[3]

Husband Their ears are pressed against the door.

Wife I can almost hear their breath robbing me of mine.

Husband They only steal their own, not realizing our breath belongs to us.

Wife My mother pleads for it.

Husband And my mother looks for it.

Wife My father hides his knife above the pillow.

Husband A spot.

Wife A mere spot swallows their souls.[4]

Husband They're the ones devouring the silence.

He covers her face again. **Wife** *takes off* **Husband***'s shoes, brings a warm water bucket and places his feet in it. She looks up at his face.*

Wife A big chicken too.

Husband (*laughs with great delight*) And a chicken as well.

Wife And a big bucket.[5]

Husband (*lifts the wedding veil from her face again*) You're as beautiful as my luck.

Blackout.

Husband (*the husband's voice heard from afar*)   Cloth.

Wife   Father.

A female robot appears, carrying a water bucket, pours it under the door, then returns to the wall, holding the bucket in her hand.

Robot   Sacrifices, sacrifices . . .

The sound of women cheering is heard from afar.

Scene Two

The kitchen of the house. The wife stands next to the robot. A teapot whistles steam, and the robot produces the same whistling sound. The wife stands with a loaf of bread in her hand, then, takes the teapot and the bread, and approaches the husband. She pours tea on the ground and eats the bread eagerly. The husband takes his empty teacup, sits on the ground, trying to gather the spilled tea. He looks at the wife who is crouching behind him.

Husband   The needle is still in the haystack.

Wife   Yes, in a haystack.

Husband   Did you look for it?

Wife   I looked for it yesterday.[6]

Husband   Did you find it or not?

Wife   We will search for it again. We must find it.

Husband   You will search for it again. You must find it.

Robot   I will search, I will find, I will search, I will find.

Husband   I bathed in my sweat yesterday until the fever broke, and you were not there. Did you catch the fever?

Wife   You know . . . she[7] is my ultimate enemy.

Husband   She is my first enemy.

Wife   Don't try to create an enemy for yourself. (*She moves away, then returns.*) But you always create enemies out of nothing.

She goes away from him, goes to pick up the teapot, puts it back on the fire, and the whistling starts again.

Husband (*addresses the robot behind the wife*)   Come here. (*He kneels under her feet as she stands.*) You empty yourself to fill me. (*Whispers.*) She won't say she's ill. Whenever she gets sick, I find her standing tall, torn inside, smiling, and hiding the agony. Do you know why she does all this? So I won't replace her with a healthy woman. (*The robot moves away. He runs to kneel beside the robot.*)

Robot Good health. Good . . . good . . . prevention is better than cure.

Husband (*addresses the robot*) She's perfect . . . too perfect. (*He becomes furious.*) It drains me from the inside.

Robot She's filling herself. Filling herself.

Husband She wouldn't be like this if not for the cats and the red sheet.

The robot makes a cat sound, intertwining with the sound of the teapot whistling. The sounds become louder. The husband spins with force, holding his head, then screams.

Husband Enough of cats and sheets![8]

The sound disappears. The wife disappears. The husband stands up with joy and happiness, dusting off his shoulders, shouting.

Husband Now we stop, head toward what should be.

Robot Should be . . . should be.

Husband As it should be.

Robot (*follows him, repeating his words*) As it should be . . . as it should be . . .

Husband Everything is not as it should be . . . even when you decide it should be, you wake up in the morning to the sound of the vegetable seller shouting.

Robot Fresh vegetables, fresh fruits.

Husband Spirits were never meant to be frozen; they must remain fresh.

He lies on the ground, the robot lying beside him.

Husband I dreamed a beautiful dream, and its voice entered my ears, screaming . . . A losing game is the game of dreams.

Robot Losing game.

Husband What do you think about playing hide and seek today?

Robot Hide . . . seek.

Husband Yes, the same game we've been playing for years. (*Leans on the robot's shoulder.*) Five years, and I've been playing hide and seek so all of them will deem me worthy.[9] And in the end, the gods celebrate *their* sacrifices. They don't celebrate those of us who make the sacrifices, but the ones who receive sacrifices, the ones who always clink their glasses. And I'm still ringing doorbells, wearing formal attire, combing my hair, and applying a stinking fragrance to my body.[10]

Halal . . . Halal . . . Haram . . . Haram.[11]

Robot Haram . . . Haram.

Husband Every day, you find me in the first hiding spot.

Halal . . . Haram.

Robot (*stands behind him, echoing*)   Haram . . . Haram.

Husband   It's always the shortest way.[12]

Wife appears.

Wife   What do you want to eat for lunch?

Husband   Halal, halal, halal, anything.

Robot   Anything.

Wife   Anything.

She turns her back to the husband and writes in the air.

He does not like this.

This makes him bloated.

This makes him sleepy.

This isn't cooked the way his mother cooks it.

She looks at him.

Anything.

Robot   Anything.

Wife   Glory to the things we don't understand.[13]

Husband   Let's play a game.[14] (*She looks at him with surprise.*) Yes, play a game, any game. (*He screams behind her while she turns her back to him.*) Just a game, a mere game.

Wife   I don't play games. Your relationship with my things isn't the same as my relationship with yours.

Wife *exits.*

Husband   Play with myself and win myself. It's better than playing with her and losing to her. She always wins, but I tell her that the rules of the game are reversed, and that I'm the one who wins despite my loss.

Wife *exits and reenters, carrying a plate of food, placing it in front of the husband on the ground, then disappears followed by the robot.*

Husband (*checking rice grains*)   Even the rice and salt grains complained about me. They didn't rise, refusing what's around them.[15]

Glory and eternity to the machine who doesn't complain and doesn't resent.

Open mouths accepting defeat with joy,

Gazing eyes looking above, tears soaring to the heavens.

A body that aspires only to sleep. Fingers that embrace but only curl up in the palm of my hand, unable to beckon.[16]

The wife returns, takes the husband's plate, and sneaks to the end of the kitchen.

Husband Wonderful, this rice is just as I've always liked it, my love.

Robot My love, my love.

Scene Three

A small room with a large bed, black curtains.

Husband Why is the room so dark?

Wife I chose the sunset and the night.

Husband Where is the light?

Wife You like darkness.

Husband Because of the darkness around me, I can't be sure that dawn has broken.

Wife I'll remove the curtains tomorrow and light the lamps for you.

Husband Run to light the fire . . . Hurry to burn incense in my clothes, burn them well while they're inside the clothes. Rebel against it, rise against what's inside me until even my body rises to the heavens. The fools will rush to extinguish me, just burn it. Hold your matchstick like you hold the meat knife. Shall I beg for death?[17]

Bread is gone.

Water is gone.

Charcoal is gone.

Candle is gone.

And her voice didn't go away

Wife So, stop, don't water these seeds. They don't need water.[18]

Husband And are there seeds?

Wife Its branches always spring forth.

Husband Wretched are the branches that don't bear fruit.

Wife And your branches are fruitful, go forth with them, declare the hour of their harvest, let the others eat abundantly until their bellies swell.

Husband Will you rise today? Your rising has no value anymore.

Wife My seeds realized you are not their water.

Husband Rather, your seeds are dry, they can't grow.

Wife You couldn't climb the hills. Stay on your plains. You're as hunched as ever.

Husband   I still rain.

Wife   And the soil still rejoices at the rain.

Husband   Laboring every day, we give birth to a loaf of bread and tea in the morning, and the sun looks at me as if saying, "The loaves thrive under your shade and your pride."

Wife   Thriving under your fires and God's praises above the houses.

Husband   And God's praises above the chimneys.

He tries to hit her; she disappears under the bed.

Husband   Come out. I won't hit you. In fact, I've never hit you.

Wife   But your whips wound my soul.

Husband   Come out now, or I'll call her.

Wife   I won't come out.

Husband   I'll call her. You've started rebelling.

Wife   I won't come out.

Husband *calls the robot.* **Robot** *enters and lies on the bed.* **Wife** *comes out and sit next to the robot.*

Husband   Will she stay here?

Wife   She'll stay here.

Husband   Ask her to leave.

Wife   You're the one who should ask her. You called her.

Husband   No, you made me call her.

Wife   You.

Husband   You.

Wife   You.

Husband   You.

Robot   You. You. He. She. Sleep. Bed. Sleep. Bed . . .

The husband lights a candle.

Husband   And you still excel at the role of a wife.

Wife   And I still . . .

They lie on the bed with the robot in between, darkness, the sound of the robot's parts creaking. An old child's lullaby:

Oh Wannas[19], oh Wannas,
With gray in my hair, you came to be.

Barren they said, not fertile.
Oh child, oh child,
Barren they said, not fertile.[20]

The robot appears to be nursing a child while lying on the bed. The husband is asleep. The wife sings the song repeatedly. Blackout, except a spot of light on the robot, she places her head on the wife's pillow. The wife places her head on the same pillow, facing the robot.

Scene Four

A large room, an old couch, a robot. An elderly man sits on the couch, and the robot, shaped like a broken man, is on the floor with the husband sitting on top.

Father   Where is your heir?

Husband   Where is your wealth? I am your heir.

Father   My name . . .

Husband   All of them carry names, even those who sleep by the mosque's door at dawn, and on the riverbanks, and inside the dumpsters.

Father   Their names are borrowed.

Husband   And our names disappear behind us. You still search for legacy.

Father   And who will inherit from us after you?

Husband   Shall we bequeath that old, worn-out wooden couch with its mattress turning to desert sands? Shall we inherit its musty gray covering? Is this the throne that spans from your grandfather to your grandson?

Father   Wisdom lies in the body.

Husband   Wretched is the throne, wretched are the sands, and wretched is the wisdom. (*He kicks the broken robot underneath him forcefully.*) And this is also a body that possesses wisdom greater than the wisdom of thrones, but I am not satisfied with a wise man who doesn't understand walls unless he understands what curtains and cushions are.

Father   When water springs from the muddy drains, neither the cushions nor the lips will be quenched.

Husband   And the deserts, heavy with sin, will nurse these bastards.

Father   It's enough that it's pregnant.

Husband   Listen, you storeroom rats, who give birth to more and more of your pups every day . . . (*He shouts*) It's enough that you're pregnant.

Father   The hills are barren, only giving birth to thorns, and the plains, extraordinarily swollen, have become a snake that consumes everything around it.

The gravel and volcanoes caught in its gullet, and you're still screaming that the rats are pregnant and will give birth to flowers for us.

Husband The earth won't stop shaking and shedding gravel one after another. What's wrong with us and the gravel? Let's stay in the thorns. (*He stands up, turning his back to his father, trying to leave.*) Don't turn your back on me and leave, leaving your long shadow winding around me. (*He falls to the ground and curls up.*) He's trying to strangle me, trying to sap me from the insides.

Father is silent.

Husband Take your shadow with you. I don't want it here.

Father *laughs and turns his back.*

Husband Turn towards me, the volcano will calm, the earth will stop trembling, and my voice will be heard.

Father You have no voice.

Husband Your voice rises.

Father The voice of God rises more and more.

The sound of the call to prayer "Allahu Akbar." Blackout.

A bent figure, whose face is not visible, appears in the shadow of a headless man praying.

Lights come back up.

Husband We wake up all night, asking Heavens to bless us, as we proclaim sin near its columns.

Father Glory be to Allah.

Husband *spreads the prayer rug, shakes it forcefully, stands on it, repeats the action three times.*

Father Allah is the greatest.

Husband We shake off our sins and ascend to the heavens, and we bow (*Bows.*) and bow (*Bows.*) and bow (*Bows.*), and we no longer have the strength to raise our heads.

Father Praise be to Allah.

Husband We won't ascend again.

Father Don't ascend. Your burdens are heavy; you can't ascend with them, but praise be to Allah.

Husband Praise be to Allah . . .

He gets closer to his father's face forcefully.

Father Praise be to Allah . . .

He raises his voice very loudly, his face pressed against the husband's face.

Husband   Praise be to Allah . . .

He gets his nose close to his father's nose.

Father   Praise be to Allah . . .

He breathes heavily, his eyes staring intently at the husband, noses close together. Both scream "Praise be to Allah", the father forcefully pushes the husband, he falls to the ground. The father screams "Praise be to Allah". The father exits, the husband breathes in relief and places his head on the broken robot.

Husband   Praise be to Allah . . .

Scene Five

A large courtroom, a single bench, two robots sitting on it, and a large box containing the husband.

Judge   You have a chance to confess.

Husband   What chance do I have while I'm receiving these lashes?

Judge   Where did you hide her body?

Husband   She's sitting right in front of you. (*He points towards the second robot.*)

Judge   Who is this?

Husband   My wife!

Judge   Don't pretend you're a madman to escape punishment.

Husband   I'm not mad, and I'm not a killer.

Judge   So, where is your wife?

Husband   She's right in front of you. I'm not lying. Ask her . . .

Judge (*to the robots*)   Which one of you is his wife?

Both Robots: (*in the same tone*)   I am his wife . . . He is my husband. (*They repeat in unison.*)

Judge   This machine just repeats what it's told.

Husband   My wife turned into a machine. I didn't kill her . . . (*He shouts.*) She turned into a machine! I loved her deeply. How could I kill her?

Judge   I'll talk with you according to your irrational logic, just stay calm. How did you reach this point?

Husband   We rode the sea's back . . . and the sea rode on our backs, taking the cruelest retribution from us.

Judge   You must return.

Husband   When you return inopportune, your legs carry you into exile. You'll ride naked wings that rain without clouds.

Judge   A madman's nonsense.

Husband   I'm not crazy; I am aware of what's around me.

Judge   Your circumstances tell me you're unaware. So why did your wife turn into a robot?

Husband   She was a human being, then she gradually turned into a robot.

Judge   How gradually?

Husband   Her mind turned into a robot's, then her perception of the world changed. After that, her body changed, and here she is, sitting in front of you. (*To the robot:*) Speak, can't you? Tell them I didn't kill you. Tell them you willingly turned into a machine, and I didn't turn you into one.

Judge   And which one of them is your wife?

Husband   The one on your right is my wife; the other one isn't.

Judge   How did the other one come between you and your wife?

Husband   On the first morning of our marriage, we found shadows behind a pile of cushions that towered over the couch. My wife told me she was a ghost but went towards her. My wife brought her to me and told me she wasn't a ghost.

Judge   And how did she agree to live with you?

Husband   She had no voice, and she didn't say no.

Judge   Because she didn't say no, you kept her.

Husband   I didn't fear her voice.

Judge   Did you love her? I mean, your wife.

Husband   Did I love her, or did I love my love for her, or did I love her love for me? My sword had three fangs, and my failing stick inclined to the right and left. I saw my stick as a snake, and she told me it was a snake. She feared it, and I looked at her and took pride in my actions.

Judge   Did your snake bite her?

Husband   I did not allow it.

Judge   Did she love you? I mean, your wife?

Husband   She loved me and blessed me in her prayers every day, until she tore up my prayer rug, took my essence, and coiled in the henhouse, so I wouldn't hear her blessings anymore, only the sound of eggs hitting the bottom of the roost.

Judge   How did you kill her?

Husband   I didn't kill her; she poisoned me and I slowly swallowed it. I rejoiced while swallowing, again and again, until my insides burst in front of her. I dozed off and woke up to find her gathering my remains and restoring me once more.

Judge   So, she killed you?

Husband   Yes, she killed me, and she curled up inside the pile of iron.

Judge   Where is your body?

Husband   It rests beneath my father's shadow, that long shadow that stretches out endlessly.

Judge   And to where does your shadow stretch?

Husband   I have no share in this void.

Judge   Did you ride the void, or did she?

Husband   We were afraid to dismount it, fearing that we would land and discover where the void hides.

Judge   Whom did you both fear?

Husband   I fear the person of the long shadow, and she fears the person of the red rag.

Judge   I don't understand you, but I'm trying to find a useful language for you. Why did you kill her?

Husband   I was not walking on the ground; I used to ride the wings of the air and sit in my place as I always did. I whip myself, then return to ride and whip myself, whipping until I stop the iron's punishment.

Judge (*laughs*)   Sitting is the escape from standing.

Husband   I did not sit, and I will not sit, and I will not escape. I did not kill her.

Judge   But everyone says you killed her.

Husband   It's the one looking at me; ask her if I killed her.

Judge   How can I ask her when she is a pile of iron?

Husband (*screams loudly at the wife robot*)   Don't make me move you by force like a bird in a cage.

Judge   Be silent!

Husband   Be merciful. Ask her. (*He approaches her.*) Ask her if I killed her. How can I kill iron? Shall I stab its heart, suffocate it, cut it with a knife, or put poison in its food?

Judge   Today is your final hearing. Since you insist on denying everything, I'll do as you ask. I'll give you one last chance to confess. I'll ask your wife if you killed her or not.

Husband   I beg you, do it, and she'll tell you I didn't kill her.

The judge walks toward the robots and places a chair in front of them.

Judge (*looks at the husband*)   Which one of them is your wife?

Husband (*points to the one sitting on the right*)   This is my wife.

Judge (*approaches her*)   Did he kill you?

She does not answer.

Judge (*repeats his question*)   Did he kill you?

She remains silent.

Husband (*screams*)   I didn't kill her! I didn't kill her!

Second Robot   He killed her, he killed her . . .

Wife Robot (*looks at the second robot*)   He killed her, he killed her . . .

Judge   This is the evidence, and a witness from her own people has testified.

Husband (*screams*)   No, I didn't kill her! I didn't kill her! She's right in front of you!

Judge (*pointing at the husband's face*)   You killed her . . .

The judge's hand appears as steel, almost like a robotic hand.

Husband (*surprised, addressing the judge*)   Who are you?

Judge   I am the judge.

Husband   But you're also a robot!

Judge   I'll remain a judge despite that.

Husband   And what's my fault? Why am I judged by a robot?

Judge   That's your fate, oh murderer . . .

Husband   I didn't kill her! I swear I didn't kill her! Don't believe her; she doesn't know what she's saying . . .

Judge (*sits on his chair, strikes the table with his iron hand*)   And we have judged that he killed her!

Notes

1   The white sheet alludes to the practice of verifying a new bride's virginity by checking for blood from the wedding night to prove that the hymen was intact before consumation. Similar practices have been documented throughout the world, including Europe, and date back to at least the Jewish Torah (see Deuteronomy 22). It is still common practice, though not universal, in Iraq for the family of the bride and the groom to inspect the wedding sheets. Where no blood is present, husbands may have legal recourse, and courts can order medical doctors to certify women's virginity (even though such exams cannot be

conclusive). The opening scene also refers to the husband's family waiting outside the door and listening to ensure there are no problems with consummating the marriage.
2. A metaphorical sacrifice that symbolizes the wife's refraining from raising her voice and being forced to remain silent.
3. It is not uncommon in Iraq for brides to face violent repercussions, even death, if their virginity comes into question after the wedding night. A rejected wife may face this violence from her own family, whose honor is thought to be impinged by her perceived lack of virtue.
4. In these lines, the spot, referring to the spot of blood on the wedding sheet, has a totemic power, representing the Wife's virtue, her family's honor, and the Husband's masculinity and virility. The knife also symbolizes the threat of violence to the wife referred to in note 3.
5. Chicken alludes to the traditional dinner for the newlywed couple; in the second instance it may represent the wife's sacrifice, submission, or fear. The bucket is for washing the husband's feet, a symbolic act of submission but one that is not common in Iraqi society.
6. The "needle in a haystack" suggests the husband is looking for something essential in his wife. The wife appears to understand the needle literally, missing the husband's symbolic meaning. The haystack may symbolize the traditions and norms of society.
7. Fever. The wife does not want to show her illness (weakness) fearing the husband will replace her.
8. In the eyes of the husband and the robot, the wife paradoxically "fills" herself through self-sacrifice and submission to the husband, playing the role of a perfect wife, even hiding her illness (weakness). The husband experiences this as draining him. The robot blames the wife's behavior on social and cultural norm, metaphorically the cat and the red sheet (referenced earlier in the play).
9. Hide and seek refers to social and political games. "Their" refers to society, and "gods" refers to corrupt politicians and those in power who exploit the people through the game of halal (permissible) and haram (forbidden).
10. He is just following empty traditions and customs of society.
11. Children use these words to indicate the beginning (Halal) and ending (Haram) of the hide and seek game. However, the literal meanings of these words are sacred and forbidden, alluding to the larger theme of social pressure for conformity.
12. Haram (the forbidden) is always the quickest way to gain something.
13. Refers to things done in the household by the wife and which gives the wife a value.
14. Sexual intimacy.
15. He complains of her perfection and total obedience.
16. Wife's complete submission in bed.
17. Refers to the bedroom rituals. In subsequent lines, "bread," "water," "charcoal," and "candle" refer to the absence of romance.
18. The wife is infertile.
19. Name of the mother's child, and the name means a loving and kind companion.
20. The lullaby is a mother's lament at having endured rumors of barrenness and pressure from her husband's family to divorce until she finally gives birth to her child. The grey hair is not from old age but pressure from society to have a child.

Introduction to *Women of War*
Jawad Al-Asadi

Women of war, with their oppressive circumstances, displacement, and migration to lands other than their own, write their lives in exile. They struggle to find acceptance in a new society and adapt to exile while longing for their homelands, from which they were forcibly driven away during times of social deterioration, the disintegration of human values, brutal repression, and free horizons closed off. In their struggle for a new life in foreign cities, with new traditions, and new ideas, the women find themselves living a more refined and less harsh life, and with more freedom to enjoy artistic and intellectual pursuits, freedoms they lacked in their homelands. However, they experience a psychological conflict when narrating their lives and trying to make sense of the violent and harsh realities they endured in their countries: the brutal abuse that left unprecedented torment in their souls. These women come from different homelands and, thus, have diverse expressions of their oppression and injustice, which color the play and give it a distinctive character.

Women of War

Jawad Al-Asadi

Characters

Maryam
Adele
Fatima

Scene One

A house shared by three female refugees: a large living room with a huge, titled antique mirror that has been there for many years, a wide couch, and coffee table stacked with plays, novels, a record player, and CDs. Also on stage, a small dining table with three chairs, three beds, and a bathroom.

When the women testify to the asylum investigators, a large drape descends to mask the house.

Jazz music plays. The three women stand waiting together, along with a few other refugees, in front of the drape and take turns speaking before a microphone. They introduce themselves to the investigators and give their testimony.

Maryam   Mr. Investigator, my number is four, four, four. I was born at dawn on Wednesday at a quarter past four, in the year 1949. I descended from devout parents. Since my childhood, I was raised to read the Quran, recite it beautifully, pray, and supplicate, and visit sacred places. I grew up in a strict upbringing. I willingly wore the veil on my head from a young age. Friday was a sacred day for me. I spent it in the nearby mosque, praying and reciting with pleasure until my voice became hoarse and my body tired from bowing. My father died at the age of forty-seven while my mother is still in her prime! I am the youngest in the family, with six siblings. One was executed, and he was only twenty-four years old. The second was abducted because of his religious identity and was summarily killed, while the rest were scattered seeking asylum in countries like Germany and Sweden! As for my mother, she remained alone, without any support or security to speak of, except for the mercy of the Lord of the Worlds. Mr. Investigator, please, I beg you, please, please hurry up in— (*Pause.*) Yes?! Okay, I'm here, I'll wait. Oh, I forgot to mention that I became a widow three years ago!

She stands with the refugees waiting for her turn again.

Adele   Mr. Investigator, my number is nine hundred and thirty-three. In my city of Latakia,[1] I left behind on the balcony of my home bright flowers that will not live without me to water them. Honestly, I'm not sad or concerned about anything. I expected what happened in my country. I'm not in a hurry for anything! If you grant me asylum, okay. If you don't grant me asylum, okay! I have plenty of time, life is ahead of me and not behind me! I have been infected with the virus of excessive optimism since I was a child! So, I dance, I sing, I listen to music, I walk in the streets without a purpose or goal— (*Pause.*) Yes, okay. I'll smoke a cigarette and wait until you ask to see me again.

Fatima   Mr. Investigator, I will once again remind you of my number, two thousand, two hundred, and fifty. Many women, who applied after me, have been granted asylum. However, I have been waiting here for a year with no decision!! I can no longer tolerate your indifference, your tedious questions, and your excessive hostility toward me. I demand a swift resolution to my case, or else I will leave for another country, alright? Do you understand? (*Pause.*) Sure! Great, excellent. I hope so. I will wait with my friends until it's my turn.

Fatima *stands beside* **Adele** *and other women.*

Maryam Of course, I'm a Syrian. What did you say? Oh, yes, originally from Aleppo, yes, from Aleppo! But I was born in Hama! And I consider it a paradise on Earth! If you knew, Mr. Investigator, how the people in my city live, you would be completely amazed, especially when you see the crowds of men and women who prostrate in the mosques and pray all day long to the Lord of the Worlds! Especially the young people who have embraced Islam sincerely, and paradise is a blessing for their hereafter! You should see their tender, radiant faces overflowing with faith, and their nobility and unity under the message of the Prophet of Messengers, peace be upon him! (*Pause.*) What did you say? Okay, alright! May I go to the restroom, please? Thank you.

Adele I think you've heard of Latakia. Yes, yes, it's right on the edge of the sea. I spent my childhood and my entire adolescence in the mountains and on the coast. People in Latakia, Mr. Investigator, are friendly, civilized, and not fanatical. Of course, we have theatres, cinemas, bars, and nightclubs. Every Thursday evening, Mr. Investigator, I used to go to the nightclub with a group of young men and women! We would dance and drink until dawn, then go to the beach and swim until noon. Some of us would return home, while others preferred to stay at the beach all day.

Fatima I'm certain you forgot that I'm from Baghdad. You know, Baghdad is the city of life and culture, people from different nationalities live there. Of course, everyone lives as if they are one big family! There is no distinction among Baghdadi people between Palestinians, Somalis, Iraqis, Moroccans. Everyone has their rights equally, until the dirty war that came and destroyed and divided everything! Tell me . . . Why are you burning our paradises? One after another, yes? What are you saying?? Why and how did I come here? (*Laughs sarcastically.*) I flew through the clouds on the magic carpet, then landed at your magnificent airport with a forged Danish passport, which I bought for ten thousand dollars from Ali Baba and The Forty Thieves. For the thousandth time, you ask me how I came here? It's like you have Alzheimer, Mr. Investigator! You keep repeating the same questions! Please—! (*Pause.*) Okay! I'll go out to smoke a cigarette until you ask to see me again. And my request to you is not to repeat the same questions.

Maryam I arrived at the airport in Germany with a forged Swedish passport! Mr. Investigator, I didn't say Syrian, I said a forged Swedish one! Yes! The story of my arrival here could make for a sad and funny movie at the same time! Do you want me to tell my story now? No, alright! Later, later! Okay, okay, okay . . . Later

Adele I turned myself into the German police upon landing at the airport. Honestly, I didn't expect the police to treat me with such exceptional kindness. They put me in an air-conditioned room, offered me orange juice, and one of them even gave me a cigarette that I smoked! In less than three hours, they took me to a wonderful shelter, where I met many other refugee women who made me forget the fatigue of the long journey. Oh, how happy I am now! Mr. Investigator, on the way from the airport to the shelter, I saw with my own eyes the beauty and charm of the city. I saw the clean streets, the underground and overground bridges, balconies adorned with flowers, pampered dogs walked by pampered humans. I saw a lady washing her cat with shampoo and brushing her teeth with tenderness and affection.

Fatima   Unfortunately, my journey from Ankara to Germany wasn't easy at all! I faced significant difficulties and went through many dangers. Do you want me to explain the details of the journey? No? Okay, please forgive me if I say anything harsh— No, not at all, I'm not as sharp-tempered as you might think! Let me say, I regret choosing your country as my place to live! I believe that the Swedish, the Dutch, and Austrians are more kind than you are! Because they understand what it means to be an artist and to be an actress! (*Pause.*) Okay. Nevertheless, I will wait and wait, but beware if my patience runs out, then . . . I will explode dramatically and you will hear words you've never heard before, alight?

Maryam   My profession? Well, I'm almost a nurse. I learned to administer injections from my mother, as I was trained at home. My reputation spread in the city of Hama! So, I started working day and night to save money and buy a passport from one of the forgers! Here in Germany, I also do injections, for just one euro. A little prick and, with Allah's help, everything will be over! You don't care about these details, huh? You want information about me leaving Syria and arriving here? Alright! I swear by God Almighty, every day I write my testimony, but I tear it up, then I write it again and tear it up, sometimes I get so nervous from the interrogation and the investigators that I get severe abdominal cramps. Like now, for example, as I speak to you, the cramps are starting to hurt me. So please allow me to go to the bathroom again.

Maryam *hurries to the bathroom, making noises due to the intense cramps.*

Adele   Mr. Investigator, to be completely honest, my journey was not complicated at all. I took my place on the plane posing as a Dutch lady because I had a forged Dutch passport and I speak English fluently. During the flight, I got to know the pilot, who found me attractive and gave me his business card! I am very happy to be here, yes, very happy, and I am flying with joy. (*Pause.*) Excuse me? My profession? I don't have a profession. I left school early and got married! I worked as a saleswoman for clothing, then suddenly the war broke out, and within a year and a half, everything collapsed. The streets were no longer the same, houses were destroyed! People's spirits crumbled, prices skyrocketed, most people left their homes and fled. Syrians ended up on the borders of Lebanon, Jordan, and Turkey. Bodies filled the streets, panic and fear everywhere. Life was no longer possible at all. I felt suffocated, my nerves shattered. I escaped to Turkey and then came here!

Fatima (*strongly*)   Please, Mr. Investigator, don't treat me like I'm nothing. True enough, I left my country under threat, but you need to know who I am and what a rich civilization I come from. My memory is filled with a history of great scholars, artists, thinkers, and innovators like Al-Jahiz, Ziryab Al-Kindi, and Al-Khwarizmi.[2] Have you heard of them? You spied on our civilization and stole our innovations, and now you boast about what originally belonged to us. You need to understand that I am the descendant of an ancient country with a rich theatre tradition. And you need to understand that I am one of its most prominent actresses! People used to come from across Iraq just to watch me perform! Why are you surprised? People used to come from Mosul, Karbala, and Babel to watch my plays! I am the daughter of the paradise you turned to ashes. Have you forgotten how you stole the statues of the god Marduk from the Baghdad Museum and shattered the statue of Hammurabi?[3] How your tanks invaded the Museum of Antiquities and turned it into a parking lot for your armored vehicles? You destroyed Ishtar, Gilgamesh, Damuzid, and Inanna,[4] you demolished our entire history and displaced people from their homes. *Ich bin nichtdaraufim Berlin.* You know, I'm forced to speak your onerous German language, and the bitterness is killing me. Do you know what it feels like when you can't even sleep in your own bed, in your own home? When you talk to me, you must remember that I am the leading star of the theatre in the Arab world—rather, in the whole world. Do you understand who I am now? Excellent.

The three refugees step forward to the microphone, and they gradually speak fast, making it difficult for the investigator to understand what they are saying. Their speech speeds up as the music rises.

Scene Two

The three women are in the living room. **Maryam** *prays,* **Fatima** *holds a radio and listens to the news, while* **Adele** *hums in a foreign language.*

Adele (*addressing* **Fatima**)   Seriously, don't I look like a movie star? Don't be angry with me, I couldn't resist the temptation to raid your closet full of dresses, shoes, and hats. Wow, wow! I was torn between which dress to choose. Look, look what I'm wearing, Juliet's robe, Juliet, Juliet. This dress used to cling to your body, and this gown is magnificent. Didn't you wear this in the Bernard Alba play? Wow! I also took possession of these clogs; I love the sound of their heels when I strut in them. (*She taps her shoe heel on the floor and struts.*) Fatumti,[5] I discovered the makeup stash and wigs. I stole your fiery red lipstick. Look, look at my lips, aren't they appetizing, as captivating as you always were on stage? (**Fatima** *remains still, as if frozen.*) Fatima, can you hear me? (*Angrily.*) Aren't you always like this, lost in your thoughts and delusions? I'm tired of your sorrow, anxiety, and always listening to bad news. (*Turns away, then returns.*) I know, I know that you didn't sleep at all last night and kept listening to the bloody news from your country. (*Brings a chair and sits beside her.*) Fatima, my dear, from now on, I won't let you sit disheartened like this.

Fatima   I feel guilty being away from my family.

Adele   Alright, let's imagine you're with your family right now. Would you be able to heal their wounds and stop their pain?

Fatima   At least I could care for my mother if something happened to her.

Adele   There's nothing for us to do from here on out except adapt to the conditions of this country and make a life for ourselves here. We have to forget who we were.

Fatima   My body is here, but my soul is there.

Adele (*laughs*)   So, didn't I come here too? Why are you acting like you're the only one?

Fatima   I wish I hadn't come.

Adele   Pack up your things and leave if you regret it so much.

Fatima   It's too late for such talk.

Adele   Then change your mood to fit in with people here.

Fatima   Oh, I regret being here in Germany.

Adele   You're mistaken, my theatre star.

Fatima (*sighs*) (*sarcastically*)   Theatre star. What theatre star are you talking about?

Adele   At least here we can reveal what's stirring in our souls. I'm certain that the safety of this country will offer us great opportunities to live luxuriously, which we didn't have in our country. When you think about returning to the theatre, ask yourself, "Where is the audience? Where are the theatres, and what is the fate of the artist!?" Ha! Oh, if I were a star like you, I would build my stage here in this house, on this table, between these old walls, and I would reclaim my roles, especially those that tell about violent, passionate love that drives lovers to obsession, madness, and rebellion! And I'm sure the refugees here will be your eager audience, waiting to hear you.

Fatima   Fiery emotions do well up inside me, but they are for the soil of my homeland where my art flourished.

Adele   As for me, I've settled these mixed feelings. In time, I'll have a house in Germany and a wonderful German dog and a blond German boyfriend. I'll walk it in the street and kiss him in front of everyone like this. (*She starts kissing the air and laughs.*) I will do everything to forget my country, which I'll toss into an ancient history museum. I'll erase from my mind the massive curse of my home country, even if doing so fills me with bitterness. Now, I have nothing to do but dance, yes. (*She laughs hysterically.*) I'll dance, I'll dance until I go into a coma.

She turns on the music, then starts dancing on the table until she gets tired and lies down on the couch. Silence.

Scene Three

Fatima *and* **Adele** *are in the living room.*

Fatima (*anxiously*)   I'm worried about Maryam!

Adele   Don't worry about her. She'll be back soon. You need to prepare for your meeting with the investigator. Are you ready?

Fatima I don't know! I don't know.

Adele Use all your skills as an actress. Inspire them with your performance and get their approval.

Fatima I don't know why but I become confused and can't organize my thoughts, especially when they sit there with those cold, fake smiles and ask their ignorant questions. In front of them, I look like a simpleton with no past or direction for the future. So, I'm sarcastic with them, and I have fits of laughter as if I'm addled brained!

Adele Did this confusion happen after you came here?

Fatima No, my nerves gave out in prison back home.

Adele When did that happen?

Fatima They arrested me on the street while I was going to the theatre to perform in *Bernarda Alba*. Ten days of abuse and beatings. They wanted to get information from me about one of the actors I was close with, but I didn't tell them anything.

Adele How did you get released?

Fatima By pure chance.

Adele You see, you could have been among the dead.

Fatima That would have been kinder than witnessing the crimes committed against my people.

Maryam *enters, slamming the door behind her, her clothes wet from the rain outside.*

Fatima Where were you?

Maryam *(flustered, she rushes to drink water)* I'm parched!

Adele Where were you, my dear?

Fatima *gets water for* **Maryam.**

Fatima Drink, why were you late?

Maryam *drinks water, looking confused and trembling.*

Fatima Maryam, Maryam, speak, what's wrong with you? Talk, Maryam, calm down, Maryam.

Maryam *(breathing heavily, fearful and confused, she throws herself into* **Fatima's** *arms and then they both sit on the couch)* Afraid, I'm afraid . . .

Fatima Afraid? Afraid of what?

Maryam Afraid, afraid, afraid of the test results.

Fatima Don't be afraid. Everything will be okay.

Maryam I wish I hadn't gone to that damn hospital.

Fatima What happened?

The rain is getting heavier.

Maryam   In the hospital, I saw lots of women from different countries, suffering from weakness and chronic illness. Others had experienced horrors and nervous breakdowns from being here, away from their children and husbands.

Adele (*enters, smoking a cigarette*)   You always bring us depressing news!

Maryam   Continue with your dancing, makeup, and preoccupations!

Adele (*laughs sarcastically*)   My dear, admit that you were at your lover's house, not at the hospital.

Fatima   Leave her alone.

Adele (*laughs*)   Would it be inappropriate to hear about your love affairs from another female refugees or from you directly?

Maryam   Your spite and jealousy will consume you.

Adele   On the contrary, I'm impressed with your two sides, the veil on your head and the fire of love burning inside. Modesty and shyness on the surface and intense desire hidden inside. Mmm, I love this combination.

Maryam (*irritated*)   I'm free, and I'll always do what I want.

Adele   I'm just teasing you!

Maryam   Where is my prayer mat?

Fatima   I don't know.

Maryam   Where is the prayer mat, Fatima? I want to pray. (*Searching for it.*) Okay, found it!

Fatima   Please, pray quietly, alright?

Fatima *tries on a dress.*

Maryam   Alright.

Adele   Fatima, wow, what an elegant dress. Shall I iron it for you?

Fatima   Here. (*She throws it to her;* **Adele** *catches it and gets excited.*) Be careful with it, don't burn it. It reminds me of my best characters' roles.

Adele   Juliet's dress! Wow! "My love, Romeo, don't die. Oh, my love!" (*She holds the dress against herself.*) You know, someday I'll steal it from you and wear it on my birthday? (*She laughs.*) I'll memorize some of your lines, climb on the table, and scream, "Take me into your arms, my love, Romeo." (*She sings in French.*)

Je t'aime, je t'aime,
Comme un fou, comme un soldat,
Comme une star de cinéma.
Je t'aime, je t'aime,
Comme un loup, comme un roi,

Comme un homme que je ne suis pas.
Tu vois, je t'aime comme ça.[6]

Maryam *prays quietly while* **Adele** *sings loudly.*

Maryam   My dear, must you go through an acting fit while I'm praying to my Lord? Can't you try to understand the difficulties I'm going through?

Adele   Alright, alright.

Maryam (*gently*)   More than once, I've asked you to be considerate of my situation!

Fatima   I apologize to you on her behalf.

Maryam (*to* **Adele**)   Listen, you need to change how you treat me because my patience is running out.

Fatima (*to* **Maryam**)   Come on, I know you're tired. Rest here in my arms. Listen, the rain is pouring outside. Does it remind you of anything?

Maryam   I don't know.

Thunderstorm begins with rain intensifying. The music gradually rises as **Adele** *appears, carrying a long transparent cloth.*

Adele   I love the rain pouring on me, so I threw all my umbrellas to the wind because the wind challenges me and carries me upward. I burned all my skirts because I wanted to walk naked and barefoot over the seas in a fluttering shirt and with a free soul. Who knows? Maybe hope will grow in my fallow field, and then I'll say, My homeland, my homeland, my homeland, good morning, O exposed poems of my homeland!

She exits while laughing as music fades completely.

Scene Four

In the same living room.

Fatima   Adele! Where are you? (*She washes her face with water.*)

Adele (*enters, carrying an ironing board, an iron, and some clothes*)   Did you have a good time, Fatima?

Fatima   Shh, speak quietly.

Adele (*whispers*)   Aren't you hungry?

Fatima   There's nothing left in the kitchen except some old cheese and a few olives.

Adele (*hears* **Maryam** *praying, sarcastically*)   Shh, she's praying.

Fatima   She's praying for God to relieve her pain!

Adele   She's not the only one in pain.

Fatima She came back from the interrogation last night tense and defeated. She said the investigator was harsh and belligerent with her.

Adele Because she thinks everyone is against her. That's why she takes everything the wrong way! The investigator who questioned me was very polite and courteous.

Fatima Not all investigators are the same! The ones who questioned me so far have been unprofessional and ignorant about how people live outside of Europe. I wish I had an investigator who understood anything about our countries! Maybe we made a mistake coming to Germany. They say the Swedish and the Dutch are more compassionate than the Germans, especially when it comes to burying the dead. In the Netherlands, for example, they put the deceased on a cart pulled by two delicate horses and parade them through the city. Afterward, they bury them. In Germany, they place the deceased on a cart pulled by blind horses, circling with it until dawn in celebration of their death. Afterward, they place the deceased in their grave.

Adele As an actress, can't you shine a light of hope on us?

Fatima (*acting*) Hope? Where are you, O Hope? I'm looking for you! I'm searching for you!

Adele I really feel everything will be okay! I want, I want to live my normal life, to drink, to dance, to stroll in the streets, to go to movies. I want to take my share of this world. (*As she sits on the couch, placing the gown on her shoulders with the music playing louder.*)

You know what? I still feel strong, capable of holding the whole world in the palm of my hands, like a colorful balloon. (*Laughs.*) I didn't leave my homeland to bury myself in mourning and cry over the ruins. No, no! This time, I will plan the life I want for myself, no matter how enormous the disappointments are. Oh, oh, if only I were an actress!

Fatima What would you do?

Adele I'd create new characters, characters who are happy, free from persecution, and free from despair and depression. Fatima, why don't you do the same and improvise a scene about love, longing, and affection?

Fatima In those special moments in my life when I was on the stage, my voice echoed loudly. I would immerse myself in the role I portrayed, to the point of getting goosebumps, even fainting. I was beautiful, desirable. Men swarmed around me with flowers. At home, I had so many dates, the phone kept ringing, ringing, ringing. Here, everything has come to a halt.

Knocking on the door.

Adele Alright, alright, coming.

Adele *goes to open the door, and* **Maryam** *enters.*

Fatima What happened? Tell me! Speak! What happened?

Maryam Nothing!

Fatima Speak.

Maryam It's one of the refugees.

Fatima What happened to him?

Maryam He had a psychological breakdown. (*Laughs.*)

Fatima What happened to him? Speak, tell me. Did he die?

Maryam (*laughs*) What if he did? His heart will be at peace!

Fatima Where will they bury him?

Maryam Where will they bury him? In the refugee cemetery. (*She laughs and withdraws quietly to a corner.*)

Fatima Do they really call the cemetery that?

Adele They'll invent it. (*Singing.*) Create a refugee cemetery, and I'll send you many refugees from Baghdad, Lebanon, Palestine, and Libya. (*She laughs.*)

Fatima The worst thing in the world is when people are laid to rest in exile without a word, without wails or mourners, not even family members!

Adele Don't exaggerate. Death is death, whether a person is buried here or there.

Fatima Listen, if I die, carry me on your back and take me quickly to my homeland! (*Laughs.*)

Adele Actresses are immortal; don't worry.

Fatima *looks around but doesn't find* **Maryam**.

Adele Where's Maryam?

Fatima Maybe she went to pray. Don't worry about her; let her deal with her pains.

Adele Do you believe her?

Fatima Why wouldn't I?

Adele She claims her breasts are swollen, meanwhile there in the park, under the pine trees, is Sasha the Bosnian . . .

Fatima Shhh! She'll hear you.

Adele Let her hear me. One day, I'll tell her everything that's on my mind.

Fatima Don't accuse her unfairly.

Maryam Fatima, where did you put the test results?

Fatima I don't know.

Maryam I want to go to the doctor.

Fatima Weren't you at the doctor's yesterday?

Adele (*sarcastically*)   Listen, to get to the doctor quickly, my advice is to go through the park!

Fatima   Come back before dark, okay?

Maryam (*to* **Adele**)   I heard everything you said to Fatima!

Adele   I don't care.

Maryam   Why are you so hostile to me, huh?

Adele   On the contrary, I loved you before and still do!

Maryam   So, why do you meddle in my life?

Adele   I barely think about you!

Maryam   Of course, because you're a trivial woman!

Adele *laughs.*

Maryam   Why are you laughing?

Adele   I'm laughing at the dirty coincidence that brought us together!

Maryam   Speak your mind. Don't be afraid.

Adele (*sarcastically*)   Look at me. I am trembling out of fear!

Maryam   You are a bitch!

Adele   Nobody here is more of a bitch than you!

Maryam   One day, I'll crush you under my feet!

Maryam *exits the house, then returns. Long silence.*

Maryam   I've decided to stay and not go to the doctor.

Scene Five

Maryam *is praying loudly,* **Fatima** *is lying on the couch reading, while* **Adele** *is still ironing clothes.*

Adele   What's with her? Why doesn't she pray quietly?

Fatima   Her condition seems to get worse every day.

Adele   We've tolerated her long enough. Which one of us hasn't gone through tough times, huh?

Fatima   I think she's going through a serious breakdown. I've tried to find out several times what her life was like before she came here. It seems like she doesn't want to talk about her past or has decided to bury it deep inside.

Adele Yesterday, she spent over an hour in the shower, shouting, sometimes crying, and sometimes laughing hysterically. I honestly can't keep up with her mood swings anymore!

Fatima I know! She's started to annoy me as well.

Adele I don't even know who she was talking to.

Fatima I don't either.

Adele Every day the hot water runs out because she uses it all without giving a thought to us. Please talk to her!

Maryam *continues praying loudly.*

Fatima She doesn't listen to me anymore!

Adele It's like she doesn't want to hear either of us.

Fatima Yes, she hears but she seems to ignore us.

Adele Then why should I be the one cleaning the kitchen, doing the dishes, and putting the laundry in the washing machine? I didn't come here to be her servant.

Fatima Please, ignore her.

Adele Fine.

Long silence.

Adele What's this book you're holding?

Fatima I woke up early this morning longing for the plays I used to perform!

Adele I'd love to see you on the stage, performing one of your great characters. I've been begging you for a year!

Fatima It's too late for that now. I've turned into an idle actress here.

Adele Never. You just need to put on some of the costumes from your wardrobe, and I'll be your audience!

Fatima Don't open my old wounds. The sounds of the people rushing to buy tickets still ring in my ears. It tortures me. At one performance, the audience kept applauding for more than twenty minutes. I would bow to them while they threw flowers at me. Sometimes, I would cry tears of joy because of how devoted to me people were. At the end of each show, they would climb on stage to kiss me and talk about my character. Where did all that go? Look at me now. Loneliness and emptiness eat at my bones. Trust me, every day that passes here, away from my audience and the theatre, is a dark day. Imagine, after my name was on every tongue, and my image on the front page of all the newspapers, everything vanished. Now, no one knows me!

Adele Your efforts won't be in vain, ever! I'm certain you'll return soon to your former glory, and your fame and name will echo even one day here in Germany.

Fatima Last night, I lost my temper in front of the investigator when he ignorantly asked me, "Do you have theatres? Is there an audience for theatre in your country? Do you know who Schiller and Goethe are? And Shakespeare?" I told him, "When your audience knows who Al-Mutanabbi, Al-Maghut and Badr Shakir Al-Sayyab[7] are, then our audience will know who Schiller and Goethe are!" They are fools, thinking we have no history, no culture, and no arts! They sanctify their culture as the highest and most refined while looking down with contempt on our culture!

Adele Forget the investigators' nonsense and bragging now! I'd be happy if you read me a passage for one of your beloved characters.

Fatima I'm not in the mood for that right now, Adele, please.

Adele I'll kiss your hands.

Adele *kisses* **Fatima**'s *hands.*

Fatima I'm very tired today. I'll do it another time.

Adele No, today means today! Read it without any emotion or drama, just a simple reading.

Adele *kisses her again and insists.*

Fatima Okay!

Adele (*excitedly*) Wow, wow, wow . . .

Fatima Fine, give me that shawl!

Adele Alright, the great actress!

Fatima I think this wig is suitable!

She places the shawl on her shoulder and the wig on her head.

Fatima Where are my glasses?

Adele Okay.

She hands **Fatima** *her old glasses.*

Fatima I'll read you a passage from the epic of Gilgamesh! Alright?

Long silence, the lighting changes, soft music, and **Fatima** *starts to adapt herself to look like a theatrical character.*

Fatima Many years ago,
I learned from loss that
Love is snatched from
The depths of our hearts
Leaving neither beloved nor lover!
Understand, Gilgamesh,
What I want most is
To drink from the eternal well,

River of everlasting life,
For this would mean the dead rise from their graves,
Prisoners freed from their cells,
And sinners absolved of their offenses.
I believe that the kiss of love
Kills our physical heart!
It is the only way to attain eternal life,
Which cannot be endured amid withered flowers
And loud farewells, extended arms reaching for our corrupt ambitions!
I believe emotion is the pure act of God,
The emotion that always burns, never extinguishes,
Even if it is in hell or heaven!
It makes no difference to me
Because hell is the eternal gift!
It reveals the presence of God
To only the heart that longs
Among decaying ghosts
And care for no other eternity
Except being alone with the sacred.
This solitude that God enjoys inside and outside His creation!
It's enough for those who love to find only one, just one, within themselves.
That is the cup of immortality!
Time and place are infinite,
Nothing burns them except the exhaustion of patience.
Many came to help me build the ship of eternity,
With its seven decks, each with nine rooms.
The shape of the ship was square and sturdy,
Containing food and precious metals.
We gathered everything living inside,
Then my family climbed into the ship,
And we took anyone who wanted to come with us . . .
Prey and sheep were also there,
As well as the city's craftsmen and its sailors.
Then the door was closed, and the time for the terrifying rain came.
Oh, there was a warning, the storm approached.
The winds blew, then roared,
And houses were uprooted as if swept by a broom.
People clung to the branches of trees until they were uprooted and floated on the water, along with possessions and debris into the barren emptiness.
The shores failed to curb the water's fury,
Even the gods became like dogs, barking and howling and decaying like dead fish!
I looked at the land now shrouded in silence and devastation.
The bodies lay like dead sardines in the mud.
I fell on the ship's deck and cried!
Why were we condemned to die like this?
I asked questions without answers, like a child whose parents died for no reason!

I permitted myself to shun all my eyes beheld,
Because sometimes we long to abandon the human,
Because nothing can be endured except the solitude of, the one and only, my heart.
I'm miserable for what I've seen!
Youth lost and not to be reborn of its mother's womb,
Children who didn't return to their remains,
Lost wives,
An entire country collapsing as if it had never existed!

Adele   Bravo, bravo, bravo!

Adele *screams hysterically, and there's recorded applause and shouts of "Bravo!" Then there's a long silence.* **Adele** *helps* **Fatima** *remove the shawl, wig, and glasses. Then she hugs her tightly.*

Fatima (*bitterly*)   My mouth is dry. Can you get me a glass of water?

Adele   Of course, a glass of water for the greatest actress of our lifetime.

She brings her a glass of water.

Fatima   Adele, I feel hungry. Do we have anything to eat?

Adele   Of course, sure. In a few minutes, I'll set the table.

Adele *immediately starts arranging the table with enthusiasm.*

Fatima   Ask Maryam if she's hungry or not!

Adele   You ask her!

Fatima   Okay! Maryam, the food is ready. Come here!

Adele *prepares the table, placing plates and utensils, then pours the soup.* **Fatima** *takes her place behind the table. Both* **Adele** *and* **Fatima** *start eating before* **Maryam** *arrives.*

Fatima   Maryam, the soup will get cold. Come on, aren't you hungry?

Silence.

Adele   Eat or not, it's up to her.

Fatima   She didn't sleep all night!

Adele   Of course, due to her longing for the Bosnian guy!

Fatima   What Bosnian are you talking about?

Adele   The man you met at the previous shelter!

Fatima   The tall, blond one?

Adele   Yes, him!

Fatima   I don't think there's anything between them besides a casual friendship.

Adele   They meet in the park every day!

Fatima   It's normal for a man to meet a woman! In the park or anywhere else.

Adele   Sure, but in this house she acts like a veiled, dignified, aloof, chaste, disciplined, and ideal lady; meanwhile by the river in the park she takes off the veil and her clothes to wallow in vulgar fornication with that man!

Fatima   Did you see it with your own eyes?

Adele   Most people have seen it!

Fatima   I think it's just women's gossip. Maybe because some of them wish they were in her shoes. Jealousy among women leads to wicked rumors.

Adele   The real problem is her flagrant sexual behavior with her lover.

Fatima   I don't believe a word of it. Anyway, here she is.

Maryam *sits and starts eating in silence.* **Fatima** *pours soup for* **Maryam**.

Fatima   What's new with you, Maryam?

Maryam   Nothing.

Fatima   Did you go to the hospital yesterday?

Maryam   Yes.

Fatima   Did you get an X-ray of your chest?

Maryam   Yes.

Fatima   What were the results?

Maryam   I'll get the results tomorrow.

Fatima   Have you been to the old shelter recently? Have you seen your old friends?

Maryam   Why are you asking?

Fatima   Just because I miss going there. I've lost contact with them, especially that African lady who plays the saxophone.

Maryam   I never see her anymore. I don't have enough time.

Fatima   I also miss Rubika, the Iranian, and Lena, the Ukrainian, and many others. Honestly, we shouldn't have agreed to live in this shelter. It's far from life there. Sometimes I want to roam around the nearby park. Maryam, have you ever been to the park?

Maryam   Never. I've become programmed to stay at home, go to the hospital, and to my appointments with the investigator.

Fatima   I feel nauseated just hearing the names of the investigators and the detectives.

Adele   Two days ago, they rejected the asylum applications of ten women.

Fatima   Why?

Adele   I heard that all their testimonies were fake.

Fatima   Speaking of asylum and refugees, if a refugee dies without completing their asylum paperwork, where will they be buried? Have you thought about this?

Adele   The VIP refugees, the veiled ones, have their own graves! (*She laughs provocatively.*) That's what I heard!

She continues laughing, which annoys **Maryam**.

Maryam   Watch yourself and watch your tongue.

Adele   No, you watch your tongue. I wish your tongue could be surgically removed so that we wouldn't have to hear your hymns, moans, and fake pains!

Fatima   Adele, please stop it!

Adele   From now on, it's better if you recite and pray in your room. Do you know why?

Fatima *moves away from them.*

Because your voice is grating and repulsive.

Maryam   No, I will pray here, and I'll pray loudly. Anyone who doesn't like it can bash their head against the wall.

Adele   Okay, I'll also listen to music whenever I want and turn up the volume like this.

Adele *turns on the music and listens to a pop song. She starts dancing enthusiastically.*

Fatima   Adele, please turn off the music!

Adele   Okay, okay, okay . . .

Adele *turns off the music.*

Maryam   Listen up, if you don't like me and my prayers, move to another shelter, where you'll find other women like you.

Fatima   Maryam, I think it's almost time for your appointment with the investigator.

Maryam   Leave me alone, I don't want to go!

Adele   Fatima, I'm going to buy a pack of cigarettes and a bottle of wine. Do you want anything?

Fatima   No.

Adele   I'm going to get drunk tonight! Okay?

She leaves and closes the door.

Maryam   Oh, I wish that whore wouldn't come back! Honestly, I can't stand her because most of the refugee women see her as a prostitute. She keeps going to nightclubs in alluring makeup and clothes. She has nothing to do except entertain foreigners, especially the Germans! You've noticed how she disappears for long periods because she is sleeping with German men and spending the night with them. She's beyond filthy, and I'm ashamed to live under the same roof. A month ago, I asked the housing management to transfer me to another shelter!

She is in pain.

Fatima   What's the matter?

Maryam   An intense pain.

Fatima   Where?

Maryam   Here, in my chest!

Fatima   Where exactly?

Maryam   My breast!

Fatima   Come, sit down. I'll get you a glass of water.

Maryam   I'm scared!

Fatima   Don't be afraid. Everything will be okay!

Maryam   Why did you come here?

Fatima   We all know why we're here! We're not tourists. We have to stay in a country that we have no connection to.

Maryam   Yesterday, I got an email from my sister. She says our village has been completely demolished, and everyone has fled to dangerous places. I'm worried about my brother, Husam!

Fatima   Where is he now?

Maryam   He left Hama three months ago, and we lost contact with him.

Fatima   Maybe he went to Beirut?

Maryam   I don't know!

Fatima   My sister and mother have also been trapped in the house for six months now.

Maryam   What should we do?

Fatima   I don't know!

Maryam   My pain is increasing.

Fatima   Should I take you to the emergency room?

Maryam   No, I'll wait for the X-ray results tomorrow. My God, how will I face the investigator today!?

Fatima   What time is your appointment?

Maryam In two hours.

Fatima Don't worry!

Maryam I am extremely nervous.

Fatima Don't worry, you just need to keep your composure and provide your testimony with supporting details and specific dates.

Maryam I always get flustered and lose control of myself and become confused!

Fatima Write down key points on a piece of paper to make your statement coherent. It's better if you bring some pictures if you have them.

Maryam I'll try my best! Ow . . .

Adele *enters.* **Maryam** *moves away from the door and* **Adele**, *and* **Adele** *talks to* **Fatima** *and laughs loudly.*

Maryam Don't spew your venom on me!

Fatima What bothers me is that you both act like belligerent teenagers. Enough, please.

Maryam I know she keeps smearing my name in front of you and the others!

Fatima She's never told me anything like that.

Maryam Of course, you told her about my relationship with the Bosnian!

Adele I can't even listen to you; your voice annoys me!

Maryam You should know that my relationship with the Bosnian is pure and genuine. Is it a crime for a woman to love a man here!?

Fatima No one has the right to interfere in your personal matters.

Adele *laughs sarcastically.*

Maryam He hasn't even touched me.

Adele *laughs loudly.*

Maryam Believe me, Fatima, he hasn't touched my body. Just so you know, this shameful woman who sleeps with every German Tom, Dick, and Harry wants to make me out as a slut in front of you! (*To* **Adele**.) Get this straight, I'm not some slut like you. I'm madly in love with him.

Adele You're lying!

Maryam I am not!

Adele Even the words you tell the refugees about your love for and union with God are lies. Your story about your illness is made up! Why are you trying to deceive yourself and others? Tell the truth, the pain in your breast is because . . .

Maryam Because of what, you slut!

Adele Because your lover sucks on them until you faint. That's the truth!

Maryam Where's the knife? (*She screams.*)

Maryam *raises the knife, trying to attack* **Adele**, *while* **Fatima** *prevents her.* **Maryam** *explodes, breaking plates, throwing books off the table, and then she sits on the couch and cries bitterly. Long silence.*

Fatima (*calmly*) I've never seen women so savage in my life! Why did either of you come here? To seek asylum? Asylum from what? Why? It would have been better if you'd stayed where you were, so you don't air your dirty laundry in front of strangers. I've tolerated your childishness and belligerence more than I should. I've endured this foolishness and ignorance. No, I won't stay here a single moment longer. I'll pack my things and live with the animals; that's better than staying with you!

Fatima *starts gathering her belongings and tries to leave the house.* **Adele** *and* **Maryam** *try to calm her down. She is calm, sitting on the couch.*

Adele I will leave with you!

Fatima I don't want to hear either of your voices. Okay? Back off, both of you. Move away from me. I thought you would be more compassionate and more understanding. Why are you poisoning my life? Isn't it enough that I live here without my family, without my audience, all the time trying to regain my balance and collect myself? Why this excessive hostility? Why? It's a farce! I've never seen anything like this in my life! A knife? Have we reached this level of savagery? To solve our problems with violence and profanity! Isn't there another way to communicate and resolve conflicts? In any case, I can't bear to hear the voice of either of you anymore. I'll turn off the light and go to sleep, and if either of you makes a move, I'll leave immediately.

The three of them stretch out on their beds, and there's a long silence. Thunderclaps and light rain. The lighting changes to a nighttime mood.

Fatima (*whispering*) Maryam . . .

Maryam Please, I want to sleep.

Fatima Please, I need to talk to you.

Maryam Fatima, leave me alone!

Fatima I won't sleep before talking to you. Come, please . . . sit on this chair.

Maryam Fine, go ahead.

They sit facing each other on the chairs. The rain intensifies, and thunder can be heard.

Fatima Can you answer some questions honestly and frankly?

Maryam (*bluntly*) As a friend or as an investigator?

Fatima No, as a friend who has perhaps seen more of the world.

Maryam *laughs.*

Fatima I want to know, from you, why did you choose this country and this shelter? Why are you here?

Maryam I'll ask you the same question: why are you here?

Fatima Did you come to Germany searching for freedom and security you didn't have in your country?

Maryam Of course, I lacked many things in my country. Who knows, maybe I'll find some of them here.

Fatima Like a man, for example?

Maryam Like a man.

Fatima Did you find one?

Silence.

Fatima Why are you silent?

Maryam Yes, there's a man in my life.

Fatima Is he Arab? Eastern? Indian? Serbian?

Maryam No, Bosnian. (*Laughs.*)

Fatima Why are you laughing? Did you sleep with him? I promise I'll keep your secrets.

Maryam Please, don't upset me!

Fatima Did you sleep with him or not?

Maryam Honestly, yes, I slept with him.

Fatima How many times?

Maryam Once.

Fatima Just once?

Maryam *laughs.*

Fatima Where did you sleep with him?

Maryam In the park.

Fatima The park near our house?

Maryam No, there's another park about an hour from here.

Fatima Is there a hotel or a resting place in the park?

Maryam No.

Fatima Then?

Maryam On the grass.

Fatima And people!

Maryam It happened at dawn on a Sunday when everyone was asleep.

Fatima Did you enjoy it?

Maryam Madly.

Fatima And him?

Maryam More than me.

Fatima How?

Maryam When we were making love I felt like he was devouring me, breaking into me, biting me, hitting me more violently than I've ever experienced before!

Fatima Did you have a relationship with another guy?

Maryam Yes.

Fatima Oh! So, you were sleeping with two men at the same time.

Maryam I didn't intend to have two men at the same time, but . . .

Fatima The first one, from Bosnia, and the second one?

Maryam The second one was from Pakistan, a Pakistani refugee, exceptionally handsome.

Fatima *laughs.*

Maryam Why are you laughing?

Fatima I'm laughing because you were hiding all this from us.

Maryam (*sarcastically*) Maybe because I'm naturally shy.

Fatima Did you love them both equally?

Maryam Yes, I was sincerely in love with both of them.

Fatima I can't believe what you're telling me! Honestly, you've shocked me!

Maryam Am I the only woman in the world who's been with two men? For your information, most of my veiled friends do the same thing! And I've never felt like I was untrue to myself, committing a sin, or deserving of punishment. I always confess to God during my prayers. God knows everything about me.

Fatima (*laughs in surprise*) Alright . . . Tell me, which one satisfies you more sexually?

Maryam Both of them!

Fatima (*laughs loudly*) Alright . . . What's the difference between them, my horny friend?

Maryam Honestly, with the Bosnian, I have orgasms quickly! But with the second one, it takes more time. The first one knows from experience how to awaken me as a woman! He enthralls me by playing with my nipples! Then, he passionately bites my chest like no man before. Whereas the Pakistani has no experience in . . .

Fatima Okay, okay . . . excellent, you mean the second one needs more practice.

Maryam (*laughs*) That's what I was trying to say!

Fatima And what would you say if both men asked for a serious relationship?

Maryam No.

Fatima Why not?

Maryam Neither the Bosnian nor the Pakistani can tickle my fantasies!

Fatima *laughs.*

Maryam Why are you laughing?! I'm really . . . I'm not in love with either of them. The truth is I'm looking for another man now!

Fatima Do you ever feel that your incessant prayers are at odds with your desires?

Maryam No.

Fatima Are you proud of the veil on your head?

Maryam I've gotten used to it.

Fatima And when you recite prayers every day, who are you reciting to? Who are you addressing?

Maryam To the Lord of the Worlds!

Fatima Has a doctor ever told you that you suffer from schizophrenia?

Maryam Never.

Fatima Hasn't he diagnosed your talent for deception?

Maryam I'm not deceptive at all. I do what pleases me, especially what brings me comfort and pleasure.

Fatima I'll be straightforward with you.

Maryam Go ahead.

Fatima Why do you behave so selfishly inside the house? Are you convinced that we exist just to serve you? For instance, during your period, why do you fill the house with screams and break things in the kitchen and the window? Why do you make the atmosphere in the house so foul? Just a few days ago, you threw my books on the ground and tore some of them. It didn't occur to you that the books are precious to me?

Maryam Consider me a troubled woman, insane!

Fatima You claim to be ill! You don't like meeting the investigators, you put on the veil to display wholesomeness and modesty, but at the same time, you sleep with men who are filthy sadists! Who are you, tell me! Hanging between God and the devil, between the veil and counterfeit, between love and lovelessness, half a believer, half a dreamer, half a liberal, half a radical! Half devout, half slut! Honestly, I can't stand your duplicity anymore! And let me tell you . . . either change your ways or get out of this place! Find another shelter, alright!

The rain continues to pour heavily outside. Long silence.

Maryam (*contemptuously*) Alright, madam of the theatre, star of the masses, I also can't stand your whining, your impartiality, your dissembling! You provoke me with your silence and your collusion with that bitch Adele! I am not impressed that you're an actress. To me, an actress is half prostitute, half fraud, half clown, half crazy! I don't care about your audience's admiration or your stardom or the characters you want to reclaim or even the lowbrow books you stack on this couch!

She throws the books on the ground.

To be honest . . .

The only thing that we have in common is that we're in the same shelter. My bad luck has thrown me between the whore Adele and a wicked, heartless actress. You are neither a sister nor a friend . . . You are like a lifeless heap, stuck in a ridiculous past! This place has become empty and repulsive to me. Every day, my fear of you both increases. What should I do? Which shelter should I go to? I've asked the investigators more than once to move me to another shelter or transfer me to another city. Oh God, to which city should I turn to? Which country will shelter me and free me from the misery of this shelter!?

Sound of a new email arriving. **Maryam** *heads to the computer and reads to herself aloud.*

Maryam "My sister Maryam, I'm writing you this message as our brothers are organizing the funeral for our brother Husam, who died by a gunshot from unknown individuals! (*A long silence.*) We are living in a state of panic and fear. Our city has turned into a ghost town, the neighbors have all fled, and there's no one left here but me and your mother, as well as our neighbor Abu Adham and a herd of cats and stray dogs. My advice to you is never, ever return to this wretched country."

With deep sadness, **Maryam** *goes to her bed and covers herself with a thick blanket. She falls silent as the rain intensifies, accompanied by violent thunderclaps. The light changes towards daylight.*

Fatima Adele, please give me my coat and hat. It's time for my meeting with the investigator.

Adele *helps her put on the coat and places a hat on her head.* **Fatima** *puts on her glasses.*

Music plays, and the lighting and setting change. **Fatima** *walks quickly towards the investigator's office. There is a change in the lighting as she approaches the investigator's office.*

Fatima (*addressing the investigator*) While the actors and actresses were putting the final touches on their makeup, waiting to enter the stage and perform *Bernarda*

Alba, suddenly three men entered my dressing room. They grabbed me by my hair, shoved me into a Mazda car, and drove me to an unfamiliar place. After a series of beatings, questions, and insults—all in an attempt to extract information about my political stances and affiliations because I come from a left-wing family—I passed out in solitary confinement. After a while, I found myself dumped on the airport road. (*Pause.*) My older brother helped me get a forged passport. I crossed the border for Ankara. From there, a smuggler helped me, arranging for me and more than ten families to go to Prague by air. Indeed, we arrived there, where we were handed over to another smuggler who organized a risky overland journey for Germany.

At dawn, they loaded us onto a large truck filled with sheep, goats, and other animals. They smeared our faces with mud, threw straw on our heads, and asked us to lie face down while we crossed the borders. A large bribe to the border guard allowed us to cross safely. The smuggler asked us to get out and head deep into a dense forest. We had to evade patrols active in that forest. The temperature was thirty degrees below freezing, and we were a procession of women carrying their children and bags, traversing a cold, strange land, navigating between dense trees that stood like spears in our faces. Hours passed as we followed one smuggler after another until one of them said, "You are now in Germany." In that moment, several women fainted from exhaustion and the overwhelming feeling of salvation. As for me, I no longer knew who I was. I forgot myself, my family. I couldn't remember if I was really a woman or had turned into a crushed ant, an animal, a tree, or a stone. I felt in that moment that I had become nothing. Nothing at all. (*Strongly.*) Do you understand now who Fatima is?

The lighting changes. **Fatima** *returns home exhausted, received by* **Adele**, *who helps her remove her clothes and offers her a glass of water.* **Fatima** *sits on the couch.* **Maryam** *asks her to read the letter that arrived. She reads it, and* **Adele** *also reads it.* **Fatima** *embraces* **Maryam**, *and* **Adele** *also hugs her tightly.*

Long silence.

Maryam (*quietly*)   I want to go back to my homeland.

Fatima   No, I won't allow you to leave here ever.

Maryam   I want to be with my mother.

Fatima   Your brothers will be with her.

Maryam   I want to attend my brother's funeral. I want to bid farewell to Husam.

Fatima *embraces* **Maryam**. **Adele** *gives her a thick blanket to keep her warm as the rain continues. Music plays. The weather is still rainy.*

Scene Six

The next day.

Adele *washes the white sheets and hangs them on the laundry line.* **Maryam** *enters, holding her X-ray reports.*

Adele Anything new?

Maryam Nothing.

Adele No news at all?

Maryam None.

Adele What's the result of the X-ray?

Maryam I don't know.

Adele What's wrong?

Maryam I feel disgusted living here, but I don't want to go back there. I've never felt so lost before. Even this scarf feels heavy on my head and my soul.

Maryam *removes the scarf from her head.*

There's something fading inside me. Even my faith isn't the same. I pray in the morning and forget it in the evening. I no longer feel like I belong with anyone. I've lost faith and hope in everything.

Adele Speak, tell me everything that's inside you.

Maryam I feel intense anger.

Adele Why?

Maryam I'm mad at myself! Leaving my country seems to have broken me. Now I always feel that leaving my country was like contracting an incurable disease.

Adele Doesn't God see our countries? Our butchers?

Maryam God sees everything!

Adele Then why doesn't He punish them?

Maryam I don't know. He may punish them, or He may not. Perhaps He will punish them in the hereafter.

Adele The hereafter! Isn't our life here the same as being in the hereafter?

Maryam Honestly, I no longer know anything.

Adele I suppose you've heard that Sasha, the one you gave everything to, married a German girl and moved to another country?

Maryam I heard about it.

Adele That's not fair, is it?

Maryam Fair? What fairness are you talking about?!

Adele *hugs* **Maryam**, *then she feels something in her pocket.*

Adele What's this?

Maryam Sedative pills, the doctor prescribed them to me.

Adele Sedative pills or something else?

Maryam Leave me alone.

They argue over the pill box, which **Maryam** *takes and rushes upstairs to the bathroom. She swallows the pills. Silence, then the light goes off over* **Maryam***, only to return after a while, indicating some time has passed since she took the pills.* **Maryam** *laughs hysterically and mumbles incomprehensible words, then pours water over her head.*

Maryam My body will soon decay. My hair will fall out! (*Laughs loudly.*) Oh God, I'm not doing well, and tomorrow I have an appointment with that vile investigator. What will I tell him?

The lighting changes, and we see **Maryam** *carrying her personal papers and testimonies, running towards the investigator's office. Mixed music with sounds of cars, trains, and street noise escalate as* **Maryam***'s pace quickens until she enters the interrogation room.*

Maryam (*rapidly*) To the investigator, on Friday, May 10, 2013, while I was heading home after prayers, a young man stopped me. At first, he expressed great admiration for me, especially because I'm a veiled girl. He walked beside me and talked about his great respect for me as a devout Muslim girl, mentioning that he had been observing me for a long time and asked the neighbors about me. He praised my dignified bearing and how the light of Muhammad (peace be upon him) shone from my eyes. He expressed an intense desire to marry me according to the Sunna of Allah and His Messenger. I gave no response and had no desire to talk to him, so he hinted that Allah had thrown me in his path, and I was destined for him. At that moment, I was afraid and hurriedly tried to escape from him, but he followed me, reached out, and touched me. I tried to call for help from passersby, but suddenly more than five men, who he must have conspired with, surrounded and abducted me. Indeed, they put me in a Peugeot car and drove for more than an hour and a half. Afterward, they took me to a place I didn't recognize. The young man who had admired me before said that he would marry me in accordance with the Sunna of Allah and His Prophet. Then he began to explain to me the meaning of jihad by marriage, or marriage as a form of jihad.

He began to read aloud a paper, claiming it to be a hadith specifically addressing the topics of marriage and intimacy. Suddenly, he shouted with fervor, 'From now on, and by the guidance of Islam and the Messenger of Allah, you are mine!' I couldn't believe what was happening; I screamed loudly, blood rushed to my head. In a fleeting moment, I found myself thrown to the ground and naked, my clothes and veil stripped away, before this man who violated my body in the name of jihad. I pleaded to God, to the Prophet, to the people, but no one answered. With brutality and savagery, he assaulted me until I began to bleed.

The next day, while I was still bleeding, another man entered. He repeated what the first one said, adding that he was acting in accordance with religious custom and to further thier inevitable victory. He assured me that I would be rewarded and perhaps have a place in paradise, and who knows, maybe I would dine with the Prophet's Companions.

Over ten days, ten men violated me in the name of the same cause. I collapsed mentally and physically, and they took me to a remote hospital, then disappeared. Since that day, I still feel defiled, and all the waters in the world cannot purify my body! This is my testimony, esteemed investigator.

Scene Seven

Adele's Birthday

Adele *enters from outside, carrying a bottle of wine, some fruits, and a little food, while* **Maryam** *sits with deep sadness.* **Adele** *tries to create an atmosphere resembling a party and plays loud music.*

Adele   Today is my birthday, and I'm far away from my homeland. Maryam, help me set the table. Fatima, I bought red wine and chips. Fatima, come here.

Fatima   Coming, coming.

Adele   What kind of music do you prefer?

Fatima   Play whatever music you like.

Maryam   Lower the volume; I can't stand loud noises.

Adele   Fatima, set the table.

Adele *drinks the wine quickly.*

Maryam   Slow down, Adele. You're drinking too fast! Give me a glass of water.

Fatima *gives her a glass of water.*

Adele   Maryam, have a sip of this wine, don't be afraid!

Maryam   Impossible!

Maryam *removes her headscarf.* **Adele** *sways from drinking too much wine.*

Adele   Come on, join in the birthday celebration.

Maryam *is silent.*

Adele (*dancing*)   Fatima, come dance with me! (*Loudly.*) A toast to Maryam!

They dance with great joy. **Adele** *pulls* **Maryam** *to dance, but she doesn't respond.* **Adele** *drinks too quickly and becomes drunk. She falls on the couch.*

Adele   None of you asked me why and how I came to Great Germany! Perhaps you thought I came to play with the fancy dogs the Germans walk on the streets or to marry a blond German man to have blonde children! All I wanted was to walk down the streets in the rain without an umbrella! And to accompany a circus clown who pulls an elephant behind him and carries colored roosters on his shoulders. Today, I will reveal my secret to you, the one I've kept hidden for so long. I will tell you my story about the boy of my dreams, who I once saw standing in Salhiyah, Damascus. His long hair fluttered high, carrying a bundle of books, and he stared at me eagerly and desirably. I fell under his spell immediately, and he dragged me to his bed in his house! He made love to me, married me, and then he traveled to Rome, and I followed him! After a year of our life together, I got pregnant, and at that moment, I felt a happiness I had never known before. My body transformed into a womb, a heavenly playground for my child. Later, I found out from the doctor that it was a girl, and my joy only grew. Every day, I felt her movements, her head, up and down. There's no feeling gentler than carrying another body inside you, a person growing and taking shape within you. Heartbeats next to your heart, a soul floating within your soul. She moved inside me, creating a delightful commotion, sounds, giggles, and cries, and then sleep. My whole life became her playground; I would go out to the market, only to pick out colorful clothes for her. The whole house filled up with her socks and her lovely dresses, her bed in the middle of the room, teddy bears here and rabbits there, a small donkey here and a sleeping deer there. I was about to give birth, close, within an inch or less, I approached the moment I had dreamed of my whole life!

I left no street unexplored; I mingled with people as if I were carrying all of life beneath my skin. The doorbell rang, my daughter was battering my womb. The nurse wheeled me in the carriage amid my screams, tears, and pleasure. The whole world was between my thighs. After giving birth, I lost consciousness, fell into a deep sleep. I woke up to the sounds of nurses and the doctor, who whispered in my ear, "Your daughter is incredibly beautiful, her body is healthy, except for a hole in her heart. In four years, she'll need surgery." Then my husband left, disappeared forever. (*A long silence.*) After exactly four years, my daughter sailed away with no return ticket. As if the entire world had fallen upon my head.

Gradually, peculiar music starts playing, and the large mirror is pushed to the front of the stage. **Fatima** *appears with her face painted white, wearing clothes similar to those in the Japanese kabuki theatre.*

Fatima Do the dead have festivals? I always hear the festive noise of what they call the Day of the Dead. While my homeland, my country, stretches out on a wide carpet of dust, I always asked my dead-living lover to tune his strings while listening to my violin. I kiss him fiercely every day and pluck the chords of his soul in the darkness of crowded dungeons filled with warriors!

My love, my husband, Romeo of my dreams, and my son asked me every day before performing on the stage: "Will you play the role of Juliet straight, or will you secretly twist your fingers in the text's air, hoping to catch the sleeping bulls within its lines?" I told the actor in front of me, the one who was playing Romeo, "Why are you alone? Where are the female guards of your lust, the ladies of your bosom, the spinsters of your desires? Why do you train them to depose me? At first, you held them in your womb, and then you expelled them. You carried me, then you expelled me! They search for me in the bedrooms with their slippery breasts pointing towards the bathtub. Oh God, how much you resemble me tonight! I am like you! How can you and I resemble each other when you are my sin? How?" I was beautiful in your womb, beautiful next to your marble body. Your fiery kiss seared my characters on the stage. Oh Romeo! Am I not your Juliet? Aren't I the worshipper of your scent, a kiss on your handkerchiefs? Talk to me, wake up from your sleep, Romeo . . . Romeo . . .

Fatima *bursts into tears. Both* **Maryam** *and* **Adele** *comfort her, then they sit her on the couch.*

There's a knock on the door. **Adele** *goes to open the door, then returns holding a letter.*

Adele   A letter addressed to Fatima Salim Awad, Maryam Mohammed Yassin, and Adele Antoine Dib . . . The committee of investigators decided that . . .

Fatima *takes the letter, and* **Maryam** *also reads it eagerly, then a long silence.*

The three of them sit on three chairs at the front of the stage and quickly present their testimonies before the investigators in a caricatured manner, as in the first scene of the play. The music accelerates with their pace.

Adele   We will keep knocking on the doors.

Fatima   No one can bend my neck and defeat me.

Maryam   Tomorrow to another land.

Adele   The bicycle is my horse.

Fatima   The sun is my hat.

Adele   We will fly like birds.

Fatima   The three women and the flying up high.

Adele   The bicycles are ready.

Fatima   My suitcase is ready.

Maryam   I am ready too.

The three of them scream, whistle, and laugh hysterically. **Fatima**, **Adele**, *and* **Maryam** *all ride their bicycles with unprecedented joy and sorrow.*

Notes

1   A city in Syria on the Mediterranean coast.
2   Scholars, artists, scientists, and mathematicians who during the Abbasid Caliphate lived in or were born in modern day Iraq. Fatima's references to these figures reflects the pride that many Iraqis feel at Baghdad having been the seat of the Abbasid Caliphate and the center of learning during the so-called Golden Age of the Arab-Islamic Empire. Among other things, Al-Khwarizmi was one of the chief innovators in the development of mathematics, including algebra, a term in English partly derived from one of his treatises.

3 In 2003, following the US invasion, amid widespread looting throughout the country, tens of thousands of items were stolen from the National Museum of Iraq, including unique treasures from ancient Mesopotamia.
4 Ancient Mesopotamian gods and heroes.
5 Diminutive of Fatima, meaning "my little Fatima."
6 The song "Je T'aime" (1997) is by Lara Fabian, a Belgian-Canadian pop music singer-songwriter.
7 Al-Matanabbi (915–965) was a revered Arabic poet from the Abbasid Caliphate period. Baghdad's book market is on a street named after the poet. Muhammed Al-Maghut (1934–2006) was a Syrian poet and playwright known for his innovation. Badr Shakir Al-Sayyab (1926–1964) was among the most famous of modern Iraq's poets at the forefront of the free verse movement.

Introduction to *The Mug*
Amir Al-Azraki

First presented in 2017 at the University of Waterloo and later echoing through the airwaves as an audio play during the UNESCO Short Play Festival in 2019 at the University of Otago, New Zealand, *The Mug* unveils a poignant narrative inspired by the harsh realities of an Iraqi artist refugee. In Canada, Arab refugees navigate the complex challenges of settlement, acculturation, and assimilation. This short play depicts the experiences of a theatre artist in his early 60s, grappling with the scars of a tumultuous past while navigating the challenges of a new life in Canada.

I had the pleasure to visit this artist in his temporary residence in Kitchener, Ontario. Observing an array of mugs adorned with various university logos in his home, my curiosity about their significance unraveled a deeply moving tale. Each mug, a token bestowed upon him after sharing the harrowing chronicles of his life in Iraq, became a tangible repository of his tribulations and triumphs.

The artist's wry comment about using these gifted mugs to sip Arag (a liquor), a bitter nod to the irony of solace found in such simple tokens, resonated with profound implications. As he uncovered his history, a mosaic of wounds and trauma emerged. Invited to speak at various universities and cultural events, he returns home to his wife and children, who are now struggling with linguistic and cultural dislocation in Canada, including the challenge of losing their proficiency in Arabic and his own difficulty in securing employment and learning English to communicate with his family and the community. Each night, grappling with disappointment and a sense of helplessness, he pours himself a drink in a university mug, listens to music, and immerses himself in memories of the past. The nightly ritual of pouring Arag into one of the university-branded mugs became a cathartic act, intertwining with the strains of music and a nostalgic journey into his bygone life. Against the backdrop of a family struggling with fractured communication and unmet aspirations, the play unfolds a poignant narrative of agony, alienation, exploitation, nostalgia, desire, and despair.

The Mug is inspired by the artist's moving story. It sheds light on the journey of an Iraqi artist tortured in Saddam's regime, who witnessed the loss of his sons during the American invasion, only to find refuge in Canada. The play serves as a testament to the enduring human spirit, encapsulating the universal themes of resilience and the search for meaning amidst the ruins of a shattered past.

The Mug

Amir Al-Azraki

Reprinted by permission of Waveland Press, Inc. from
Weiss THE PERSECUTION AND ASSASSINATION OF J-P MARAT AS
PERFORMED BY THE INMATES O.T.A. O.C.U.T. DIRECTION OF THE
MARQUIS DE SADE
Long Grove, IL: Waveland Press, Inc.,
© 1981; reissued 2002 All rights reserved.

Um Kalthum music.[1] **Majeed** *enters. He sits on a table holding a mug of Arak in one hand and a cigarette in the other.*[2]

Majeed

A poet's tears, a mug, a story . . .
The residue of memories distilled in his drink.
 Chugs it till he chokes,
the story spews forth . . .

A lifetime on the stage, for decades I have performed for crowds, the multitudes, for you! (*Indicates the audience and takes a drink from a mug.*)

I have embodied the grief and loss of Hamlet, the anguish of Othello . . . I sang for the revolution in
Marat/Sade.[3] (*Sings:*)
Marat we're poor and the poor stay poor
Marat don't make us wait any more
We want our rights and we don't care how
We want our revolution NOW!

And I danced with Mack the Knife in *The Three Penny Opera.*[4] (*Dances and sings:*)
You gentlemen who think you have a mission
To purge us of the seven deadly sins
Should first sort out the basic food position
Then start your preaching that's where it begins.

Yes, I have been poor, destitute, in *Ba'e Al-Dibs al-Faqir* and also played a King in *Al-Fiil Ya Malek Azzaman.*[5] I have breathed life into these roles for audiences around the world . . . Underneath it all . . . below the surface of these great roles . . . underneath these facades, I ask . . . who am I?

Pause.

(*sarcastically*) "Son of Sumer and Babylon," lost son of the "Cradle of Civilization . . ." Ruins! Grief, loss, anguish . . . these are not strangers to me . . . they are my familiars . . . my closest companions . . . Yes, over the years I have enacted the lives, the trials, the tribulations of others, of characters, but . . . where do I find my own voice? Who hears it? Who cares? Who am I? I am! I am . . .?

Takes a slow drink, followed by a pause.

A fraud! A collection of obsolete, worn out memories. (*Drinks.*) Memories and grievances . . .

After the war, I arrived in Canada hoping for, for . . . something better. If not happiness—happiness may be too much to ask for—then something . . . something stable, a place to put down roots, a new future for what was left of my broken and battered family . . .

Drinks and continues in a reflective voice.

Yes, I arrived here . . . well, my body did . . . my heart, my mind, my soul crippled by the war we were fleeing . . . My hopes and happiness stamped out, crushed by the oppressive regime and by the American invasion that murdered my two dear sons . . . (*Pause.*) A father's heart can never, never be whole again after such a loss.

Even so, to tell the truth, a tiny shred of hope did remain . . . a tiny spark in the depth and darkness of my despair. Yes, hope . . . not for happiness but for a measure of peace, quiet, for the possibility of building some kind of future for my remaining children . . . Was I a fool? Am I?

Yes, an old fool. What followed after I landed in this 'free' country attests to my foolishness, my naiveté. Let me tell you how stupid I was . . . (*Pause and continues slowly.*) how I sold what remained of my pride, my soul, to the vultures and opportunists who used my tragedy to line their own pockets.

My life story, my deepest pain, become fodder for so-called artists and academics. Rich material to exploit at conferences, workshops, universities . . . they used details of my life to peddle their art . . . used me! I was used, disposable . . . another caricature like Hamlet or Othello, an imitation of life! But I? I? Where was I located in their projects, their seminars . . . where was I when they held my story up for the analysis and dissection of students and academics and so-called artists? Exploiters who appropriated my life and my terror and my pain and my dead boys and made it their own! Deceivers! Who take for granted their own peaceful existence, who've never feared for their safety and who know nothing, nothing?!? Where was I? Lost! Buried alive!

Deep silence, trying to collect himself.

Without realizing, fool that I am, I was tricked into performing a caricature of myself, of imitating my own life!

For my trouble, for my contribution, they presented me with a coffee mug, see it has the university logo on it . . . sold my soul for a mug. (*Points to logo on mug.*)

I fill it with Arak, at least it's good for something. (*Tops off mug from the bottle and drinks.*) I am alone. Night after night I sit with my mug, and try to make sense of it all. Everything is gone. That tiny last spark that I carried over here, that precious shred of hope imported all the way from the ruins of Iraq, hope for a better future, is now snuffed out . . . it wasn't for me. I find no solace in my work or my family . . .

I contemplate my mug, fill it with Arak . . . fill it with my tears . . . I repeat the same stories, count the same losses, bewail the cruel injustices of this world until I think even this mug is tired of my lamenting. Who wouldn't be? I am tired of myself! My family and friends have heard it all before a million times but still I cannot stop telling the story . . . of my imprisonment . . . imprisonment then, in a prison . . . and now in 'free' Canada . . . the internal prison of isolation and hopelessness.

Takes a slow drink.

I sleep sometimes. Sometimes I have vivid dreams . . . they're not nightmares exactly although they are confusing . . . scattered impressions of a past life; the voices of the southern birds' singing, explosions in the distance . . . the scent of myrtle and ambergris in my mother's scarf . . . the smell of gunpowder . . . the swirling dabka dance and the dance of torture . . . What a life . . . Sometimes I am overcome by nightmares of violence and destruction that pursue me relentlessly through the night . . . I wake disoriented, weeping, cursing it all. Then I ask myself, how long can I carry on? How long? Even my family . . . my wife, my children are becoming strangers. "You always smell of Arak," she complains . . . disgusted. Our children don't even speak Arabic anymore and I refuse to learn English, why should I?

I thought I had already lost everything but there were still a few things left to go . . .

Of course, they all think they know what is best for me, get busy, get a job, go give a seminar, do a play, learn English, do a monologue about your pain and inner conflict . . . .! Ha! (*Laughs ruefully.*)

I am an actor, this is my craft and sullen art, I will play my part. Cheers. (*Holds up mug.*)

Notes

1   Um Kalthum (1904-1975) was the most famous and celebrated female Arab singer of the twentieth century.
2   Arak (or araq) is a spirit traditionally produced and consumed in the Levant made with anise, giving it a liquorish flavor.
3   *Marat/Sade* refers to the play *The Persecution and Assassination of Jean-Paul Marat as Performed by the Inmates of the Asylum of Charenton Under the Direction of the Marquis de Sade,* which was written in 1963 by German dramatist and novelist Peter Weiss.
4   *The Three Penny Opera* was written in 1928 by German playwright Bertolt Brecht in collaboration with Kurt Weill.
5   *Bā'i' al-Dibs al-Faqīr* (The Poor Date Molasses Salesman) and *Al-Fīl Ya Malik al-Zamān* (The Elephant, Oh King of All Times) are plays written by celebrated Syrian playwright Saadallah Wannous.

Introduction to *Azrael*
Mithal Ghazi

Azrael is an attempt to delve into the meaning of life and death in a country where the essence of meaning is lost amidst the contradictions in our lives. *Azrael* is a scream in the face of death, an attempt to make sense of this life that is precious to us as Iraqis. The play introduces Azrael, the eternal symbol, as a way to reckon with the profound political, social, and artistic significance of life. It is a life whose constant tumult never ends, for nothing is worse than death.

Life is more beautiful when our eyes are fixed on its last light as we leave it unwillingly. In the mad cities where the power over life flows from the power to kill, the dividing line between life and death becomes blurred. It is necessary to unravel this conflict by defining the space between these two worlds, and thus, the play becomes a platform for an immense philosophical debate between the Angel of Death, who is akin to a postal worker unaware of the joy and sorrow contained in their deliveries, and a comedic actress who plays many roles on stage, as a queen, a princess, and a pauper. However, her great roles cannot help to save her from death, as death is an authoritarian power that does not heed or succumb to the numerous rationales of living.

Yet, the play tries to shift the power from the realm of death to the realm of life, allowing life to triumph in the end with Azrael taking on the burdens and aspirations of those whose lives he takes away. The play is an invitation to life more than it is an invitation to death. It is life—the most beautiful, the sweetest, and the most exemplary.

Azrael

Mithal Ghazi

Characters

Man
Woman
Nurse
Doctor

A hospital room, dimly lit, with only one bed occupied by a patient. We hear the patient's cries and groans of pain. Near the bed, a doctor and a nurse are attending to her. They look at her, then inject her with a sedative.

Nurse   Poor thing . . . She's in so much pain. Doctor, is there any hope?

Doctor   None at all. Death is creeping upon her, little by little. Poor soul won't live to see another dawn.

Nurse   Will she die?

Doctor   Inevitably. Her time has come.

Nurse   Is there any way to save her?

Doctor   There's nothing we can do. We must let her face fate peacefully.

The doctor leaves, and the nurse looks at the patient one last time before exiting. Blackout

We hear heartbeats and a pulse-monitoring device. Suddenly, everything stops, announcing the patient's death. Then, we hear a massive rusty iron gate opening with a terrifying, eerie, and horrible creak. Smoke pours out as the gate opens, revealing a giant, imposing figure followed by a group of terrifying creatures. Their faces are hidden. We hear a slow, ominous voice from the giant figure . . .

Man   The time has come . . .

Suddenly, the horrifying creatures pounce on the dead patient with ferocity, as if they were a pack of wolves tearing her apart, piece by piece, to extract her soul from her body. We hear the sounds of nerves, veins, and arteries being torn away, and then the extraction of the soul from the body. The sounds are gruesome, as if something sticky is being pulled from a rough surface. The patient screams and writhes in extreme agony, causing her to bolt from her bed, still screaming.

Woman   What's happening? Who are you? Get away from me! What do you want?

He gestures to the creatures to back away from her, as the patient sits terrified and bewildered in a corner of the room.

Man   Calm down. The time has come, that's all. Life is over.

Woman (*skeptical*)   This can't be real. I must be in a nightmare. It will end. It has to end. (*Notices the giant man in the room and asks.*) Who are you, and what are you doing here at this late hour? Who gave you permission to enter my room like this? The hospital administration should have informed you that no one can enter my room like this. (*Threatening him.*) You should be aware you'll face consequences, sooner or later. However, I'll give you a few moments to leave me in peace. (*Waits for a while.*) Well, I believe the time I was willing to spare for you has run out. (*Screaming.*) Doctor! Nurse! Where are you? Hospital administration! Guards! Curse you all! Is anyone here? One of you needs to come here immediately! Can you hear me?

Man (*calmly*) No one can hear you tonight.

Woman And who are you?

Man Perhaps I am the only one in this world who hears these screams every night without interruption.

Woman So, you hear me clearly. Maybe it's best for you to leave, and this can end.

Man I can't.

Woman Then it's up to me to call for help, and you must leave immediately.

She attempts to leave.

Man You can't do that either.

Woman Maybe I should ask you again, why are you here?

Man I've come for you.

Woman Are you one of the doctors in this hospital?

Man No.

Woman A nurse?

Man No.

Woman The hospital manager?

Man No.

Woman Then who are you?

Man Just a visitor.

Woman But these aren't visiting hours. I don't even know you, and I've never seen you before. Please leave now.

Man Very well, I will leave, as ultimately I must, but perhaps we should leave together . . . and immediately.

Woman (*surprised*) You're joking. I don't know you. Why should I leave with a stranger?

Man You must simply submit to this.

Woman I don't understand.

Man That's fine. I have no intention of engaging in debates, discussions, or justifications with you.

Woman How dare you sneak into my room like this, coming and going as you please, without permission? Don't you feel any shame for your behavior? Who are you, anyway?

Man You only need to prepare to leave, as the journey is long, and you will find the time for it. There are more important things for you to worry about who I am. It is my duty to take you tonight.

Woman I don't understand what you're saying or what you mean. Maybe there's been some mistake, confusion, or misunderstanding. Perhaps I got the room number wrong. Maybe I'm not the one you're looking for. You don't even know who I am.

Man I know you, and there's no need to introduce yourself.

Woman What if I asked you who I am?

Man Something whose time has passed.

Woman (*puzzled*) Time . . . What time are you talking about?

Man Your time in life.

Woman So, you believe my time in life has ended?

Man And that means your time in the afterlife has begun.

Woman And does this mean that I . . .

Man Dead.

Woman (*laughs*) Dead? I'm dead? Soon you'll claim to be the Angel of Death and say you've come to escort me to one of the pits where you spirit away those you visit during their last night alive.

Man I am the Angel of Death.

Woman Is this a joke? (*Laughs.*)

Man (*gripping her forcefully, leading her towards the massive gate*) Laugh all you want. Your soul and body will feel grief without measure. Perhaps we should leave now and reach the grave before your absence causes more pain and sorrow for your loved ones.

Woman (*slipping from his grasp*) Please, let go of my hand. You're causing me pain, a nightmare to these eyes. Is anyone trying to wake me up? (*Screaming.*) Doctor! Nurse! Is anyone here going to wake me up and free me from this nightmare?

Man I told you before that everyone is waiting for you. It's not appropriate to make them wait any longer. Just let us leave now, without delay. We must reach them before their tears run dry.

He takes her forcefully, but she slips away again.

Woman What tears are you talking about, and who is waiting for me there? Where are you taking me? Who are you, for God's sake? Who gave you the right to terrify me like this? I beg you, leave me alone.

Man (*angrily*) You should believe that I am him.

Woman So, you are Azrael?![1]

Man (*loudly*) You must believe that I am him.

Woman Who am I to you?

Man Just a dead woman.

Woman (*suspicious*) So . . . I am . . .

Man Dead.

She listens to her heart, then goes to the heart monitor and finds that her pulse has stopped. She goes to her bed and lifts the covers, surprised to find a dead woman.

Woman This is me . . . isn't it? Dead? (*Breaks down.*) Impossible . . . impossible. (*Cries.*)

Man (*tries to take her forcefully*) We should leave. There are others waiting to be taken tonight.

Woman (*resists*) Please . . . What if you gave me some time to believe that I'm dead? You can't just snatch me from life like this without a chance to understand the idea.

Man But you were ill.

Woman Hoping to recover.

Man Were you meant to live forever?

Woman I always dream of a long life.

Man What about death?

Woman Believe me . . . I never dreamed of a day like this. Every day the sun rose was a dream to me. What death are you talking about? There's no place for death when you're thinking of life.

Man (*looking at his watch*) You're wasting time, woman. You must leave with me immediately. Enough of your stubbornness, debates, and discussions. I've spoken to you more than necessary. I'm not interested in hearing what you want to be. You've wasted more of my time than I expected. They're waiting for you there, and I'm the only one entrusted to bring you to them for your departure.

Woman (*angrily*) My departure . . . What if the people rushing along my departure just want to move past their suffering, past their grief, and quickly return to their happiness, to eat and drink, and to live long after me? What about me? Who thinks of me? No one . . . They'll leave me alone in a world I don't know, alone in the darkness, alone with the walls of the grave closing in on me, alone with the earthworms feasting on me. They'll hurry to bury me just so my odor doesn't offend them, just so my rotting body doesn't disturb their eyes for too long. (*Hears digging sounds.*) They're digging so much . . . They dig and dig, all for me, as if I'm one of their misfortunes, just so they can rush to be rid of me. (*Screams.*) Enough . . . Enough digging. (*Begging.*) Please, ask them to stop digging.

Man I have no power to stop them.

Woman What if you gave me some time to believe that I'm dead?

Man But my orders don't include granting you this time. I came to take you, and the time is now.

Woman What if I pleaded?

Man I can't.

Woman What if I prayed to God to grant me this time?

Man That's up to you. You've lived your life as it was meant to be. What you ask for won't help.

Woman What if we talked for a while?

Man It's not allowed.

Woman (*frustrated*) Why is it not allowed? Just because you're Azrael?

Man No, it's because I am Death itself.

Woman Don't those sentenced to death have the right to talk, even a little?

Man But you've talked enough.

Woman But I didn't believe it until this moment, that I'm dead.

Man (*shouting*) You must believe it . . . (*Calming down.*) It's my duty, entrusted by God, to remove the souls of people, kings, princes, ministers, the poor, the rich, prophets, saints, etc. I had to attend their final moments, and in their eyes I saw the same questions, the same requests, and the same pleas for something I could not grant.

Woman So, you listened to them?

Man (*shouting*) I didn't listen to their wishes.

Woman What about the fear and terror you brought into their hearts? What's left of the light that used to shine in their eyes? What did you leave them with in their final moments? (*Looking at him.*) Look closely and contemplate my eyes. (*Looking in his eyes.*)

Man What are you looking at?

Woman I'm looking at the fear of millions stored in your eyes. Look at their pleading and submission before you, small and fearful. Please, I don't want to leave with you, and I'm afraid. Please, don't pour all this terror into my heart. Have mercy, I beg you.

Man How do you expect me to welcome you? I am the Angel of Death, and I must evoke fear and dread. I'm here only to take your soul tonight.

Woman Do you know anything about the life I've lived?

Man I don't care about your life. I am here to take your soul.

Woman But you should have cared about my life. I'm an actress; I've played all the roles, whether poor or rich, sad or joyful. I've experienced all of life's miseries and its joys on stage. I've cried, I've been angry, I've danced, I've leaped on the stage. They called me an artist. Do you know what it means to be an artist? In society's eyes, I am a woman of no value, living life freely without constraints or boundaries. (*Laughs.*) Have you ever tried being an artist? Do you understand the misery I've lived through? To be deserted by your loved ones just because you're an artist, to face death multiple times on stage while they abandon you. Do you think you can comprehend what it means to be an artist? What kind of misery I've experienced? The thousand lives you've lived on stage can't save you when the execution order is given. Well, what if we made a deal, you and I?

Man (*surprised*) A deal?

Woman Yes, what if I exchanged my journey with you for a smile on your face?

Man You must be mad.

Woman What if you smiled a little?

Man I can't.

Woman What if you tried . . . something very simple . . . (*Gesturing with hands.*) Just raise the corners of your mouth like a boat in the middle of a calm, beautiful night at sea.

Man You're delusional. The fear of death seems to have driven you out of your mind.

Woman Do you think . . . Do you think I should tell a joke or a witty remark to make you laugh? It seems to be quite challenging for you. (*She thinks.*) I have an idea . . . What if I perform Charlie Chaplin taming a mosquito in a circus? (*She acts it.*)

Man You're wasting time, woman.

Woman No, it's you who's making this difficult for me. It's just a smile before departure. Smile . . . Please, smile, for the sake of the victims who are consumed every day with the fires of cannons, barricades, explosives, and unjust killings. Smile for the children devoured by the fires of sectarianism, brutality, hatred, and animosity . . . Smile for those from my homeland who die, and there's nothing left in their final moments but astonishment and disbelief at what's happening to them. Smile for this burning country, which suffers every day. Smile, please. I implore you. All I want from you is to bid farewell to this world with a final smile on the face of the last person who sees me, even as I act the role of the clown while I'm dying. (*Suddenly bursts into tears.*)

Approaching her, attempting to touch her but hesitates. Finally raises her head towards him.

Man You're crying . . . and asking me to give you a smile in exchange for taking your soul, for your departure. Don't you see that it's you who is making this difficult for me? You're lying; what smile are you pretending to have? It's just an image of sadness deeply rooted in your soul. God charged Adam with all of His creatures, and He granted him His gardens, love, and peace. He placed him in His paradise and gave him whatever soothed his solitude. But, Adam made a mistake.

Woman (*sarcastic*)   So, he ate an apple, big deal.

Man (*startled*)   It's not just an apple, as you think. It's the seed of evil that grew into wars, killings, destruction, cruelty, and ruthlessness beyond measure.

Woman   So God expelled him from His heavens.

Man   God didn't want His Heavens to become a battlefield. He didn't want His Heavens to be filled with prisons, gallows, and executioners. Instead, He wanted His Heavens to be blue, where He could find solace when He looks upon the sins of humans on Earth. He created everything but evil. Evil has its tyranny and power in all of you. Adam was banished when he betrayed his homeland. Adam was banished when he allowed his sons to kill each other. Adam was banished when he allowed injustice between humans.

Woman   So, what we're experiencing is punishment for those betrayals?

Man   I know why I'm here. I'm the one who brings safety and peace. Surrender to my purpose. Let's go, woman.

Woman   How can I leave this burning place and abandon my hopes, dreams, and happiness here? Every day on Earth holds a dream beyond description. What if you let me return to my life for at least one day?

Man (*attempting to lead her to the gate*)   No, it's not allowed.

Woman   A few hours?

Man   It's not permitted.

Woman   What if it's just for a few minutes?

Man   There's no point in asking, woman. Time is passing quickly.

Woman   Please . . . I beg you.

Man   No, it's me who's begging you. Time is passing, and the gate might close . . .

Suddenly he hears the clock striking midnight, indicating it's 12:00. He urgently takes her towards the gate.

Man   Come on, before the gate closes!

Suddenly, as he takes her toward it, the massive gate closes. He becomes furious.

Man   You ruined everything, woman! What was I thinking, listening to your delusions and chattering? It was never supposed to happen this way! Damn you, woman!

Woman (*approaching him*)   Calm down, please.

Man (*sits on a chair*) Leave me . . . Stay away from me . . . Don't approach me like this. I am . . . I am Azrael, woman. I am Azrael in the flesh. I am Azrael who throughout history has inspired fear and terror. No one has ever done this to me before. Shame will befall me because of you. If it weren't for you, I wouldn't have been delayed . . . What am I going to say to my Lord, the one who controls my destiny and yours? Please, my God, forgive me . . . Your mercy, my Lord . . . Your mercy . . . (*Tries to calm down.*)

Woman This is better.

Man (*yells in her face*) But you . . . You . . . Who are you?

Woman (*tries to calm him*) Shh . . . Perhaps you should calm down. You're here against your will. The place might seem strange to you, but you have to stay here whether you want to or not.

Man What do you want from me?

Woman Just calm down. Take your time. Relax. Breathe deeply, and then let it go and also let go of all your worries and troubles. You're here by His will, and you'll leave here by His will. This is His will manifest as His judgment.

Man Are you saying I have to stay here?

Woman No, I mean you're delayed here, maybe there's wisdom in it known only to the Almighty.

Man (*starts to get agitated*) But rest assured, when these gates open for me, you'll leave with me, no hesitation. I won't allow you to utter a single word then.

Woman (*smiles*) You'll get what you want. Just calm down.

Man You are cunning and deceitful. You lured me into this with your words, and now I'm stuck with you. Perhaps you tricked me like Adam, to draw me into your games and cunning.

Woman laughs.

Man Is there anything funny in what I'm saying, woman?

Woman You should be happy because you've started saying things that amuse me.

Man As if there's any humor in what I'm saying, woman. I am so angry with you.

Woman This is how a man always is when he makes a mistake or gets entangled in the web of his problems. He inevitably looks for a woman to hold responsible for what is happening.

Man Isn't that what's happening to me now?

Woman Would you like something to drink?

Man *looks at her in silence without answering.*

Woman What if I prepare something for you to eat?

Man *is surprised.*

Woman   I apologize . . . I forgot that beings like you, angels, don't drink or eat . . . (*Sarcastically.*) and don't feel.

Man   You should be careful with your words from now on.

Woman   You failed to lure me into death; it's a feeling that bothers you, isn't it?

Man   And you succeeded in luring me . . . into . . . into . . .

Woman   Into life.

Man   A word that holds no meaning for me.

Woman   Perhaps I should impart that meaning to you in the time left between you and me.

Man   What if I refuse?

Woman   You can't, because you're experiencing it now. You're here with a woman, and this is the life you refuse to believe in.

Man   When a man and a woman meet, does life flourish beneath their feet?

Woman   Perhaps that's what's happening now. Have you ever sat with a woman? It's a feeling you've never experienced before.

Man   I don't want it . . . The one thing I don't want to forget is that I am the Angel of Death . . . the angel of what you despise and fear . . . the angel of what you refuse to believe. Remember I am Azrael!

Woman   And I am just a dead woman. We've known that, but that was in the past. In the future, you might have to live it as a man. And when you're a man, you should possess a heart.

Man   Why should a man have a heart?

Woman   Because a woman cannot live without a man's heart. It's her rightful place, where they come together.

Man   How does that happen?

Woman   Give me your hand.

Man   For what purpose would you give me a heart?

Woman   Just reach out your hand, and don't be afraid.

Man   Do I have to do that?

Woman   Yes, you must.

She touches his hand, heartbeat echoes in the room.

Man (*looks around the room*)   What is this sound? Where is this sound coming from? It's a strange sound I've never heard before. (*Searching.*) Is it here? Is it there? (*Points to her chest.*) Is it here?

Woman (*points to his chest*)   No, it's here, beating within you.

Man   And what is this sound doing inside me?

Woman   It rejuvenates your spirit and nourishes you, giving you a soul for the time that remains.

Man   So, that means you've given me a heart and life?

Woman   And happiness you've never known.

Man   Do you know . . . I've heard you wishing for death sometimes. Why do you reject it now when it comes to you?

Woman   That's only when I feel confined. There's nothing easier for us humans, when we feel helpless, desperate, and dejected, than to wish for death. It's an escape from facing problems.

Man   But you've uttered it before saying, "Oh Lord, how I wish death would come and free us . . . Oh Lord, take me so I can find rest!"

Woman (*laughs*)   And you can't wait to respond to my wish.

Man   And that's what happens every time you utter it. I try to seize you to take your soul . . . but there's always someone reminding me that it's just a false wish that humans sometimes ask for to escape life's difficulties. So, I stop and leave you be.

Woman (*laughs*)   Can you offer any other options in death?

Man   Like what?

Woman   Like dying happily . . . or dying in love. Perhaps I need a thousand years to find the happiness I've sought on this Earth because the years I've lived haven't been enough to find it.

Man   Do you know death from before?

Woman   Perhaps I know it better than you do. When conscience dies, you see people doing the most terrible things before you. When feelings and emotions die, you see in death the most repulsive thing you can find. When loved ones die, you realize there's no chance after them in life but to wish for death after their departure.

Man   So, what keeps you from accompanying me?

Woman   My dreams . . . Living with my hopes is more beautiful than moving on and leaving them behind.

Man   Haven't you lived to achieve them?

Woman   What I've lived isn't enough to achieve them . . . because we're in a country where the years of my life were insufficient to realize the happiness we dream of. What if I ask you one last time?

Man   Maybe I should submit to your desires for this night only.

Woman   What do you know about death?

Man (*hesitates*) Death . . . means . . . death.

Woman (*surprised*) Seriously? You hesitate to define death when you're the Angel of Death. I can hardly believe that you're unaware of what you do and what you represent.

Man I am not what you think I am. I am just an entity entrusted with taking out people's souls and transporting them from one place to another. From a place they know to a place they are unfamiliar with due to their fear and loathing of it. It's illogical for people to hate what they don't know. So, I am tasked with bringing them trembling and fearful. I can't lead them any other way if they are afraid of it.

Woman And what do you know about those whose lives you take away? I mean, what if it were the opposite, where the dying takes your role when death comes to you?

Man It's a feeling that doesn't concern me, and I'm not tasked with understanding it.

Woman What if you felt it?

Man I don't know.

Woman (*shaking him*) What . . . if you felt it?

Man I don't know . . . I don't know . . . I don't know, I swear, I don't know.

Woman You must know. You don't understand the meaning of life until you understand the meaning of death.

Man Where do you see life, in your opinion?

Woman It's out there, in the outside world. You'll find everything outside. You'll find life in the squares, in the streets, in the theaters, in the cities. You'll find everything you need there to understand the meaning of life, happiness, and sorrow. Misery and joy, love and hatred, hope and work, all of these are found in life. You'll find children when they're joyful, lovers when they're in love, mothers . . . You'll find an endless number of stories. Perhaps we should go out together for the time that remains, just to witness it.

Man (*resisting*) That's impossible.

Woman Nothing is impossible.

Man This isn't allowed.

Woman It's allowed. What if you were forced into it? (*Tries to pull him outside.*)

Man (*pulls away*) I can't. I can't. I told you before I can't. You must leave me to my own devices for the time that remains. I am Azrael . . . Azrael, woman!

Woman And are you afraid of life?

Man I don't know it, so I fear it. It's the opposite of what you feel as a member of your kind. You always fear what you don't know.

Woman What if you knew it? What if you opened a window to look at it, just to understand why humans are so keen not to leave it?

Man But you've always talked about life outside, about human injustices towards each other, about the sudden decisions to cause death for the most trivial reasons. Now, you're the one talking about the beauty of life. You're living in confusion and chaos, woman.

Woman Nevertheless, we insist on loving it. Life is more beautiful than thinking about leaving it. No one here ever thinks about leaving it willingly or by choice. Anyone who loves it isn't ready to trade it for anything else. All those who leave it have their eyes fixed on it from a distance without ever looking away. (*Pleading.*) Please, time is passing, and these minutes may never come before you again.

Man Do I have to do that?

Woman Yes, come on. To see what life means . . . Life . . . Life . . . Trust a woman who has been wronged by Adam, or even by God. Eve wanted to give Adam a real life—a life where he could experience sadness and happiness, make mistakes and learn from them. To turn the darkness into light within himself to create a beautiful life.

Man So, this is the life we must bite into to taste its sweetness?

Woman That's right. Believe me.

Man laughs heartily.

Woman (*surprised*) You're laughing, aren't you?

Man (*continues laughing*) Yes, can you believe it?

Woman (*laughs with him*) I can hardly believe it. This is impossible. Azrael is laughing?

Man I came here to take your soul, and now you're taking mine.

Suddenly, the massive gates open for Azrael to fulfill his mission. The two exchange affectionate looks and hold hands before departing.

Man Perhaps the time hasn't come to know life outside, but it's enough for me that I've come to know it through you.

Woman *lowers her head shyly.*

Man (*raises her head with his hands*) I'm afraid everything between us has just been a small part in a play you performed expertly.

Woman It is the most beautiful and magnificent role. It's my final scene that perhaps everyone who sees it should applaud for a long time.

Man That might happen after I finish my task.

Woman Is it time?

Man Is there one last request?

Woman Don't forget my condition: raise the corners of your mouth when you take out our souls, to at least make it less costly to leave the life we love.

Man Maybe that's what it will be like from now on.

Woman So . . .

Man So . . .

Woman So let's do what I came for.

Man extends his hand to her.

Man May I?

She holds his hand, and they walk towards the massive gate, leaving life behind.

Notes

1   Although the Angel of Death is present and the name Azrael appears in both Christianity and Judaism, Azrael is more established in Islam, where he is one of the archangels alongside Mikhail (Michael), Jibril (Gabriel), and Israfil.

Introduction to *Almas*
Muhaned Al-Hadi

I wrote this play in 2019, as an artist-in-residence, funded by the Nora program at La Chartreuse Cnes de Villeneuve lez Avignon in France. The work was first performed by students of the Conservatoire à rayonnement régional de Lyon. It was later nominated for the best translated play in Rhone-Alpes and was presented as a theatrical reading with professional actors in Théâtre Nouvelle Génération, Lyon.

This play is about the enslavement and captivity of Yazidi and Christian women in northern Iraq by ISIS in 2014. When I was in France, I spoke with the dramaturge about my intention to write about a real event that occurred years ago in Iraq. He was shocked and said he had heard nothing of it. The group of students who presented the show thought the play was a product of imagination. It came as a huge shock when they learned that these were real events. Thus, this play provides a much-needed documentation of this unknown tragedy amidst the silence and indifference of Arab theatre.

The world fell silent about the genocide of Yazidis and Christians, including Arab writers. Very few novels and plays attempted to address this tragedy. In total, there were five plays and two novels. Arab theatre artists are afraid to address this story for many reasons, foremost among them is the artists' sectarian prejudices. I was unsure if this play would see the stage, not because of the complexity of the text, but because the play would not sell in the Arab world. *Almas* is a painful story that reflects an opportunistic world, and if it were in any other country, it would have gained wide recognition.

Almas

Muhaned Al-Hadi

Characters

Almas
Director
Fouad
Susan
Janet
Abdullah
Father
Man

The stage is a gray fabric box. In the middle of this box, there's a transparent fabric window facing the audience, allowing them to see what's behind it. Behind it, there's a window similar to American interrogation rooms, transforming later into various shapes including a door, a prison, and multiple rooms. On the ceiling, there's a net dripping with red and black colors. Through the fabric facing the audience, there's a person in the center of the box who can be seen through the windows. This person starts speaking as if they're continuing a conversation.

Director's Voice Individuals who commit terrorist acts are usually part of a familial network and have affiliations with closed groups, which can be tribal, cultural, national, religious, or political. The conditions for killing innocent people through acts of terrorism, genocide, or the abduction and rape of women historically occur when a certain group faces the fear of being annihilated by another group. It is a means of self-defense. But you say there was no separatist sentiment in your village, so how did all these killers and thieves emerge?

Almas That's the truth, everyone in the village was surprised by what happened.

Director Then . . . (*Silence.*) then . . . (*Silence.*) and then?

Almas When the black cars armed with weapons came and took us to a large schoolyard . . .

Director Stop. You jumped ahead in your story; I'll remind you of what you were talking about.

Replays the recorded dialogue of **Almas***'s voice.*

Almas's Recorded Voice There were no signs of division in our village before . . . We were all united, and each of us worshiped God in our own way. In our village, the Muslim calls to prayer mixed with church bells and the voices of our Yazidi preachers.

Almas On a summer morning, I was ten years old. The villagers were sleeping on the rooftops because of the intense heat. At dawn, I heard the Eid prayer call: "Allahu Akbar, Allahu Akbar," announcing the Muslims' Eid. No, no, it was our Eid, it was the Eid for all the people of the village.[1] I placed some bricks next to the wall to climb on,[2] looked out onto the street, and saw large crowds heading to the nearby mosque. Among them were my father and uncles, standing at the mosque's door. My father, who was the eldest among his brothers, would put on his best clothes and cologne and go out with his brothers at dawn, congratulating each other on the holiday. My mother woke up before us, preparing the holiday pastries.

Director Stop. Could you . . .

Almas It's a morning dish made of milk, rice, and some sugar. I would carry the plates with joy, knocking on doors to deliver them to the neighbors. And in the morning, I would put on clothes my mother bought for me for this occasion and run to the large square. By the way, the large square wasn't really large, but it seemed big in our eyes as children. There we, the children, would play our favorite game, hide and seek. I'm no good at this game, and they always found my hiding spot easily. It was a strange moment; I was afraid of losing and having to search for others. He was with me. (*Silence.*) He held my hand and said, "Don't be afraid, I'm with you." It was Fouad, our neighbor. He was around the same age as me. I didn't know that many years later his hand would again hold mine, but in a different way and be more cruel!

Director (*interrupting*)   Stop. Can you repeat the last part?

Almas   He held my hand and said, "Don't be afraid . . ."

Director   . . . and after that? Cue.

Almas   It was Fouad, our neighbor. Back then, we used to go to school together along with my cousins, both boys and girls, in the alley where our house was.

Director   Stop! Before we move on to talking about your going to school and coming back, tell us . . . what happened when you were hiding? Cue.

Almas   He held my hand and said, 'Don't be afraid, I'm with you', and he pulled me up the hill. It was the first time I climbed to that place. Oh God, what a magnificent view. How small my village looked. I saw the houses, streets, and minarets from the top of the hill. As we continued to climb, the sounds started fading away gradually the further away we got. He said to me while holding my hand: 'Do you know, Almas?'

Director   Stop.

Almas *turns to him, annoyed.*

Almas   That's my name. I didn't tell you that.

Director   Cue!

Almas   He came closer to me. I wasn't afraid of him for many reasons, first because he was my neighbor, and we spent time together from morning till evening. His voice was trembling, and his breath was getting heavier as he spoke to me. I could feel his heartbeats, and I heard them from a distance. He told me he loved me. I told him I loved him too. He kissed my cheek. His lips were warm and trembling. He said again, "We'll get married when we grow up." I laughed. I was very happy, even though I didn't know what marriage meant. After the game ended, we ran back home.

Director   Scene: Outside, Night, the rooftop of Almas's house, Almas and her mother.

Almas   Like every night, I go up to the rooftop with my mother, father, and brother. I clung to my mother. My brother clung to my father. My mother taught me that if I couldn't fall asleep, I should count the stars and write my daily message to God asking Him to protect our home, then place it under my pillow. But I couldn't sleep that night. My mother woke up to drink water or maybe to use the restroom. She noticed me and said in a hushed voice so as not to wake my father, brother, and the neighbors . . . By the way, we used to hear the sound of the neighbors' son and his new wife when they were together. I didn't understand what those sounds meant, but I learned when I grew up . . .

Director Stop!

*He replays **Almas's Voice** from the previous dialogue.*

Almas's Voice She noticed me and said in a hushed voice so as not to wake my father, brother, and the neighbors.

Director Continue. Cue.

Almas "My dear, why haven't you slept yet?" my mother asked me. So I said, "Mom, what does marriage mean?" She laughed softly and said, "It means you leave us and go to another house with a husband, and you give birth to children and become a mother." "Will I become a mother?" I asked, and she laughed with a slightly higher pitch, causing me to put my hand over my mouth so my father wouldn't wake up. (*Light laughter.*) "Why did you ask that?" my mother said. I replied with fear of her reaction, "Fouad told me he loves me and he'll marry me when we grow up." My mother pulled me close to her chest and said in a tender voice, "Fouad, our neighbor?" I nodded. "His father is a friend of your father, and his mother is like my sister. We know them well. But you can't marry him." I imagined myself in an Indian movie, and in the end Fouad would be my brother. "Why, Mom?" I asked. She said, "Because our religion doesn't allow us to marry outside our religion." I reflected, "Religion? Our religion? Outside our religion?" "What does religion mean, Mom?" "It's the path to God," she said. "Don't Fouad and his family know this path?" I asked. She responded, "Yes, they know it, but in a different way. Listen, my daughter, we have our own religion, and they have theirs. That's what I can tell you. Sleep and don't think about these things. You're still a child in these things." I didn't sleep that night. Our village remained the same; nothing changed. Fouad would still look at me from a distance and do anything I asked. But I remembered something important. (*She falls silent.*)

Director What is it? Almas, where did your thoughts wander? Speak, what have you recalled?

Almas The occupying army had settled in our country, and we saw them everywhere. One morning, as we walked towards school like any other day, Fouad told me: "My mother told me I'll have lunch at your place today. My parents went to the city for medical tests." I wouldn't see the city until I grew up, when they hung a piece of cardboard around my neck that had written on it a number and a price.

Director Cut. (**Almas** *looks towards the window.*)

Almas I apologize . . . Maybe that day was the most beautiful day of my life. We had lunch together and studied together. By the way, my mother no longer remembered our conversation about marrying Fouad. That night Fouad slept at our house. The next morning, the news spread in the village . . . On their way back, a U.S. patrol killed Fouad's parents. The next day, I saw their bodies being carried and the village bid them farewell in a solemn funeral attended by everyone. There was no separate cemetery for Muslims, Christians, and Yazidis. In death, all were equal before just as they were in life . . . Nothing differentiated or divided them. Fouad stood by my side, I held his trembling hand . . . I embraced him, and we cried together. Fouad took his suitcase and went to live with his uncle in the neighboring village, but Fouad changed after his parents' death. He disappeared suddenly for several months! Some said he had left the country, some said he was killed, and some said he had a fight with his uncle's wife and left the house, and no one knew his whereabouts. But the truth . . .

Director's Voice "Fouad was arrested by U.S. forces after being identified by someone involved in killing a group of American soldiers. They confessed that Fouad was transporting supplies for them on a motorcycle, and no one would suspect him due to his young age. After six months, he was released from prison." Cue.

Almas He returned to our village; everything about him was different: his appearance, his clothes, everything indicated a change. Even the way he spoke changed. He started expressing his hatred for Americans loudly, and he kept showing up at the village in different cars and playing recitations of the Quran on the car stereo, turning up the volume. When he approached me, he turned off the Quran and greeted me, his eyes fixed on the ground.

Director What happened next . . . Remember well. Cue.

Almas After several years, from my rooftop, I saw smoke rising from the neighboring villages. The surrounding villages were set on fire. My father came and carried whatever he could, saying, "Let's escape to the mountains." All the villagers were running and screaming, not knowing which path would be safe to escape from these killers. My father changed his route more than once . . . Each time we saw people running like us, telling us a different story. Dust from the car wheels covered our faces and clothes, and we headed towards the mountain. My father was behind the wheel, and beside him was my mother. My brother, his wife, and I, we sat in the back.

Director A documentary film must contain all the details of your life, but you didn't tell me your brother got married. When did he get married and where? Cue.

Almas I apologize. My brother grew up quickly, and my father wanted to celebrate his son's wedding before he died. Those were my father's words, and I left school due to the sectarian war, the bombings of schools and institutes, and the killings based on identity. My brother's wedding was the best in the village. Everyone danced and celebrated with us; we all danced as a group again and again. Then, his hand reached for mine . . . (*She smiles.*)

Director Whose hand? Fouad's?

Almas No, Karawan, the brother of my brother's wife.

Director's Voice After the arrival of the black banners[3] in the surrounding villages, he was found dead along with others from his village. Cue!

Almas (*sad*) Karawan . . . a polite and shy young man who speaks in a soft voice, always smiling. It was planned that we would get married later that summer.

Director (*repeating* **Almas***'s words*) My father was behind the wheel, and beside him was my mother. My brother, his wife, and I, we sat in the back.

Almas My father was driving the car like a madman, desperately trying to reach a safe place. Due to the abundance of swirling dust, my father stopped driving, and after the dust cleared, we found ourselves surrounded by a group of black cars.

Black droplets fall from the ceiling.

They looked strange, armed men with long hair and beards. Silence overwhelmed everything. We could hear the beats of our hearts; my brother held my hand and embraced his wife with the other hand. Minutes felt like an eternity . . . no one spoke. They were many, too many. Their faces were similar, identical in everything. They carried the same appearance, the same sound, matching movements, and even though their languages differed, their meanings were the same.

Bell sound.

Director Stop!

Almas Yes, they spoke various languages, but they had one steadfast goal—our bodies. They are many in number but one in purpose, means, and thinking. Amidst all this silence, Fouad emerged. Our neighbor Fouad, a childhood friend, had changed. He now looks like them, wearing the same clothes and carrying the same expression on his face and the same voice. Fouad said, "You're our people, and what's happening to you is happening to us too. Evil won't touch you as long as I am here. Go back to where you came from, and our men will accompany you."

Almas My father felt reassured hearing Fouad's words, as he was our neighbor and his father was my father's friend, and his mother was my mother's friend. Of course, he felt reassured. We returned home.

Silence.

Director Night, Almas's house, in her room. Cue.

Almas Fear pervades the place, the night changes, silence fades away, and now we hear gunfire and explosions. Where did all this madness come from? From which cave did these armies emerge? These faces do not know how to smile. How did this hair and beard grow so quickly? It takes months to have such length. How can they look like this? (*Sarcastically.*) Is it possible they are wearing wigs? I search for something that proves I'm dreaming. How can a person sleep, only to wake up in a different place and time? My message to God will be different tonight. It's not just our house that is in danger, but all the people in the village. No one can sleep in our village . . . not even the grandmothers. Sleeplessness and fear are haunting us. Why doesn't nightfall bring calm? Nightmares roam freely, dancing around me. Dreams, on the other hand, have left and don't return. Only people living in fear can understand what I'm saying. I am scared. My father smokes in the courtyard, my mother puts the edges of her headscarf in her mouth as if chewing on it and my brother and his wife are clinging to each other. I want to sleep, I used to sleep like a flowing river . . . How can you sleep or find solace when you hear death walking in the corners of your room and hiding in your closet? After hours of anxiety, exhaustion takes over, and perhaps I dozed off from sheer fatigue.

Father's Voice Running from death is death, seeking death is life, fearing weariness is weariness, and embracing weariness is rest. Freedom is the tree of eternity, and its water is drops of spilled blood.

Almas I woke up with this saying echoing in my mind accompanied by my father's voice. (**Almas**'s *voice mixed with the father's voice:*) Running from death is death, seeking death is life, fearing weariness is weariness, and embracing weariness is rest. Freedom is the tree of eternity, and its water is drops of spilled blood. I woke up from a sleep of unknown duration. My father was predicting the future to us. I cried then because my father was clearly worried about my mother, my brother, his wife, and me. My mother worries about my father, my brother, his wife, and me. My brother worries about his wife, my father, my mother, and me. My brother's wife worries only about my brother. But as for me, I fear losing everything: my father, my mother, my brother, his wife, her brother, our house, and everything that makes me feel that I'm still alive. I remembered Karawan at that moment. I don't know why I remembered him. Is it fear? Karawan was a human being. (*Interrupted by an external voice.*)

External Voice All residents are ordered to the large school on the outskirts of the village—men, women, children, elders. House inspections will follow, and those who fail to attend will be held responsible.

The announcement is repeated as a background to **Almas***'s speech.*

Almas In that exact moment, I wondered if it is possible for us to finally live in a world that is free of all these difficulties? I asked my mother that day, "Mother, is that possible?" But my mother didn't answer me. My father stood in the middle of the street with the pride and dignity I knew, his cane creating rhythm as it hit the ground. Behind him, my mother walked, followed by my brother and his wife, and me.

Black droplets falling from the ceiling.

I repeated my question to her: "Is it possible for us to finally live in a world that is free of all these difficulties?" I asked my mother that day, "Mother, is that possible?" She didn't answer me! I should've told her, too: "We're travelers in the desert of this life, women traveling in a stormy night, subject to being abducted by this thief or that! Have you experienced fear? A woman walking on the street, for example, hearing hurried footsteps behind her? She hears shoes clacking on the pavement, speeding up if she speeds up, slowing down if she slows down. Feeling eyes, eyes like those of predatory animals, observing and stalking her, glowing with an eerie brightness in the darkness? Hearing the night's whispers as she walks, her heart pounding, fearing even her own heartbeat? Imagining lifeless things moving? Hearing voices from everywhere? The school isn't far, yet it's become farther than a dream or its realization."

Director Cut. School courtyard. A group of men and women.

Almas They separated us into men on the right (*Gestures the men's area.*) and women on the left (*Gestures the women's area.*), armed men surround us from all sides. (*Gestures to the position of the men.*) All the villagers were looking, waiting for

Fouad. But he didn't come. Fear and anxiety started growing among the villagers. Maybe Fouad would arrive any moment now. They led out all the men and elderly women from the school. But Fouad didn't come. We heard gunshots . . . (*Red droplets fall from the ceiling.*) but Fouad didn't come.

Man Quiet . . . Quiet . . . Married women, stand on the right, unmarried women on the left. Whoever lies will be punished; after a few minutes, there will be a doctor to examine virginity.

Almas Some women switch lines. The moment I cannot forget and will never be erased from my mind, how can a man take a girl who isn't even ten years old away from her mother? How? How can a man shamelessly run his hand all over your body while you are silent and unable to object or speak? How? Their filthy fingers, like claws, tearing into your flesh as they pass by. Cries of women and children mix with each other. They start to take virgin women first. The screaming continued . . . A thick hand reached out for me, grabbed me by the chest and pulled me along. It had an odor I had never smelled before. I screamed at the top of my lungs, "Mother, save me, oh Mother!" My poor mother was also desperately looking for someone to save her. My screams mingled with the screams of other girls and children. Suddenly, another hand pulled me as if I were inside a cage, and this hand was the one that set me free. Oh God, it's Fouad's hand. I cried when I looked at him, "They took my mother and father, Fouad! Please, Fouad, save my father, mother, and brother!" He turned to me and pulled me by the hand, leading me out of the school. On the way, I saw black cars brimming with weapons filling the area around the school. I was speaking and crying, "Fouad, please, why don't you answer me? Fouad . . . Fouad!" I looked out of the car window and saw a mound of bodies. I couldn't distinguish who was in them, but I saw . . . (*Red droplets start falling on her body. And she begins to dance, but in a lamenting way.*) I saw it. It's my father's cane lying near that mound.

"Fouad . . . They killed my father!"
"Fouad . . . They killed my mother!"
"Fouad . . . They killed my brother!"

She dances until she falls to the ground.

Director Fouad's house. A room. There's nothing particularly noteworthy in this room, except for writings on the walls, probably left by people who used to live here. Stains of blood are everywhere. In the background, Fouad has set up a basin of water and started washing.

Almas *regains consciousness after being violated by* **Fouad**. **Fouad**, *naked, pours water on himself.*

Almas How could you commit such a heinous act? Your action resembles your pitiful face. How could you forget our love and closeness? Aren't you ashamed of my father's joy on your graduation day? Aren't you ashamed of my mother's bread when you were hungry? Aren't you ashamed of my tears when I bid your parents farewell? Will you remain silent? Speak! Answer me!

Fouad I fulfilled a childhood dream . . . and now I'm done with it.

Almas   Those childhood dreams were beautiful. Why did you tarnish them? You were, for me, the memory of my innocent childhood. Could it be that you're the same Fouad I knew? The one I wanted to be close to more than anyone else?

Fouad   That time is gone, never to return. Now . . . you're my captive.

Almas   I'm your captive?

Fouad (*putting on his clothes*)   Yes, you're mine. I'll do with you as I please, and you must obey my orders whenever I ask. There are a thousand sharia boundaries you must not cross with me.

Almas   I don't belong to anyone, and I never will. I won't obey anyone's orders.

Fouad   Each time you resist me, a trashing from my switch will be waiting for you.

Almas   If my body awaits your switch, in time my body will triumph over you. Hit me whenever you want, but I won't be anyone's possession.

Black droplets fall from the ceiling. **Almas** *is alone in her place, and in the background,* **Fouad** *is dressed.*

Almas   I couldn't imagine you would become like this . . . unleashing the whistle of death everywhere, giving out death shrouds as gifts to everyone. What happened to you? Why did you turn from a lover into a gravedigger? You've lost your mind. I waited for you to save us. I wasn't the only one waiting for you. We all waited. What's wrong with you? What changed you?

Fouad   Praise be to God, I seek God's forgiveness, God is great.

Almas   God is great . . . Do you often remember hearing 'God is great'? I also remember it.

The sound of Eid prayer echoes, and she dances as she did in childhood.

Fouad (*praying*)   Allahu Akbar!

Almas   It used to be followed by the joy of Eid.

Fouad (*kneels, prostrates, and stands*)   God is great.

Almas   It used to mean new clothes.

Fouad (*kneels, prostrates, and stands*)   God is great.

Almas   It used to be joy and caressing for both young and old.

Fouad (*kneels, prostrates, and stands*)   God is great.

Almas   The Eid swing set is replaced by . . .

Red droplets fall from the ceiling.

Fouad (*kneels, prostrates, and stands*)   God is great.

Almas   . . . explosions . . .

Fouad (*kneels, prostrates, and stands*)   God is great.

Almas ... killings ...

Fouad (*kneels, prostrates, and stands*)   God is great.

Almas ... rape!

Fouad (*kneels, prostrates, and stands*)   God is great.

Almas   Who stole "God is the greatest" from the joyful Eid and joined it to death and blood? Who restores your soul that has turned into graves, coffins, bloodshed and death?

Fouad   I ask forgiveness from God!

Almas (*laughs*)   You rape and ask for forgiveness, kill and ask for forgiveness?

Fouad   I've done nothing to ask forgiveness for! Forgiveness is a word that is always on the tip of my tongue.

Almas   And what wisdom do you have that permits you to murder the entire universe?

Fouad   I am slaughtering in order to clean this world of its dirt. The world is sick, lying on its deathbed. The earth is waiting for me to make a billion coffins for it, and one coffin big enough for its infection. It is an epidemic of infidels that must be incinerated.

Red droplets fall from the ceiling.

Almas   Who will bring you back as you used to be? You are the story of my childhood that for years I tell myself every night and sleep in its warmth. You are the child in love wearing Eid clothes (*Yelling at him.*) and now I do not know this thing standing in front of me. Your eyes don't look like his—a distorted image, remains of a story!

Fouad (*looking up*)   He wanted me to be like this, so I was!

Almas   Who is he?

Fouad   God. I am a fire of his creation.

Almas   You are a fire made by your own hands.

Fouad   I implement the law of mercy ... I purify this universe by killing.

Almas   And who made you God, the One, Independent and Besought of all?

Fouad   I don't care about your words.

Almas   How sad it is to believe our own lies?!

Fouad   I want the afterlife, oh ...

Almas (*interrupting*)   What? Say it.

Fouad (*with difficulty*)   O infidel!

Almas   Infidel? Go ahead and shed my blood, take out your knife and slaughter me. I am not your captive, I am a woman who left your place, time, face, and language, and no longer belongs to you. What are you waiting for? Come on, take out your knife and slaughter me facing the Qiblah here. (*Pointing to her heart.*) This is our Qiblah for people with no guardians.[4]

Fouad Almas, tomorrow morning you will leave this house.

Fouad *disappears.* **Almas** *begins to draw.*

Director's Voice All the events of this film were taken from real stories that took place in an identifiable place and time. On the third of August 2014, many women belonging to the Yazidi religion were taken captive. Human Rights Watch issued a new report stating that more than 3,000 girls were kidnapped and taken by ISIS as captives. ISIS members took turns raping these women, buying and selling them, and killing them if they no longer needed them. The prices for Yazidi women in the ISIS market varied according to several factors. The price ranged from a thousand dollars to two cigarettes for a girl. And because we want to treat the topic comprehensively and not only associate it with that particular region—and, at the same time, what happened here can happen to any other minority in the world—we decided not to specify the place and time of the events within the film so that the story is not limited by any given date.

Director shifts. **Fouad***'s house. Living room.* **Almas** *sitting alone at home drawing shapes and dreaming of them. Three men enter. She gets up frightened.*

Man You will come with us!

Almas Where?

Man Your master has sold you to another master.

Almas Can I speak with Fouad for a minute?

Director's Voice Fouad was arrested in Berlin after being identified by a woman he raped, and he is now in prison awaiting sentencing.

Man He has become forbidden for you, and you are not allowed to talk to him. You have to get up quickly, and if you refuse, I'll drag you by your hair. Come on get up!

Director Stop! Almas, would you . . .

Almas *starts an expressionistic dance with movements on the ground, expressing what she went through with these men.*

Director I know that this scene is one of the most difficult scenes that you will perform. You told me that there were three men who pulled you by your hair because you refused to go with them, and they blindfolded you with a black scarf after your face was covered in blood from so many punches, then they brought you into a place that looked like the room you were in before. The three of them took turns on you. You were in pain, but they didn't care. You were screaming in pain, but they thought you were enjoying the sex. They took showers before and after raping you. Why? I know there's no answer, and I know that the reality you experienced was unbearable and horrific. I know that creating a scene like this one, with whatever directorial ingenuity, can't capture or reflect that reality, so we decided to turn this scene into a news report that will say you were raped by three men in one day.

Almas *falls to the ground after the end of the director's speech.*

Director   Almas, are you okay? Can we continue the story? Do you need a break?

Almas   I need two minutes alone.

She sits on a chair in the corner of the stage facing the audience to take a break . . . Silence . . . Nothing moves, and after exactly two minutes we hear the director's voice.

Director's Voice   The market in the city, Almas with an armed group. (*Addressing Almas.*) After you were in the house with the three men for about a month, they took you from the house and to the market. What did they do?

Almas   Before we left, they took off all my clothes, put me in the bathroom, and they sprayed me with a water hose as if I were a building on fire. The sound of their reckless laughter and guffaws at my fear still rings in my ears. I never imagined that these were human beings. They dressed me in black, with nothing showing but my eyes, and we walked downtown. The big city that I used to hear about, the people of the village used to go there whenever someone fell ill because our village didn't have a single doctor. The people of the village . . .

Director   Stop! You are now in the city, your story with the village is over.

Almas (*gets angry and screams*)   My story with the village did not end! Every day I miss and yearn for it and its narrow alleys, which seemed so big in the eyes of its people. You control me completely, just like them. You want things to satisfy you, there's no difference between you and them. You exploit my story while they exploited my body. They took everything from me, and you want to take what's left of my soul, my memories. I'm tired, I don't want to continue the film. I want to leave this place.

Director   Almas, I don't control you, and I don't mean to provoke you. I'm afraid of losing the audience's focus. This is the first film about the captivity of women and your village. I'll be the first director to work on this story. That's why I've come up with an excellent strategy to make the film and present it accurately and objectively, befitting the events. We're not talking about that beautiful village now. I want your story to be intense, seen and heard far and wide. I just need you to talk about what happened to you later, with you and your friends.

Almas   You know I wasn't wrong when I compared you to them. I don't understand you. One moment you say you want a sequential narrative, and now you want me to leave behind everything that happened to me in the market and jump to talking about my friends. Tell me what exactly do you want?

Director   I apologize, my dear. Shall we return to the chronological order of events, if you wish?

Almas *nods her head, indicating her agreement to continue the story.*

Almas   Having no doctor in the village, Fouad's father and mother did not get proper treatment and died, and in that moment, Fouad changed and died with them.

The city I had dreamed of seeing one day, I returned to as a captive. Funny how dreams work. The road leading to the big market was crowded, tall lifeless buildings, darkness engulfing the place.

Black droplets fall from the ceiling. She starts drawing shapes on the ground with her feet.

Men's and women's clothes, even their faces, were black. I didn't see a woman walking alone, nor did I see a man without a weapon. They believe a woman is a ticking bomb, and only a man can defuse it.

Director (*laughing*)   It's a joke, isn't it? Please continue.

Almas   I saw an elderly man dragging away a girl barely ten years old, she was crying and pleading with me to save her from him. (*Sarcastically.*) She doesn't see that I need someone to rescue me from those men. I saw men being whipped because they smoked a cigarette, and a woman was whipped for walking alone. A man's hand was cut off because he stole a loaf of bread to eat.

Red droplets start falling.

And one of them had his head cut off because he didn't fight for them. A woman was killed because she was seen with a man without a veil. And a family was stopped and beaten because their children watched cartoons. Of all these cases the one that surprised me most was the man whipped eighty times for smiling. What a joke and what a punishment! Smile . . . Imagine being whipped because you smiled. (*Laughs hysterically.*) What kind of religion and culture hate smiling? (*Laughs and then stops.*) At that moment, I wished to laugh hysterically.

She laughs quietly, then gradually starts laughing loudly.

Director   Stop!

Almas *returns to her story.*

Almas   They stopped me in the middle of the square; they exposed our faces and placed small signs with our prices on them. (*Painful sarcasm.*) I'm worth $1,000, that's the price for anyone who wants to buy me. Numbers . . . now I am just a number.

Seller (*loudly*) You need to forget your name, your birth, your religion, your history. Now, you're just a number. Remember your number. You're number 214. (*Calling out loud.*) This blonde captive looks like a German girl, her hair is blonde, and her eyes are blue. Check her out. Only a thousand US dollars. Examine her with your hands. Purchased goods are neither returnable nor exchangeable. Our product is intact.

Almas   The hands that reached out to examine my body were like knives. It was painful. They reached everywhere on the body, nothing was forbidden, and no action embarrassed them. Everywhere, above, below, a hand extended to . . . (*Gestures downwards between her thighs.*)

Director   Stop! What happened next? Cue.

Almas A procession with the provincial judge passed by. The city seemed calmer when he came. An old sheikh, his beard colored like a rainbow, reaching his navel. I smiled secretly because he reminded me of a cartoon character David the Gnome.[5] He turned to me, perhaps sensing my hesitant smile. His gaze was foolish in my eyes, and before he could ask about my price, the seller shouted at the top of his lungs, "It's a gift!" He gave me to him as a gift, relinquishing a thousand dollars just to gain favor with the judge. I was given away for free. (*Laughs.*) How can someone imagine that they are worth nothing?! Perhaps having a price is painful, but the most painful thing is that I am worth nothing. Damn you and your father! You dog, you son of a dog! Selling me for free, you son of a bitch! Didn't your mother teach the value of a woman?! Or perhaps you never had a mother to begin with. I'm for free?! (**Almas***'s voice comes from offstage, and she starts moving and drawing.*) I was scared, Mom, when my feet stumbled upon their many slogans on the narrow pavement. Each slogan carried the voice of its speaker, and people trampled on everything without noticing. I was the only one who noticed me sitting beside an old tree, and I cried. I cried bitterly, Mom, because I mourned for memories and homes. I feared for the fading colors, mourned the tearing of your dress. I remembered my old messages to God. Perhaps they never reached Him or got stuck in place. I was scared for my voice that got lost in betrayals. Nothing matters to me anymore, neither my body nor my memories. All of it shattered. I remained alone. I used to boast about every kick to my stomach by the bearded man, as if they were a badge of honor for me. Today, I'm here. No one kicks me anymore because I'm in a safe place, but I'm afraid, Mom, for . . .

Director Stop! Judge's house, a room in the house, Almas, Susan, Janet. Action.

Almas The judge had many guards. They were all armed, but there was one among them who seemed closer. His name was Abdullah. Abdullah used to come to us, the three of us. There were two girls with me. In the beginning, we didn't talk to each other. Anything was possible. Both were scared that I might be a spy sent by the judge to uncover their secrets. Days passed. I don't know how much time has gone by while I'm here. The details of time don't occupy you. Whether it's day or night, all that connects me to time is the portions of food thrown at me, and I keep counting the time. When the third "morsel" is thrown, you know it's evening, and also keep a count of violations against the body . . . At that point, we became friends. I sleep here, the Syrian Susan is on my right, and Janet is on my left. At night, we used to tell stories about everything that happened to us. After that, we became friends liked we'd known each other for years. They told me what happened to them, how they were abducted, sold to several people, and then gifted like me to the judge.

Almas *lies down in* **Susan***'s place and starts telling* **Susan***'s story.*

Susan said, I come from a leftist family.

Almas (*moves to her place*) Leftist? What does leftist mean?

Susan[6] (*laughs*) I'll tell you about it another time. Then she continued . . .

Director   "A free country and happy people" was the slogan raised on October 28, 1924, when the leftist seed was planted.[7] It focused on the human trinity of "consciousness, revolution, and ethics."

Almas *moves to* **Janet***'s place and mimics how she used to laugh, then returns to continue* **Susan***'s story.*

Susan   My mother is Russian. My father married her after the Syrian government sent him to the Soviet Union in the late 1980s. My mother was beautiful, tall, like a movie star. We lived our lives without mingling with those around us, not getting into the details of religion. We had a very large library. My mother always read. We had all the books of Russian literature. There was no Quran or Bible in our house. That's what my father and mother decided. I was born into this atmosphere. My uncles disowned my father for marrying my mother many years ago. For work, my father moved to a city on the border. Our house was a socialist model. My mother and father brought our furniture from the Soviet Union. If you enter our house, it's like entering a Russian house in the late 1980s. The only difference was the weather.

Director   Stop. We're not here to describe the place. What matters to me are the actions of the characters.

Almas (*continuing without looking at the director*)   After the city was taken over, my father decided that we should leave. We got into the car. On the way, an armed group set up a checkpoint. After talking to my father and giving them our papers, we told them we were Muslims. However, there was nothing indicating that we were. They started asking us questions.

Man's Voice   Are you Christian, Shiite, Alawite, Yazidi, or Muslim?

Father   Yes, I am a Muslim, and this is my wife and my daughter.

Man's Voice   Are they Muslims too?

Susan   Yes, we are Muslims.

Man's Voice (*loudly*)   Shut up, you! I'm talking to your father. Tell her to be quiet.

Father   Yes, we are Muslims. I am a professor at the university, and this is my wife and my daughter.

Man's Voice   We'll give you water. We want you to perform ablution in front of us.

Almas   Susan told me that her father held the water bucket, but he did not know to perform the ablution.

Man's Voice   Do you know the call to prayer? The direction of the Qibla? The number of daily prayers? The number of prostrations in the Dhuhr prayer?

Almas   But her father didn't answer any of those questions. Her father and mother were killed because they were of a different faith. Susan was taken captive and passed from one man to another until she ended up in the house of the old judge.

Director   It seems you're diverging from the story, Almas.

Almas *doesn't respond to him.*

Almas's Voice There were two girls with me in the judge's house. In the beginning, we didn't talk to each other. Anything was possible. Both were scared that I might be a spy sent by the judge to uncover their secrets.

Almas (*continuing the story*) As for the second woman, that was Janet. She was light-hearted, sarcastic and funny, making us laugh with her. Even when she was in pain, she turned her pain into sarcasm.

Director Stop. Stop narrating this. I want you to go back to the core of the story.

Almas I won't say whatever you want me to. I'll say what I experienced, what I and the girls went through . . .

Director This narrative is not included in the film script.

Almas Who wrote this script? Come on, answer me. I don't care about you or your film. I'll lay bare for the world all the wounds that have scarred my soul.

Director Your voice will reach everyone in the world through this film. We're expecting festivals and major awards.

Almas You're the one who's expecting, not me. You'll be called a supporter of women's rights, fighting against discrimination, rape, and the violence that we've gone through. You'll earn millions, be interviewed, and you'll become a global celebrity. My story and my body will be a bridge to your world of fame. I will tell my story the way I experienced it, not the way you want it.

Director Please, Almas, listen to me carefully and try to understand my perspective.

Almas *continues while the director is still arguing and then he falls silent as if giving in to what* **Almas** *wants to say.*

Almas She used to call the old man the Frogman. We were puzzled by her description. She said when he takes off his clothes, his skinny legs, hunched shoulders, and saggy belly make him look like a frog. And she made fun of how he asked for a massage and then lay down snoring while she massaged him. She told me that she tried to escape once, but the attempt failed, and she was caught. The judge ordered his men to rape her. There were about ten men.

Janet I couldn't control my legs anymore. They were like hungry beasts. Just one person . . .

Director Stop . . . I don't understand. You say there were ten, and then you say one person?

Almas (*upset for being interrupted*) One person treated her with respect.

Abdullah *enters the scene.*

Abdullah Don't be afraid of me. I was forced to do this to you, but I don't want to do it.

Janet And what am I supposed to do now?

Abdullah I don't know, but I want to stay here longer so you can get rest.

Janet But you're one of them. You're wearing their clothes. Your smell is like theirs.

Abdullah I don't have to respond to you.

Janet You don't have to answer. It's the truth. You're one of them. There are seven of them, and you're the eighth. Monsters!

Abdullah If you don't quiet down, I'll leave, and someone else will come in. Please calm down.

Janet Calm down? (*Laughs loudly.*)

Abdullah Shh . . . be quiet. Don't raise your voice. Please.

Janet *laughs. There's a knock on the door.* **Abdullah** *takes off his clothes and goes out to them.*

Abdullah She's crazy. No one can sleep with her.

Janet This man tried to prevent them from violating me, but he didn't succeed. (*Sarcastically.*) I got severely beaten that day.

Almas The first time the judge called me to his room, they forced me to shower and wear transparent clothes that revealed almost every detail of my body. They all wished to devour every inch of my body. I entered the room . . . It felt like a dream. He didn't speak Arabic. He came out of the shower, with a bath towel wrapped around him. (*I lowered my head to the ground, but I covertly watched him.*) His body was hairless, and his chest was saggy . . . I saw all of that when he removed the towel from his body.

Janet's Voice When he takes off his clothes, his skinny legs, hunched shoulders, and saggy belly make him look like a frog.

Almas He thought I was happy about what was happening. His hand trembled like a bare tree, a hand devoid of human features. Every time he approached me, Janet's voice echoed in my head, and I laughed. He took my hand and placed it on his chest, yes . . . as if it were a piece of cloth. And I laughed. Everything was absurdly comical. After he finished his filthy act, he collapsed beside me. All I heard was his snoring. I didn't know where to go, whether to leave or wait. What a dilemma. I stayed in his room until dawn.

Judge I am very pleased with you. You're better than all the women I've known.

Almas (*calling loudly*) Abdullah!

Abdullah (*entering*) Yes, Your Honor.

Director Sharia Court, Action.

Almas Abdullah took me in his private car without a word or any explanation. I entered the Sharia court, a large hall adorned with pictures of many women, each with a number. They took a photo of me and assigned me a new number. Then they fingerprinted me on some papers, making me an official wife of the judge. (*Laughs.*) An official wife of the Sharia judge without him even being present or my consent as the law requires. It seems like a joke. (*Laughs, then becomes serious.*)

Director Did you remember something new, Almas?

Almas (*nods her head*) Yes. When I left the hall, among the hanging pictures, I saw Hajar's photo.

Director Who's Hajar?

Almas She's my brother's wife. Her name is Hajar. Maybe I didn't tell you her name before . . .

Director's Voice A significant reward has been offered to anyone who finds Hajar, but unfortunately, up until now, she hasn't been found. Like many Yazidi girls.

Almas She loved my brother deeply. I don't know where my brother is now. Maybe they've killed him too . . . Perhaps . . .

Director's Voice After suffering an injury due to random gunfire, and when the armed men thought they had killed all of the villagers, Almas's brother emerged from the bodies. He managed to escape. After several months, he was transferred to Europe for treatment. He is currently living alone, awaiting Hajar, and managing an organization named *Almas*, dedicated to rescuing Yazidi women captives.

Almas In the evening, they used to slide the food to us under the door. Strangely, this time, along with the food, there was a cellphone.

Abdullah No one's here tonight. You can use the phone to call your families and reassure them.

Almas Susan held the phone, looked at it, and said: "We're a proletarian family. My father refused to promote mobile companies. After the landlines went down, my father decided to buy a single phone that would be available to us." After a few minutes, she handed the device to Janet. She called a number, and for the first time, I heard her burst into tears.

Janet (*on the phone*) Daddy, it's me, Janet. Don't worry about your daughter. I'm still alive, Daddy. I'm okay, don't worry. (*She mutes the phone and speaks to* **Susan** *and* **Almas**.) They don't know what we've experienced, things no creature on this earth can bear. (*Back on the phone.*) Daddy, reassure Mom and everyone that one day I will be free. Soon, I'll attempt to escape again and again until God helps me escape. Kisses and hugs.

She puts the phone on the ground and pushes it away.

Abdullah Quickly, you need to call quickly before the guards return.

Almas My father, mother, and brother have been killed. I know this. And I saw Hajar's picture in the court. But I only remember one number, our home number. And I know no one will answer . . . (*She dials the number.*) Someone answer . . .

please . . . (*She places the phone in the tray and pushes it towards* **Abdullah**.) We remained in silence for hours . . . and nothing moved . . . except tears streaming from our eyes . . .

Susan Can someone tell me what day it is?

Voice of a Guard Sleep now. I don't want to hear any noise.

Lights turned off.

Director Almas, Susan, and Janet lying in the darkness. Nothing is clear except the guard's movements in the background. Action.

Susan (*whispers*) What day is it?

Janet Thursday, I think.

Susan I thought it's Saturday.

Almas I think it's Tuesday . . .

Susan How long have we been here?

Janet I believe it's been two weeks . . .

Susan I think it's longer . . .

Almas We've been here for three months.

Susan How do you know?

Almas I've had my menstrual cycle three times while we were here, and before that, when I was with Fouad, it happened twice.

Janet We've been here before you arrived, but this damn period hasn't come yet!

Susan Is it possible that I'm pregnant?

Janet Is it possible? I might be pregnant too. But who will be the father of the bastard son inside me?

Susan Ten men took turns violating me . . . does it belong to one of them or will all of them share it?

Almas Me, ten men assaulted me!

Janet Thank God that you're not pregnant.

Susan Do you believe it? To be carrying the child of a man I don't even love? This is something I never could imagine. All the stories I've read never wrote about this . . .

Janet What will I tell the baby when it's born and asks about its father? Should I say your father is from East Asia or North Africa? Or that he's a sectarian from my country?

Susan Can you imagine what they will look like, their smell and height? I don't want this strange creature to come into this life. We already have enough of these creatures guarding our nights with their darkness.

Janet When I was a child, I used to put a small pillow under my clothes and walk around pretending to be pregnant. But now, I don't want this memory anymore.

Director Stop. Almas, is it possible that only the other women were talking, and you were silent?

Almas I have nothing to say. I wasn't pregnant like them, and there was no light. The voices came to me. From the left I could hear Susan's voice, and on my right Janet's voice. As I turned left and right, gradually my friends' voices faded, and I dozed off. That night, I had a strange dream.

Director What is it?

Almas It's as if I escaped from this room, and they are chasing me, trying to catch me. They were a group of naked men, and I was searching for any place to hide. I ran, and they ran after me until I reached a lake. This lake had a strange shape, and the men chasing me all stopped at the edge of that lake. (*Red droplets fall from the ceiling.*) The lake's water was red like blood. After a while, I realized that it was blood. Yes, it was blood. I was in the middle of a lake of blood, but this time it was the blood of my friends. I screamed . . . I cried. Janet died by suicide. She killed herself while laughing, just as she had lived. Susan, the Syrian intellectual, killed herself. I was lying among my dead friends. My dress clung to my body; my body fed on the blood of my friends. I was struck by a strange hysteria. They killed themselves using an empty metal plate. They shared the plate just as we used to share things in life. Why didn't they tell me what they were planning? They killed themselves so they wouldn't give birth to a deformed child who wouldn't know his father. (**Abdullah** *enters.*) Janet was sleeping like this (*Imitates* **Janet***'s sleeping posture.*), and Susan was sleeping like this. (*Imitates* **Susan***'s sleeping posture.*)

Abdullah This is your only chance to escape. You must be quieter.

Almas Quieter to get out of here. At what price? The blood of my friends?

Abdullah That's their fate . . . and your fate is to leave this place because of this. If you want to get out of here, sleep among your friends and don't move.

Almas All the men stood over the three bodies, including Abdullah. The men's comments disturbed the dead more than the living. Three bodies stained entirely red were placed in the back of a pickup truck.

Man's Voice She was laughing during her orgasm, and this one was silent, and this one was gentle, and this one was cold, and this one was sexy . . .

Director's Voice Neither death nor the sight of blood made these men ashamed or even silent. Their vileness was greater than the sight of death. Almas, Susan, and Janet were in the back of the truck, and at the front, Abdullah was driving the car. Whenever he was stopped at a security checkpoint, he would tell them that there were three dead infidel women whom he didn't want to bury in the holy state. He wanted to throw them into the desert to become food for wild animals. And when Abdullah arrived in the desert . . .

Director shifts.

Director Desert, daylight, Almas stands by Susan's and Janet's bodies. Action.

Almas Why all this death?

Abdullah I apologize for all the words I said about all of you, but I had no choice.

Almas I couldn't answer him. He washed the girls, buried them, and recited the Fatiha over them. Then he came to me and gave me a bag with a loaf of bread and a bottle of water and said, "Get out of here. You'll be safe." I took two steps and then asked him.

Abdullah I know what you will ask: "Why am I here and why am I working with them?" I'm forced to. I'm from this city. I grew up here and lived my best days here . . . I love my city as it used to be, and I can't live outside its borders. That's why I put on their uniform, to save what I can save. I won't leave here until the last monster among them is out or I'm dead.

Director's Voice After several months, Abdullah was caught trying to smuggle a group of women from this state. His head was cut off in the middle of the city, with the voices of the people of that city chanting "Allahu Akbar."

Almas (*addressing the audience*) "Allahu Akbar." Fouad stole "God is the Greatest," the Eid, the new dress, and the swings. "Allahu Akbar." Who entwined the name of Almighty God with death and rape? It is war. War no longer exists . . . nor does waiting . . . I emerged from this war in this state. (*Her clothes are stained with blood and dirt.*) I am Almas, my name is Almas, which means diamond. One day I asked my father why he named me Almas. He smiled and said, "You are like a diamond. Whether circumstances throw you into a miserable or beautiful place, nothing affects you; you remain a diamond, beautiful." Despite all the pain, sorrow, and loss, my soul is beautiful like a butterfly. I left that place with my memories intact . . . but it is as if whatever's left of my life never existed . . . as if I was reading a terrifying story and dozed off to dream, not a nightmare, but a dream, beautiful. Then I woke up with only a small image in my memory . . . I see my feet walking on warm, soft sand, and the sea caresses me like a memory carried by satisfaction . . . and a great sorrow coming from a wise person's mouth telling me a story of love and betrayal. War no longer exists except in my memory and some traces on my body, but it's over, and the story isn't over yet. My father, mother, brother, friends—I don't know a thing about what happened to them. The war ended, and the loss remains. So that's how I came to be here, and you must imagine what happened to me. After you leave this place, in a few minutes, you might forget my story. Maybe, just maybe, you sympathized with it, and maybe your tears fell for what I went through, maybe. Yes, I admit that. But then? Each of you will return to your world, your life, and your daily concerns . . .

What will you do to save what's left of my friends, whose whereabouts are unknown?

Unfortunately, nothing. Silence, and nothing but silence, and then you'll applaud me and leave.

And I remain alone, just like them . . . completely alone. This is the end of the story, my story only. (*She signals to the audience.*) You can applaud now. Come on, applaud.

Notes

1 Before the 2003 US invasion, it was common for Iraqi Christians and Muslims to celebrate their religious holidays together. In this case, Almas recounts how her whole village—including Christians, Muslims, and Yazidis—celebrated Eid as one community.
2 Rooftops in Iraq have fences.
3 ISIS flew black flags and banners adorned with Arabic script during their campaign in Iraq.
4 The Qiblah is the direction of the Kaaba in the holy city of Mecca, the direction Muslims face in prayer, and a symbol of the unity of the Islamic *ummah* (community). Traditionally, animals slaughtered in keeping with Islamic halal food practices are faced toward the Qiblah. Almas suggests that for people like her, those with no one to protect or care for them, the direction to their hearts is their Qiblah.
5 The titular character from *The World of David the Gnome*, an animated series from Spain which has been dubbed into numerous languages and distributed internationally.
6 The actor playing Almas also plays both Susan and Janet throughout the play.
7 The date appears to refer to the founding of the Syrian communist party, which at its inception in 1924 was the Syrian-Lebanese Communist Party.

Introduction to *Sardanbāl*
Khazal Al-Majidi

The fall of the Assyrian Empire is considered one of the great tragic events in history. After two major Assyrian empires emerged in the modern Assyrian era (746–911 BCE and 745–609 BCE) and following the powerful rule of the Assyrian dynasty with its great kings (Sargon, Sennacherib, Esarhaddon, and Ashurbanipal), weakness suddenly crept into the body of this empire. It collapsed without passing through a prolonged period of decline or weakness. In other words, it fell while still standing on its feet suddenly.

The direct cause of this collapse may have been the series of wars it fought, its excessive use of force, the vast expanse and laxity of its army, and the enormous expenditure on these wars. Greek historians and writers of the Old Testament distorted the history of this empire, portraying the final moments of its collapse in a way that diverges completely from the truth. For instance, the Greek historian Diodorus Siculus depicted the last king of Assyria, whom they call Sardanapalus (a Greek rendering of the name of the king Ashurbanipal II), as a cowardly, weak, and effeminate figure who wore women's clothing and indulged in pleasures.

In reality, this king was attempting to rectify the damages caused by the wars and to reduce the size of the empire, which had become difficult to control due to revolts in distant regions. He was a deeply conflicted human personality, grappling internally. He was indeed a complex figure of the first order.

This play attempts to restore the reputation of Sardanapalus, whom Westerner and Hebrew authors together have maligned. It seeks to explore the real reasons behind the empire's collapse: the corrosive effect of devastating wars, the rampant treachery within its court, the difficulty in controlling revolts on its fringes, and the alliance of enemies around it.

Because this play is a work of art rather than a field of history, I attempt to move away from pure historical context to present Sardanapalus with all his spiritual and psychological tensions, making him a mirror of this end. The play also tries to juxtapose mirrors of the past and present, reflecting events between them clearly, pointing out the tragedy of wars, the dominance of the impulse for death and destruction, the lust for power, the usurpation of freedoms, and the suppression of people.

The present will be the foundation of this theatrical work, and the past will assist in revealing the flaws of this present. Sardanapalus will reveal a hidden tone of tension in the hearts of all people, their aversion to the language of war, death, killing, and destruction. This is an attempt to cleanse our souls, crowded with the pin pricks of the past and present from the games of death and the justifications for killing in the name of nation, values, honor, and principles.

Sardanapalus[1]

Khazal Al-Majidi

Characters

Sardanapalus
Oracle
Queen
Wife
Priestess
Young Priestess
King Ilani
Uballit
Babylonian
Median
Scythian
Deputy King
Army Commander
Servant

Scene One: *A throne that accommodates many.*

The coffin of **King Ilani** *appears in a grand procession majestically carried on the shoulders of soldiers and mourners accompanied by mournful drumbeats.* **Sardanapalus** *is at the head of the procession, accompanied by his mother the queen, his wife, the high oracle, his friend* **Uballit**, *and the army commander.*

Sardanapalus   A king, a son of kings, how does eternity apologize for taking us?

Oracle   The heavens weep . . . the winds mourn . . . the kingdom has passed to you, my lord.

Sardanapalus   Bring out your gold from your chest and scatter it here. (*Points to the top of the coffin.*)

Oracle (*in surprise and wonder*)   I have no chest, nor gold.

Sardanapalus   Then from your brow . . . The birds weep, and we compete for the throne and rule.

Oracle   It is wisdom to see the paths before us, not to turn back.

Sardanapalus   This is no matter of fate, only of design and planning.

Queen   So let us plan the future after the burial rites are complete. (*Kneeling by the coffin.*)
Will you be lifted to greatness, or will the heavens fall upon you?
Why do you hide in these woods?

Will you follow the ascent paths to the mines of the sky?
My moon has collapsed. O springs of nectar, dry up! O depths of water, cloud!
O veins of my conscience, open and drip!

Lays her head on the coffin.

Oracle   Let the hand of glory that your rule made wipe away your tears.

Sardanapalus   Kneel in death? On what?

On a heap of dust! Or on the ecstasy of carrying the crown!
Or on a sad stretch like this in front of the mourning?

Oracle   Be gentle with yourself.

Sardanapalus   Why do I see you exchanging my pain for my praise?
Have I become so vile in your sight?

Oracle   God forbid.

Wife   Let us focus on what must be done.

Sardanapalus   Do you mean the coronation?

Wife   It is your time indeed.

Sardanapalus   My brother's body is still warm.

Wife Do not let lamentation consume your days.

The sound of chanting and music rises. The coffin is lifted and carried out.
Sardanapalus *is carried on a moving throne and placed in the middle of the stage, and then the high oracle stands in front of him.*

Oracle Ashur is the king . . . Ashur is the king.[2]
The hand of Ashur upon your head protects you.
Ashur's bow in your hand opens the horizon of the world.
You are the deputy of the god Ashur and the divine sun for the people.

The **Oracle** *holds a large golden cup filled with perfume. He sprays* **Sardanapalus**. *Then he places the embroidered cloak of the king on* **Sardanapalus***'s shoulders, then places the crown of Ashur on his head and hands him the Anlil scepter.*

The crown on your head, may your feet and arms extended toward Ashur be blessed.
And let your offspring be blessed in your land . . . And make your straight scepter the scales of justice and peace.

The music rises, everyone exits, leaving **Sardanapalus** *alone.*

Sardanapalus Amidst this chaos, like drummers offering fanfare.
A king dies and a king is crowned.
Then, then who said I want to be a king?

I who have scattered my sins and madness along this road and width?
How can I make the stars fall on my officers' shoulders only to rob the sky of its stars!?
And the darkness of the world increases . . . What a mockery!?

Claps with his hands, and **Uballit** *enters pointing to the dress the king wears.*

Sardanapalus Closer to a clown than a king. Isn't that so?

The temple of the god Nabu, the god of divination and prophecy in Ashur.
Sardanapalus *appears wandering, surrounded by incense smoke.*

Sardanapalus (*talking to himself*) And is there anything worse than this?
Where is the gentle hand? And where are the gardens of paradise?
(*Looks at his palm.*) Your palm, if washed with the whole Tigris, won't purify.
(*Looks at his feet.*) And your feet have slipped the right path and made you lost.

Priestess (*appearing as an old woman with a stick and the censer*) Delusions . . . delusions . . . delusions . . .

Delusions paralyze and numb us before the gates of adversity.
And we no longer have the strength to swat a fly or scream.
Your forgiveness, Lord of Sublime. How high we raised you as a banner for our ambitions.

And with you, we conquered hardships to elevate our status.
Your forgiveness Lord, how you were a veil for our aspirations and pleasures!

Sardanapalus Who are you?

Priestess   Why are you wandering here?

Sardanapalus   I am the answer to horizons and scatterer of questions . . .
And these feet of mine have slipped on the path, losing their way . . .
And this hand of mine, even if washed with whole Tigris, won't be cleansed . . .

Priestess   Around you are strange symbols and charms.

Sardanapalus   I wander over a misguided kingdom, finding it silent, veiled in dust.

Priestess (*sitting on the ground with the censer in her lap, adding more incense and prophesying*)   Listen . . . I am compelled to tell you something, no matter what . . .
But your path opposes mine . . .
For every attempt to fathom your future sets back my age.

Sardanapalus (*losing patience*)   I hear you, Mother.

Priestess   Day by day darkness grows around you.
Month by month your sun rots until the tree that supports you falls.

Sardanapalus   A tree?

Priestess   The Tree of Swords . . . a tree growing from your roots.
Recognize yourself, then weave around you a woolen cloak to conceal yourself,
And go to the depth of your wisdom and hide within your shells so you may recover.

Sardanapalus   Oh falcon, return to me what has been absent since my youth.

The first **Priestess** *disappears, and a beautiful* **Young Priestess** *appears, holding a lamb's liver that she reads.*

Young Priestess   Arm the angels with torches of fire, you have become a king.
But the serpents surround you.
And this throne of yours is perforated. You cannot sit upon it!

Sardanapalus (*shocked, indifferent to what he hears*)   I hear the howl of the city.
All of it staggering under the force of the wind.
My hands are cut from excessive waving, urging it to stand against the wind.

Young Priestess   This is the howl of foxes that gnaw at your kingdom,
And the wind, a storm of temptation that will cast down Assyria.

Sardanapalus   And what next?

Young Priestess (*points to the liver*)   Those close to you, who surrounded you
And those distant will vengefully tighten the noose around you.
Your land will boil, and your earth will shrink . . . greatly . . . greatly.

She fades away with her voice.

Sardanapalus   Beneath our palaces lie graves.
And above them, unattainable banners, to turn tin into gold.
(*Laughs deliberately towards the audience.*)
Look at this obscene ambition.

Ah, if only everything could turn into gold.
(*Thinks with wonder and mockery.*)
It is impossible to eat, drink, dress, and breathe gold.
Isn't that death itself?
(*To the* **Young Priestess** *who has fallen into a trance.*) Continue . . .
Return to your youth so I may know my old age.

The **Young Priestess** *appears pouring liquid lead over the sand, then placing the vessel on the embers.* **Sardanapalus** *watches her in astonishment.*

Young Priestess (*as she pours the lead*)   I will pour the liquid lead onto the earth . . . and see what forms appear.

After pouring the lead, she kneels where the shapes are and begins to interpret them.

Where have you been?
You were absent although you were present.
You lost although you gained.
You were lost although you were found . . .
Gravel in your water bag.
In your sandals, holes for the devil.
Why are you with this caravan and what is this lament emanating from your blossoms?

Sardanapalus   For it is a bloody end.

Young Priestess   Rather, it is the end of water and fire . . . When water runs after fire, fire follows water . . . What about you? Can't you see these burning castles?

Sardanapalus   And I . . . where am I in all of this?

Young Priestess   And you, amidst this and that,
Until your eyes grow gray,
And your stature fades more,
And your legs sink in mud.
Wonder . . . And wine soaks your fingers until they turn weak, and your pens dry up.

Sardanapalus   What strange omen is this!?

Young Priestess   Hear this from me, remember this from me . . . When the Tigris aligns with the enemies . . . When the Tigris aligns with the enemies (*echoes of voices on stage*), Nineveh will fall . . . And you will burn when the Tigris aligns with the enemies!

The **Young Priestess** *begins to wither and fade gradually until she disappears completely, leaving only spots of water, the burner, the hearth, the liver, the dust, and the lead.*

Sardanapalus (*searching for her*)   Where are you? O explorer of future depths . . .? Where are you? Where have you gone . . .? What does this vanishing of yours mean? Is this my own withering and disappearance too? (*To himself.*) I am tethered to my captivity . . . present, not an illusion . . . So why don't my feet touch the ground as they should? Something has vanished within me . . . what is it? Memory will assist me in recounting all this folly . . . Were there ghosts here? Was what came forth here bound in the body of a woman . . .? Transforming from her extreme old age to her extreme youth? (*Losing patience.*) What is this, O heavens . . . and what omen are you bringing upon us? Everything I am told is distorted . . . And everything I do is lost in illusion and in the wind.

Alone, he wanders, then reclines. The atmosphere turns into a dream with trumpets announcing the arrival of **King Ilani**, **Sardanapalus**'s *brother who was killed in the last war and his predecessor on the throne.*

Sardanapalus   Even these trumpets will cease one day . . . and return as cold, shy brass.

Ilani   When will you cease your wandering in this hell of yours?

Sardanapalus   I have become estranged from this world, and my estrangement has become my homeland . . . and my homeland has been lost from me. It has unraveled like a rosary, and now each bead is in the mouth of a wolf.

Ilani (*sarcastically*)   Oh, wise one!

Sardanapalus   How many times have I asked you to restrain your inclination to war? And to let those from distant nations return to their homelands . . . and make them a wall for you?

Ilani   Should I let free the rebels against Assyria?

Sardanapalus   No . . . there's no use in carrying the legacy of war, peace is more profitable. If only you had stopped the bloodshed by breaking your pride on the plains.

Ilani   Have you degenerated to this extent?

Sardanapalus   No, rather madness screamed within you and a destroyer was among your forebears.

Ilani   Enough of this nonsense, don't make me listen to you or your position. I am going to war.

He exits. **Sardanapalus** *bids him farewell with sad looks.*

Sardanapalus   Oh, war . . . everything will perish, even heads . . . Worms have multiplied, and snakes have climbed the thrones . . . Armed ghosts heralding woe and ruin . . . Who will grasp this world when it has converged upon us from all sides? Is it screaming at us?

Suddenly, **Uballit** *appears.*

Uballit   You are of Sargon's lineage, where is that warrior lineage within you?

Sardanapalus   My wars are within me . . . I battle blindness, ugliness, and death . . . I have no enemy before me to kill . . . I am hiding in wait to attack myself if his humanity weakens . . . Where is the luxury that nature had heaped upon us? It grants us everything, and we destroy everything in it . . . Oh, our ingratitude! Why have we become like this, leaping from one war to another?

Uballit Assyria is surrounded by many enemies.

Sardanapalus And choked within by the serpents of death. What black shroud wraps around its neck . . . When I lay my ear on the chest of this sorrowful city . . . I hear nothing but a lament that does not cease until the threads of dawn.

Uballit We have raised Assyria above the nations.

Sardanapalus *turns to him with anger.*

Sardanapalus You have placed Assyria above the nations . . . But now is the time for us to place Assyria among the nations.

Uballit Have mercy on yourself, my lord.

The **Queen** *enters in her majestic black attire.*

Queen Sardanapalus. There is much that threatens the kingdom from outside.

Sardanapalus And from inside!

Queen Who are those from inside?

Sardanapalus Its people are weary, angry, mourning.

Queen (*grumbling*) Ohhhh, how long will it remain so?

Sardanapalus Until I banish the specter of death from Assyria. (*He approaches his mother with a hint of respect.*) Let us leave room for reason and politics instead of wars. Mother, we have ruled over rivers, valleys, and mountains but we have not ruled over peoples . . . all of whom hate wars . . .

Queen Is it with this broad thinking you spend your nights?

Sardanapalus It was not a night but a gathering of the souls of our dead soldiers, blackened by our denial of their beauty and sacrifices.

Queen (*yelling at him*) Sardanapalus! What has become of you?!

Sardanapalus My hands plunged into those clouds, and I did not receive the rain . . . my feet sank in the mud, pulling me to my head. I advance in my prisons like a cart descending from a mountain.

Queen The weight of a ruler's responsibility is heavy upon you.

Sardanapalus We were not born to be kings . . . Many of us became soldiers and perished under swords . . . We were not born to be lions; many of us became sheep and were eaten . . . We were not born to be figures; many of us became outcasts . . . We were not born to be victors; many of us tasted the bitterness of defeat, more than once . . . Despair . . . despair . . . despair . . . We all tore ourselves apart like this, the common soldiers among us . . . The gates of hope have been closed to us . . . We have been surrounded by our despair, so we chewed on grass and drank bitter water . . . and ate gravel with the wheat. But the calamity has not been lifted . . . What can we do except patch our swords against the darkness . . . and break free from the captivity of revolving around our despair?

Queen You conspire against us.

Sardanapalus *laughs*.

Sardanapalus Since when has another opinion been heard in Assyria? Everyone runs after the ruler's whips. Why won't you listen to me?!

Queen You want to tailor Assyria to your own desires.

Sardanapalus No, to cut injustice, expansion, and slavery from its fabric and fit it to a paradise for humanity. We defend it rather than attack it.

Queen This is intolerable! (*She pauses for a long moment, then exits angrily.*)

Sardanapalus As you wish . . . for the throne accommodates many . . . as you see.

Scene Two: *Sardanapalus' Dream, "Are we not naked under our clothes?!"*

Sardanapalus (*as he enters, indicating his attire*) Closer to a jester than a king . . . Isn't that so?

Uballit It seems you're like Ashur in his prime, my lord.

Sardanapalus Let our motto from now on be "Enough of wars!"

Uballit But, my lord . . .

Sardanapalus I know. You'll say to me, "Enemies, friends, the mummies . . ." Withdraw the army and I'll make the rivers a guide for you.

Uballit We will become naked, my lord.

Sardanapalus Are we not naked under our clothes?! Look there, a cup brimming with wine, hot like a torch . . . With it, I enter into the caves of my soul and turn over the stones of my mind.

Uballit What did you see?

Sardanapalus I saw strange butterflies flying . . .
And I saw veins of gold shimmering . . .
My broken sword was there . . .
As were my virtues and slain mistakes . . .
And I saw my drunken boat punctured . . .
And I saw my flocks and herds grazing . . .

Uballit And Ashur?

Sardanapalus I saw nothing that reminded me of Ashur.
Do not impose your infirmed imagination on me.
Let me narrate what I saw in my depths.
I saw my father screaming and my mother singing, descending towards the sea.

Uballit It will be . . .

Sardanapalus (*interrupting*)   Enough of wars . . . Let our horses be more tranquil.

Uballit   How?

Sardanapalus   I do not like the wild war horses, raging with weapons. I hate these horses.

Uballit   And what do you like, my lord?

Sardanapalus   I love the small foals that have not yet known the smell of wars and cruelty . . . I raised a very small horse in my house, and I wondered if it could grow up? Its height reached an arm's length as it ate and consumed the food of the large horses, terrified by the idea of turning into a large horse and knowing the way of wars. My desire to keep it a small horse has become a reality.

Uballit   And why did you want it to be a small horse?

Sardanapalus   To save it from wars. And that's what I will do with my people, save them from wars. And make them a living people capable of escaping death.

Uballit   Can you do that?

The oracle enters.

Sardanapalus   Perhaps I am looking for my crown in hell, and they are looking for their swords in the clouds. (*To* **Uballit**.) And now go out and tell everyone . . . enough of wars.

Silence. He leaves.

And now, O oracle.

I will follow the dream that has appeared to me more than once in sleep.

Oracle   What is your dream, my lord?

Sardanapalus   Dense vapor coming out of your temple while I am on my way to you . . . obscures me and makes me suffocate . . . While you were looking at me and laughing . . . I woke up suffocated. How do you interpret my dream?

Oracle   I do not know . . .

Sardanapalus   So why do you always appear in my dreams?!

Oracle   Are you sure I am the oracle who appears in your dreams?

Sardanapalus   You are exactly him.

Oracle   As long as this is the case, I must tell you the story from the beginning.

Sardanapalus   What story?

Oracle   On the night of your coronation as king, as the night approached the end of its last half and when I was about to open the doors of the temple, I noticed the statue of the god Ashur was moving and steam coming out of its mouth and tears were flowing from its eyes. I told some of the oracles, so they asked me to bury the matter, as perhaps it was bad.

Sardanapalus Woe unto you! Do not move!

Saradanpal *approaches the Assyrian statue, feeling it from top to bottom, then kneels before it.*

Tell me, O Ashur . . . what do you bear for us? I consider you nothing but a sultan, raising up the weak with your might and humiliating the strong among both subjects and kings. Why do I see you disheveled, pale like this? (*Waits kneeling.*) When you looked upon me, you strengthened me and said your forgiveness would rise high, O Lord. For I and Ashur are but some of your horizons.

Waiting and kneeling in vain, he then rises and is about to leave.

Oracle The statue has moved!

The statue moves and emits thick steam from its mouth.

Sardanapalus Protect us, O heavens!

Voice (*emerging alongside the steam, resembling the statue's voice*)
I hear you, Sardanapalus . . . I am the spirit of your father, Ashurbanipal . . . so listen
  to me . . .
I see neither darkness nor light . . . but I feel the surging of grim clouds in my veins . . .
And I see corpses at my feet . . . These tombs will not fly, nor will their dead . . .
The horizons are soiled as much as they are swayed by the dust of wars.

Humanity has plunged into the ashes of pain.

I returned from my last campaigns wounded by a poisoned sword.
But someone plotted against me on the night of my death and choked me.
I couldn't identify them!!
(*With a commanding tone.*) Beware of those close by . . . Beware of them all.
Beware and punish those who killed me.

For my soul will wander, appearing in the idols of the gods.
Pain consumes my spirit . . . O Sardanapalus . . . the pain . . . the pain . . .

Steam and voice gradually fade away.

Sardanapalus Woe to a sinful kingdom . . .
Woe to the killers hidden in the cloak of aid and confidant.
Pain pursues me, pain devours me,
And these sins, like rain and lightning, I feel them in my veins . . .
What shall I do with this wreckage?
Father . . . can we live amidst this wreckage?

Scene Three: *And the Dust on the Moon. Politics drove me to the outskirts and to the soothsaying of a bull that doesn't fly.*

In front of the gate of Nineveh stands the Winged Bull.[3] *The bull's large legs and hooves are visible, and between each pair of hooves there is a split leading inside the foot and leg. The leg is transparent so that the veins, arteries, and tendons appear clear, and there is a ladder ascending to the insides of the bull from the split in the hoof. The interior of the leg and foot is darkened until actors enter it. The oracle stands contemplating the planets of the sky with his hand resting near his forehead.*

Oracle   The sun and the moon each in its place await the other . . . (*Lowers his hand.*) The coming days will be decisive . . . Tribulations will come and wars will erupt. May Ashur look upon the fate of the people with mercy. How my heart breaks to look upon these trials. We have spared what we could to stabilize these pillars and edifices, but a plague of doom was climbing from the roots to gnaw at the fruit. (*The three men enter and stand before the oracle.*) I have received your message. Why do you seek entry into Nineveh?

Babylonian   For trade, we are wheat and honey merchants.

Oracle   And where are you from?

Babylonian   I am Babylonian, and this is Median, and this is Scythian.

Oracle   We are not accustomed to admitting strangers except upon solving Nineveh's riddle.

Babylonian   And what is Nineveh's riddle?

Oracle   Water in the heights, air in the stone,

Fire in the cup, and earth in the moon?

The three ponder over the riddle.

Median   Water in the heights . . . there. (*Points to Nineveh's symbol: a fish hanging above the gate of Nineveh.*) The fish Nina at the top of the gate swimming in the water.

Babylonian   Air in the stone . . . there (*Points to the wing of the winged bull.*) in the wing of the bull.

Scythian   Fire in the cup . . . here (*Points to a cup with embers used by the oracle for incense.*) in the embers of your incense.

Oracle   That is correct.

Scythian   Earth in the moon . . . look at the river's waters.

Babylonian   No . . . look at the temple of the moon god Sin, it lies buried under the dust. (*Points to a place outside the walls.*)

Oracle   Who taught you this?

They smile wickedly and clear their throats, hinting at their secret agreement with the oracle to solve the riddle.

Drop your weapons here, and you may enter.

They drop their weapons and enter.

Oracle Here is your altar . . . I present you to the fire and make with the fragrance of your incense a ladder to ascend to the heavens, an intercessor before the god so that I may obtain mercy . . . I say the heavens are here in my hand. And the time has come for me to seek mercy from the mighty outside Nineveh. Not from the weak within it. This bag of gold (*Takes it out.*) is greater to me than the gifts of the heavens, for there are days that come and others that go. And I spin in your mill, O Assyria . . . and squeeze out desire. Politics drove me to the outskirts and to the soothsaying of a bull that does not fly. So why not place the riddle in the hands of one who will pay me more? And who might fulfill a need there in the heart of Nineveh to free us from this dust? (*He shakes off the dust.*)

Scene Four: *Owners of bad chemistry. Angel wings will not protect us anymore.*

Inside the palace, they gather to conspire against the king: the deputy king, the army commander, and the high oracle.

Deputy King You were banished to the outskirts, yet you continue to blow into the sieve . . .[4]

And I tried to shield you from prying eyes, yet you left me exposed.

Army Commander I have given you the loyalty I would give no other.

And gathered for you that money that I would gather for no one else.

Deputy King And what shall I do with the money?

Army Commander We will need it to undermine the king's throne.

Deputy King The circumstances are still unfavorable.

They exit.

Oracle I know what is happening under the cover of this night sky.

They all, like me, want something and they give something.

We are in a big market, very big.

Queen *enters.* **Oracle** *bows.*

Queen Does the wheel spin so fast that we scarcely see you?

Oracle (*to himself*) They look at me as if I will save the earth from the flood.
Who am I to do that?
A big stormy wheel in the heart of the world,
Crawling toward Assyria filled with death and ruin.

Queen What are you waiting for? Why don't you open your eyes in the water,
So that we may probe the depth of what's to come?
Houses will be filled with fallen fetuses, and paths crowded with sorrows.
Winds under the shoes, and damp eyes in the hands . . .

What are you waiting for until you rid this world of its myths ... When will you begin?

Oracle (*raising the censer high*)   When this incense reaches the gates of heaven and opens them, then I see the light ... and I begin.

Queen   Every time the executioner laughs, his hand tightens and much blood spills from people.
Here are lovers of gold and its worshipers.
Masters of foul chemistry, owners of perfumed black feet.

Oracle   A hand smooth like oil hides a cudgel that will accomplish what you desire.

Queen   When?

Oracle   Has the alternative king been prepared?

Queen   Ready at any moment you wish.

Oracle   I see you are eager to have him temporary king over Assyria?

Queen   Rather a permanent king.

Oracle   You shall have what you desire ...
But beware of haste ... It will expose everything ...
The gardener will not prevail until a year after his coronation, after marrying you.

Queen   Very well ... then I shall be patient for that because you will assist me ...
But when do we start?

Oracle   I will send you a signal when the time is ripe.

She looks at him reassured by his promise, then exits.

They liked the idea of the alternative king ...
The deputy king dislikes competing with the next crown prince,
And the Queen hurries her gardener lover to become king.
We spin a wheel of destiny with our hands,
And it means nothing but full hands and bellies.
What does a queen want who was once the wife of the greatest kings ...
And now is the mother of the king?

Sardanapalus's *wife enters.*

Wife   Where are you, O Oracle?

Oracle   At your command, my lady ... and I have prepared everything.

Wife   And what are you waiting for?

Oracle   Your signal, my lady and the right moment.

Wife   If it's the signal, then here it is. (*She gestures with her hand.*)
As for the right moment, there's no better time than now.
Who is the alternative king?

Oracle A gardener from the common folk.

Wife Where does he work?

Oracle In the service of Her Majesty, the Queen Mother.

Wife And after we kill him and Sardanapalus, what shall we do, O Oracle?

Oracle I shall stand on the throne and say: There is no offspring or relative of Sardanapalus except the one in the womb of Her Majesty. Thus, Her Majesty shall be the queen and her unborn child shall be king in due time, and she shall be his regent.

Wife And I will rule Assyria like Semiramis, and I will open lands and territories anew and extend the kingdom of Assyria to Ethiopia in the west and India in the east.

Oracle Is Her Majesty still captivated by the legend of Semiramis?

Wife Is there anything greater in all Assyria's history?

Oracle She is the pride of Assyrian women.

Wife And the pride of their men.

She exits with a haughty laugh.

Oracle The wings of angels will not protect us anymore.
They all covet the throne, and we all covet the money.
My God, how does the world turn like this?
Everyone will pounce on poor Sardanapalus to win the kingdom.
And the throne will go to the strongest among them.
As for me, I will be the high oracle to whoever wins.
My hands will not smell of death.
All that matters is that this madman, Sardanapalus, will fall from his throne.
(*He thinks for a moment.*) I do not like him because he does not like me.

Scene Five: *I am the king and I hate my duty. Take my hand, O Ashur, to dance.*

Sardanapalus Oh horizons, pour fish into my eyes,
Ignited me, a hot rose here in my chest,[5] and make me fathom his complaint.
We buried the Assyrian heroes in these tombs.
Their ghosts are still standing on the walls of Nineveh.
They grow like a tree; we bury its seed to reveal its fruits.

Uballit (*hurriedly enters*) My lord . . . My lord, Sardanapalus!

Sardanapalus Yet more lightning strikes Assyria!?

Uballit A grand conspiracy, my lord.

Sardanapalus (*sarcastically*) And from which quarters this time?

Uballit Everyone, even the Queen Mother!

Sardanapalus My mother? No . . . no . . . This is the mother of forty-four!?[6]

Uballit And the high oracle, and your deputy, and . . .

Sardanapalus My mother . . . my mother . . . (*Hits his forehead and laughs bitterly.*) This is a new riddle, these are suspicions. My senses exploded as I stagger in this immense haze of yellow smoke. (*As if remembering:*) I know that thread in her, I know it. And who else?

Uballit Your wife.

Sardanapalus (*with exaggerated certainty*) And why not? How could she be different from them?

Uballit She wants to be the king.

Sardanapalus A queen and a king? Is she of dual gender?

Uballit She aims to be the sole ruler.

Sardanapalus This is a funny game! (*Laughs.*) She mimics Semiramis! (*Breaks into hysteria.*) Have you seen a horse's neck shine? She can't be a horse's neck or even its tail. Ah . . . and who else with them?

Uballit (*pause*) And the King's deputy.

Sardanapalus And you? You? Have you conspired with them? How do I know you're not with them? If the stones are with them and the dust is with them, then how do I know who is with me and who is against me? And why wouldn't you be with them?! (*Grabs his throat.*) Hah, they rushed into hate as if they were digging into the abyss. Why wouldn't you be with them?

(*Lets go of Uballit.*) Rather, why wouldn't I be with them? Why wouldn't I conspire against myself since conspiracy and hatred are the customs of this era? Why?

Father . . . Oh father, even the trees howl in your absence! And you want me to know who killed you? They all killed you. How could they not kill you when they're dripping with all this hatred? And with all these nets while you're the great king? The spirits have cried for you, wanting to confess to me who threw you into the depths of horror.

Uballit Take it easy, my lord.

Sardanapalus How would you have me live after all this farce? They all sharpen their swords at my neck, and I have no neck, but I am haunted deep within. I've surrendered myself to the springtime of the soul and basked in beauty. The flutes played, so I laughed, and time scowled, so I sang. I scooped from its simmering with my hands and the sky was my ground . . . Oh my folly!

Uballit Their souls have decayed and burned in their wickedness.

Sardanapalus Rather, say we were defeated by the face of ugliness. Yes, humans descend into ugliness when an eyelash neglects their loftiness. (*Lies on the ground.*) Knowledge alone rescues beauty from falling. How I love the fruits that fall from the heights.

Uballit   From the trees?

Sardanapalus   From the heights

Uballit   You mean the sky?

Sardanapalus   No, from the heights.

Uballit (*understanding vaguely*)   Yes, yes. I think I understand.

Sardanapalus   I don't think so. (*Listening as if to a distant sound.*) I hear swords being sharpened outside the walls of Nineveh.

Uballit   The armies of Nabopolassar the Babylonian and Cyaxares the Mede and Armand Manda the Scythian stand at the walls of Nineveh besieging it.

Sardanapalus (*puts his ear to the ground and listens*)   And from afar I hear the oracle of Judah, Nahum, proclaiming the ruin of Assyria. (*Rises from the ground.*) Leave me alone, I cannot bear this storm.

Uballit   And the conspirators?

Sardanapalus   It's foolish to interrupt their work.

Uballit *exits.*

So this is it, my mother and my wife and my deputy and my army commander and my oracle? Is this how you betray, oh rebellious horde, driven by monarchal instincts? I am the king and I hate my duty. May god help you endure all this burden! Remove the dust, my god, and come beside this unsafe throne, and send a ray from your sun to melt the chains of my throne and the iron of my wrist. Take my hand, O Assyria, to dance. And let me immerse myself in temptation.

Dances and then sings.

This rose has thorns.
This moon has ashes.
This throne is stubborn.
This bull guards a cloud.
This lion has become locusts.

A servant enters carrying a poisoned dish. Finding the king dancing and singing, she pauses until he slows down.

Servant   My lord, it's mealtime.

Sardanapalus   Food? What does food mean? Taste, greed, given . . . !

Servant (*trembling*)   I'll place it here.

Sardanapalus   No . . . you eat it instead.

Servant (*stammers, puts down the food and flees*)   No, no, no . . .

Scene Six: *Fires of Nineveh. I hate crude masculinity . . . the cause of our tragedies.*

Sardanapalus *puts his head between his hands and wanders across the stage. The scene changes as if he is in a wilderness, where he appears alone, exhausted and tired, delivering his sad monologue beneath the sky.*

Sardanapalus (*with astonishment and contemplation*)   How can I prepare while everything falls apart? How can I leap while everyone kneels? How can I calm down when the waves have reached my neck? My heart will overflow after this injustice and my pride will melt away, and I will vanish. How many times I called out to my country, but it did not answer me. Its walls fell upon my head and its paths filled with my screams, as if I am not one of its people, as if it is a foreign land. Time has passed where tides ebb and flow around me and day and night cut through me . . . and in it, fake and true news are equal. I have no energy to carry a homeland in which all the people are armed with lies, flattery, and falsehood.

He turns to the sky in supplication.

O sky, wash Assyria of its sins.
Thunder and strike and rain down in fury upon these cities filled with corruption.
Woe to those wars and to this ash!
Woe to the blaze of swords and the clang of spears.
They pray for rain, and I pray for rain to cleanse us from our sins.
If you remain hesitant, O sky,
The world will drown in a flood of hatred, tongues, hands, and worms.
O sky, rain down with your torrents!

Thunder sounds and lightning. **Sardanapalus** *puts his head between his hands and knees before the intensifying rain.*

Uballit (*enters hastily*)   Tigris has overflowed and breached the walls of Nineveh, and our enemies will infiltrate us.

Sardanapalus   What?

Uballit   We could not stand against the water.

Sardanapalus   So, the prophecy has come true, and Tigris has allied with our enemies. What kind of punishment is this, O my God? We asked for rain to cleanse Assyria's sins, not to make the Tigris our enemy! Where am I supposed to go? If neither Assyria, nor heaven, nor time, nor my people, nor my courtiers are with me, then who will be with me? So let my truth be revealed and I will shout it out: I hate wars . . . I hate death . . . I hate the crude masculinity that caused our tragedies. Isn't it better for us to be men who love? Isn't it better for us to elevate love in the face of death? Pleasure in the face of famine? Desire in the face of battle? I will speak my truth, unafraid and uncompromising. I am a man, a woman, a plant, an animal, an angel, a stone, light, and sky. I am all of this, so why do the days want to place me in their traps? And why do they want me to fight ghosts in order to die? I am defeated inevitably in these mythical wars. Yet, I will not surrender but declare my truth. I am a lover, a lover before these hated damned weapons.

Uballit *and the three enemies appear: the* **Babylonian**, *the* **Median**, *and the* **Scythian** *on the walls of Nineveh, lighting torches, while* **Sardanapalus** *watches them.*

Scythian Our armies are about to enter Nineveh . . . The way must be opened for them.

Babylonian Burn the grass, for the wind is favorable and will blow towards the people of Nineveh.

Mede The wind will carry the smoke of the grass, afflicting them with weakness, fatigue, and sleepiness.

Scythian Come on, let us exploit the direction of the wind before the rain returns.

They light the beacons on the walls.

After you finish, turn these beacons over. Let them fall into the city onto the wood we have prepared, so the smoke will fill people's houses.

They throw the beacons from above.

Sardanapalus Summon all those conspiring against me and gather all the gold, money, jewelry, gems, and artifacts. Let this place become an Assyrian museum. And let us embrace nothingness afterwards, in our finest attire. Conspirators and loyalists alike. Ask them to adorn themselves with their finest possessions. Tell them that the king will grant the greatest positions to the most beautifully adorned.

Uballit But the invaders . . .

Sardanapalus Pay no attention to the invaders. They will do their duty as insects should. Our excuses have fallen. We have brought the enemies by our own strength.

Uballit But . . .

Sardanapalus Execute, then discuss.

Uballit *exits.*

Sardanapalus (*alone*) And you, oh spirit, I will lure you
To witness my salvation and Assyria's salvation from its serpents.
I am a sorrowful king of a sorrowful land.
All that remains for me is hypocrisy and inflated praises filled with lies,
Nothing left but my dog, my palace, and my tigers.
All I see is a people torn by hunger and drought.
My ancestors have left me ruin and perpetual war,
Where there's no distinction between victories and defeats.
There is no path to victory in this world.
The victory of death is the only true victory—ruin begets ruin, ruin begets ruin.

The golden chamber adorned with the kingdom's greatest treasure of artifacts and jewelry. In the center, **Sardanapalus** *lies on a bed surrounded by women and servants, some dancing in what resembles a grand royal celebration. Some wear masks and adorn themselves in the finest clothes and accessories.*[7] *Gradually, the voices quiet down.*

Sardanapalus (*mockingly addressing those important figures entering the palace*) Come . . . come, oh overflowing courtiers, women, attendants . . . Raise the banner of life against the swords of death . . . come . . . And you too, little conspirators . . . I will save you from your conspiracy and fulfill simultaneously what you desire from these plots. Come, my mother . . . and my wife . . . and you, my servant with the poison dish . . . Come all . . . come, my deputy . . . and you, chief oracle . . . and you, commander . . . Come, you splendid ones . . . come enter this magnificent hall . . . come . . . (*They enter as the music rises again and they dance, drink, and laugh. Then the voices quiet down a bit.*) Fate is shining . . . yet it remains calm. When it becomes angry, it will take us all. Soon, it will reveal that face. How we scream with pleasure at its other face, our screams of delight. Beauty and life rise against famine, death, wars, and ruin. The bull stands at the slaughterhouse door, aroused by instincts, excited by the body's euphoria on the verge of slaughter . . . why? There is nothing we possess except this beautiful, indulgent body. We hurl it in the face of imminent death. Drink the toast of Nineveh, the cup of life. Nineveh will ignite with beauty when it rises proudly amidst the drums of war and conspiracies to slaughter . . . And there . . . there in the heights, death will be stabbed . . . And it will remain eternal in history and in the sky and in the blood of those who inherit us. Drink the toast of Nineveh.

Uballit (*enters and whispers to the king*)   My lord, enemy soldiers have entered the heart of the city!

Sardanapalus   Are they frolicking enough . . . or playing chess? Corrupt blood sweats through history from time to time. What is this swarm of worms doing in Nineveh? Have they had their fill of wars? When will humanity realize there is no benefit from wars? No benefit from killing? A single drop of blood doesn't equal all the treasures of the earth.

The revelry and celebration continue. **Uballit** *exits, then reenters.*

Uballit   The soldiers have reached the palace walls!!

Sardanapalus   It's futile, they are heading towards their death and ours. How I wish they were now in the arms of their loved ones. Raise your toast! Nineveh eternal forever! Your glory will not fade, oh Assyria. Once you ruled the world, then you loosened your grip and it slipped from your hand. This is time, it rises and falls, but you remain eternal, memorialized for all.

Uballit *exits, then reenters.*

Uballit   The soldiers are at the palace gates!

Sardanapalus (*grabs him firmly*)   Why do you hesitate? Close the gates and lock them from within. It is not wise to interrupt our celebration. (*To the revelers.*) He means our soldiers are guarding the palace gates. (*The soldiers move inside and close the room.*) Drink the toast of life! Break the sting of death!

The music rises, dancing resumes, banners are raised, laughter. Meanwhile, **Sardanapalus** *sneaks away, carrying his torches. He begins to set fire to the edges of the room. The sound of water pounding against the doors and walls of the room grows louder, mingling with the sound of the fire.*

Reveler The water . . . the water . . . a flood of water breaks the door panels.

Another The fire . . . the fire . . . it burns the palace and the people.

Sardanapalus Fire and water together, what a beautiful fate. Farewell, Nineveh . . . farewell, oh Assyria. This could have been avoided, but fate has broken darkness upon us, struck like lightning, and we met it with our chests as lovers of life, haters of death, blood, and killing.

The water continues to flow, the room burns, panic ensues among those present, and they perish amidst this grand catastrophe.

Let water unite with fire and rise to the ends. We are victims of the ghosts leaping from history to the present.

Farewell, Nineveh . . . curse upon you, oh wars. And curse upon you, oh mankind, for what you have done to yourself.

Amidst the fire and water, a strong rope descends from above with a loop at its end, shaped as a symbol of Assyria—a circle with wings, a feathered shaft, and a bow, but devoid of the image of the god Ashur. It begins to sway like a pendulum within the fire, the water, and the screams of the people as they perish. **Sardanapalus** *climbs through this loop and positions himself in the designated place for the god Ashur. He resembles it as he takes up the bow, and this symbol continues to sway within the scene like a pendulum, indicating the enduring symbol of Nineveh and Assyria in the distant horizons.*

Notes

1 The original title in Arabic read as *Sardanbāl*. The oldest surviving account of Sardanapalus, an ancient (mostly mythic) Assyrian king, is by the Greek historian Diodorus. Lord Byron's closet drama *Sardanapalus* (1821), which in turn inspired Eugène Delacroix's vivid and lurid painting *The Death of Sardanapalus* (1827), is perhaps the most famous modern dramatic interpretations.
2 Ashur (or Assur) is the supreme deity of the ancient Assyrian people. The god is proclaimed king, while the human ruler, Sardanapalus, is merely his representative on earth. Ashur is also the name of the capital city.
3 The Winged Bull of Nineveh was a symbol of the power of Assyrian rulers. These statues typically have the body of a bull, the wings of an eagle, and the head of a man. In 2015, members of the so-called Islamic State destroyed part of the face of one of these statues. The image of the statue described in the play is stylized for theatrical purposes.
4 An idiomatic expression that means to engage in pointless effort without any results, blowing air into a sieve.
5 The expressions "fish in the eye" and "hot rose in the chest" mean to awaken.
6 A "mother of forty-four" refers to a type of insect with many legs. It symbolizes predation, stealthy advancement, and the secretive pursuit of power.
7 The scene is meant to resemble Delacroix's *The Death of Sardanapalus*.

Introduction to *The Clock*
Nahedh Al-Ramadhani

At the beginning of the twentieth century, the eyes of Arab societies turned towards a class of nationalist intellectuals who, on their shoulders, carried the responsibility of uplifting Arab societies that were often impoverished, backward, and subjected to English or French colonization. In the era of English and French colonization, the elite class gained significant respect in the Arab countries. They attained a status that transcended the boundaries of their small nations outlined by the Sykes-Picot Agreement. After a struggle that persisted for five decades or more, the era of direct colonization came to an end, and Arab nations achieved their independence, albeit superficially. Soon, the military seized power in most of these countries, marking the beginning of a challenging period in the lives of these people. A catastrophic reign ensued for decades, where intellectuals became either mouthpieces for authoritarian authorities, fled in exile, or remained silent under coercion. However, as globalization extended its reach and the soft power envoys were sent to replace military forces in the region, the concerns of Arab nations were no longer the primary focus of intellectuals.

Most of the intellectuals began to hope for collaboration with any Western entity, especially after the decline of Arab nationalist parties and the fading of their influence. Some Arab dictators even turned conciliatory towards the West, seeking appeasement and attempting to present Arab nations as part of the Western project. *The Clock* revolves around the defeated Arab intellectual. Between a simple cobbler and the intellectual, the events unfold, portraying one who wants to make change in the world but doesn't know how, and the intellectual who knows how but doesn't want to, so they can stay in the same status.

The issue of the intellectual, his role, struggles, and setbacks, holds great significance in most of my writings, such as *Shahriar's Companion* (*Nadīm Shahrayār*), *'Ishtibāk* (*Clash*), *The Belly of the Whale* (*Jawf al-Ḥūt*), and *W.A.A.K.*, a novel which thoroughly explores several protagonists, each representing a type of intellectuals with diverse statuses and opinions.

The Clock

Nahedh Al-Ramadhani

Characters

Shoe Mender
Man in Dishdasha
Café Waiter
Old Man
Man in Hat
Short Man
Tall Man
Woman in Abaya
Unveiled Woman
Veiled Woman
Woman
Boy
Photographer
Intellectual
Police Officer
Interrogator
Ruler

Scene One

The stage is dark. The sound of a large clock ticking is heard: "Cuckoo, cuckoo, cuckoo." Then the clock chimes and sighs. The sound of cogs breaking is followed by creaking and ticking. Then complete silence. Gradually, the stage lights up with dim lighting. A public square is at the center, with a tall tower featuring a huge clock commonly found in a town square. Further upstage, there is a towering building with a massive anvil on its rooftop. In front of it, a police officer holds a rifle, and another holds a trumpet. Seats and small tables are arranged around the clock. The sound of a rooster crowing is followed by a distant call to prayer. Actors enter quietly, wearing various costumes: traditional robes, turbans, Arab and Moroccan attire, sportswear, and work clothes. They sit silently, chatting casually, holding teacups and coffee mugs. Some read newspapers. A large sign in the café reads "Free Smoke." The stage lighting increases until it covers the whole area. The shoe mender enters wearing a leather apron.[1] He looks around, then raises his head and shouts.

Shoe Mender   Our clock? The clock!!

Man in Dishdasha[2]   What's wrong with it?

Shoe Mender   It's stopped working.

Café Waiter   The clock? Well . . . Yes, we didn't hear any ticking or chimes.

Old Man   It really has stopped.

Man in Hat   Of course, It doesn't make sense for the sun to be in the middle of the sky and the clock to still show three.

Short Man   Don't be hasty, my friends. Let's not jump to conclusions.

Tall Man   Indeed, no need to be hasty.

Shoe Mender   There's no haste. The clock has stopped.

Short Man   Who said that?

Shoe Mender   Haven't you noticed that its hands have stopped moving?

Woman in Abaya[3]   Indeed, its hands have stopped moving.

Unveiled Woman   And it's pointing to three, when the actual time is around . . . I suppose . . .

Café Waiter   What time is it now, I wonder?

Short Man   It's the same time as it was yesterday at this exact moment.

Shoe Mender   That doesn't mean anything.

Tall Man   But it's a perfectly accurate reckoning of time.

Shoe Mender   We can't live our lives based on such reckonings.

Woman   Indeed, we need a clock.

Unveiled Woman And the clock has stopped.

Boy How will we perform our tasks?

Short Man Just as we always have.

Tall Man Yes, yes, just as we always have.

Shoe Mender And time?

Short Man Time moves forward even if we don't have a clock.

Old Man If only the State allowed us to have clocks like everyone else.

Short Man You want the State to share its temporal authority. Time is within the domain of the State.

Man in Hat And the clock is a time measuring device.

Short Man So, it's also within the domain of the State.

Tall Man Indeed, it's within the domain of the State.

Man in Hat And since the State has relinquished its autocratic authority . . .

Short Man Then we must respect its temporal authority.

Tall Man Yes, we must respect its clock.

Short Man And we shouldn't demand back what we've willingly given up.

Shoe Mender Who said we willingly gave it up?

Old Man No need to get into that. Let's try to find a way out of this situation.

Short Man I see you've rushed us to the disaster. Who told you the clock is broken?

Tall Man Indeed, who said it's broken?

All It's the shoe mender.

Shoe Mender My friends, calm down and let's review the situation from the beginning.

Old Man Listen to what he has to say.

Café Waiter Give him a chance to speak. He deserves a moment of our attention. He's our best shoe mender. Please, go ahead.

Shoe Mender To be precise, we need to agree on a few things. Let's start from the beginning. Isn't this the only clock we have to set our schedules by?

Short Man Yes, it's indeed the only clock.

Tall Man His words are accurate so far. I add my voice to yours and declare to the whole world that it's the only clock that—

Shoe Mender Hold on for a moment before you add your voice and declare anything to the world. We're in agreement that it's the only clock.

All   Yes, we're in agreement.

Shoe Mender   You all remember that the sun rose yesterday at the same time it did today, around a quarter past six in the morning, right? And we gathered here yesterday at eight in the morning?

All   Yes, we remember that.

Man in Hat   You're still speaking logically. Please continue.

Shoe Mender   Then if the sun rose today at three in the morning, it's not normal.

Man in Dishdasha   Perhaps it's by God's will.

Café Waiter   Or the clock might really be broken.

Others   How will we know?

Short Man   Let's wait for half an hour. If the clock's hands move and it chimes, then it's not broken.

Tall Man   And the problem brought up by the shoe mender will be solved.

Unveiled Woman   But how will we know we've waited half an hour?

Short Man   Then let's wait an hour.

Café Waiter   And how will we know we've waited an hour, clever one?

Veiled Woman   It's truly a puzzling matter. What's the solution?

Café Waiter   There must be a solution. It would've been so easy if each of us had a clock.

Short Man   You think so? If each of us had a personal clock, we wouldn't survive a single day. Everyone would stick to their own time, and chaos would reign in every aspect of life.

Shoe Mender   People all over the world have their own clocks.

Man in Hat   Don't forget we're a fledgling State. Owning personal clocks requires a long period of education, awareness, and training. It's not as easy as you think. Plus, it would be a huge waste of public funds.

Man in Dishdasha   Do you know how much it would cost the State to buy a clock for each citizen?

Old Man (*sarcastically*)   Haven't the education, awareness, and training periods ended already? And does anyone know where the budget goes? I've been hearing about all of this for decades.

Short Man   You're all always in a hurry. What's the importance of decades in the life of nations?

Tall Man   Indeed, indeed. It's true. I add my voice to yours.

Unveiled Woman   You've gone off-topic. Have we been waiting here for an hour?

Café Waiter An hour? It's only been a few minutes.

Short Man How? We've been standing here for over two hours.

Shoe Mender And how do you know that?

Short Man I've smoked four cigarettes, and I usually smoke one every half hour.

Veiled Woman Perhaps you were anxious and smoked more.

Short Man Anxious? I'm never anxious. I'm a strong-willed person. My wife always says—

Shoe Mender Let's not get into your wife's comments. Can you all finally accept that the clock is malfunctioning?

Man in Dishdasha You're always causing us problems, shoe mender. I'm not convinced of anything yet.

Short Man We must be cautious in all things.

Café Waiter What should we do?

Short Man Let's wait until noon. Where is the photographer?

*A **Photographer** enters carrying a massive wooden camera. He captures the scene and begins developing the image in a large water basin.*

Short Man We must be cautious about everything. We need to beware of perceptual errors.

Tall Man We've documented the clock and its hands. There's nothing better than documentation.

Man in Hat And we must be cautious of collective delusions and paranormal phenomena—

Old Man Let's wait until the sun is directly overhead.

All Let's wait.

Curtain falls, and murmurs rise.

Scene Two

*The curtain opens to reveal a crowded square. Light shines on the stage, bustling with people. The **Shoe Mender** stands alone, looking at his watch. Women in abayas and headscarves shop from wandering vendors. Young men flirt with women. Men sit in seats, sipping tea and reading newspapers. Some youth engage in sports, while others attach earpieces and dance. The space is packed except for the area upstage, in front of the towering building, where only a police officer stands with a trumpet.*

Distant call to prayer.

Shoe Mender (*addressing those seated*)   The sun has reached its zenith in the sky. And the clock has not moved.

Everyone notices the clock as if they had forgotten about it. They stand up, gathering around the clock again.

Short Man   Where is the photographer? Where is the photographer? You must document the event.

The old **Photographer** *takes another picture of the clock.*

Old Man   Did you hear the call to noon prayer? The sun is high in the sky, and the clock still points to three.

Veiled Woman   Indeed, it still points to three.

Short Man   Don't jump to conclusions. Wait for the photos.

Tall Man   Indeed, I don't favor haste and impulsiveness. I echo your voice, demanding to wait for the documentary photos.

The old **Photographer** *shows the two pictures to everyone. One of them takes the photo with interest, takes out a magnifying lens from his pocket, and studies the images. They mutter with others, then take the magnifying lens and scrutinize the pictures.*

Man in Hat   A truly strange occurrence.

Short Man   But we can't conclude that the hands of the clock haven't moved at all.

Tall Man   Indeed, the hands might have moved slightly, imperceptible to the naked eye.

Café Waiter   So, what's the plan then?

Man in Hat   The signs suggest that the clock might be malfunctioning.

Old Man   How could the clock malfunction? It's unthinkable that such a clock could break down. It has been here for a long time. It's an exquisite creation, a sturdy product of craftsmanship. It's been here since the colonial era.

Short Man   Hush, hush . . . the colonial era. How dare you utter such a word!

Tall Man   The colonial era. How dare you utter such a word!

Old Man   The colonial era . . . Ah, those were beautiful days.

Man in Hat   Beautiful days? Surely, you've lost your mind, man.

Old Man   You haven't seen anything in your lifetime. The colonial era was colorful – white, black, and red. But now, there's nothing left but . . . the color of dust.

Unveiled Woman   You must be crazy. Does anyone yearn for the days of slavery?

Old Man   Slavery . . . heh. Back then, we had something extremely precious. Something your generation knows nothing about. We had hope back then. And now . . . now we have nothing left but dust.

Short Man Dust . . . dust. Accumulated dust might have caused the clock to malfunction.

Shoe Mender You've finally admitted that the clock is malfunctioning.

Man in Hat We haven't admitted anything. It's indeed malfunctioning.

Short Man And the images and documents prove that.

Tall Man Yes, the documents prove that.

Woman We must find a way out of this embarrassing situation.

Café Waiter It's a real problem.

Man in Hat One of us should inform the ruler about it.

Short Man Otherwise, we won't be able to carry out our work properly.

Unveiled Woman Who will inform the ruler? Do you think he's been unaware of this until now?

Shoe Mender But no one has taken official action to resolve the situation.

Man in Hat There must be a plan to repair the clock. I believe the Minister of Interior will take all measures to resolve the situation and uncover the conspirators and those responsible for the clock's malfunction.

Short Man No doubt it's a conspiracy.

Tall Man Certainly, a conspiracy . . . a conspiracy . . . no doubt it's a conspiracy. And I add my voice and condemn anyone trying to undermine—

Old Man No need to condemn now. It's still too early to know the truth of what happened.

Man in Hat Do you think they've apprehended the network of saboteurs or not?

Short Man Perhaps the saboteurs are still among us.

Tall Man Be cautious. Watch everyone. Has a stranger infiltrated us?

Unveiled Woman Where is the Minister of Interior?

Man in Hat I don't think the Minister of Interior will do anything. It's the Minister of Defense's duty.

Veiled Woman What does the Minister of Defense have to do with it?

Man in Hat Don't you know that the clock is affected by a lodestone?

Tall Man The clock is affected by a lodestone. Maybe we've heard of something like this before.

Shoe Mender What kind of magnet could affect a clock of this size?

Man in Hat You're ignorant . . . you're fools . . . indeed, a colossal space magnet has been unleashed against our clock. Haven't you heard of Star Wars?

Café Waiter Cool movie. Have you seen *Who Framed Roger Rabbit*?

Man in Hat I'm not talking about movies. I'm talking about the real Star Wars. The space arms race. Surely, a space magnet has been aimed at our clock.

Short Man How will the Minister of Defense respond? Do we have deterrent weapons against satellites? Do we have anti-space magnet missiles?

Unveiled Woman There's no doubt these are military secrets. I believe the Minister of Defense will take appropriate action.

Old Man I don't think the Minister of Defense will do anything. Who said there's an army planning to destroy our clock? We are peaceful. We are bound by non-aggression treaties with all the inhabitants of the planet. And we live under an international umbrella. A sturdy umbrella that keeps us from the pull of the largest magnets. It even shields us from the sun and rain. Truly a luxurious umbrella, from under which nothing escapes but dust. Dust that fills everything around us.

Short Man I think the Minister of Health should intervene. He must save the clock and save our lives from what's about to happen. The ticking of the clock resembles a heartbeat. He must find someone whose heart beats at a rate of 60 beats per minute. To regulate the rhythm of our work hours.

Tall Man Yes, he must find someone or else . . .

Shoe Mender And how will we make sure his heart beats 60 times per minute? Did you forget we don't have a clock now?

Man in Dishdasha I . . . and I seek refuge in Allah from saying "I" . . . I think the Minister of Religious Affairs should intervene. And the call to prayer should be the marker of our work hours. So, we go to work two hours after the Fajr call to prayer. And we return from work half an hour after the Dhuhr call to prayer.[4] And so things will be organized.

Shoe Mender How can we go two hours after Fajr call to prayer if we don't have a clock in the first place?

Man in Dishdasha Indeed, indeed . . . I forgot about that.

Veiled Woman Why doesn't the Minister of Foreign Affairs do something? He could contact friendly countries and ask them about the time.

Man in Hat Yes. In such circumstances, we'll be able to distinguish friend from foe, who stands with us and who is against us.

Unveiled Woman Do you think other countries will abandon us in this ordeal?

Old Man No . . . quite the contrary. Everyone will try to help us, and that will make the situation worse.

Everyone How?

Old Man Every country will answer our Minister of Foreign Affairs' question differently . . . India's Foreign Minister will give a different answer than Canada's or

Argentina's. Have you forgotten about longitude, latitude, elevation, and time zone differences?

Short Man Does anyone have a geography book?

Tall Man Right, do you think the Minister of Irrigation might take appropriate action?

Short Man No, even the Minister of Sports won't be able to help in this catastrophe.

Tall Man So, we're in a real crisis. Why doesn't the Prime Minister take radical action?

Shoe Mender Haven't you forgotten that the Prime Minister was executed five years ago . . . and his successor's appointment has been postponed indefinitely?

Tall Man Right, let's wait for his successor's appointment then I'm sure he'll immediately take appropriate measures.

Unveiled Woman Maybe we should wait another five years . . . though it's an awfully long time.

Short Man Very, very long.

Tall Man I certainly agree with you, it's five years.

Old Man Five years of what?

Tall Man It doesn't matter. I stand with the Prime Minister.

Café Waiter The executed one?

Tall Man No. I will stand with . . . I'll tell you later . . .

Veiled Woman Will someone inform the ruler? How can we remain silent about this situation? How much longer will we live in fear? Raise your voices. Raise your voices to reach the ruler in his soaring tower.

Old Man Why don't you leave the ruler alone? Surely he's busy with video games now . . . These games have saved many of us from execution. He finds them more entertainment than executing citizens.

Man in Hat That's the benefit of knowledge and progress. I'm always on the side of scientific advancement.

Unveiled Woman Knowledge is advancing frighteningly fast.

Tall Man Indeed, modern video games are hard to defeat.

Unveiled Woman I'm not talking about that.

Shoe Mender Can't you see we're getting off-topic?

Short Man Oh, you're always reminding us of unpleasant things . . . what do you want now?

Shoe Mender The clock. Have you forgotten about the clock?

Some people turn to the clock and shout:

Crowd The clock's hands moved! It's pointing to quarter past three.

Short Man Where is the photographer? Capture these moments.

Tall Man Capture, capture, capture . . .

The **Photographer** *rushes, almost stumbling over his massive camera's legs. He takes a picture of the clock and starts printing it.*

Short Man Do you see how all this fuss was for no reason? Can anyone now deny that the clock is functioning properly?

Tall Man Very regularly.

Shoe Mender Are telling me it's currently 3:15 in the morning?

Short Man I didn't say that. I said the clock isn't malfunctioning. It's working. It's working, and everyone can see that. We have all the necessary documents to prove this fact.

Tall Man It's working. The clock is working.

Shoe Mender I'm not talking about the clock itself working. I'm talking about the time it's indicating. Is it really accurate?

Man in Hat You're just raising one issue after another. At first, you said the clock was malfunctioning, and now you're saying it's working but not indicating the time. What exactly do you want from us?

Café Waiter It's me. I. I don't want anything. I just want things to be orderly.

Short Man Who do you think you are? You're just a shoe mender.

Tall Man Indeed. You've annoyed us enormously, you insignificant shoe mender. You've wasted a lot of our time.

Shoe Mender How much of your time have I wasted? I've only taken a quarter of an hour.

Short Man A quarter of an hour? You've been bothering us since dawn. Filling our heads with your strange words and questions. And you say a quarter of an hour?!

Shoe Mender But the clock indicates that I've only taken a quarter of an hour of your time. When I met you, it was pointing at three. And now it's showing three and a quarter. Don't you believe this clock?

Man in Hat This talk is no longer productive. Let's agree again on common ground as a basis for our conversation.

Everyone Agreed. Agreed. Let's quickly find common ground. Come on. Come on, let's agree . . .

Old Man   Do you want to discuss the clock malfunction or know the time?

Short Man   The clock malfunction is more important.

Unveiled Woman   But we want to know the time. That's why the clock exists.

Café Waiter   If the clock is malfunctioning, we'll never know the time.

Shoe Mender   Wait a moment. Are we in agreement that the clock is not malfunctioning now?

Short Man   Yes, it's working. We have a document now that proves its accuracy.

Tall Man   We have documents . . . everything is documented.

Shoe Mender   So, there's no problem then. The matter is resolved.

Everyone (*relieved*)   Resolved . . . resolved . . .

The crowd starts dispersing.

Café Waiter   Wait . . . where to? The clock is not giving us the time we are used to!

Short Man   It's simple. Let's adjust our daily schedules according to what the clock indicates right now.

Tall Man   Yes, we should adapt our lives to fit the clock's current state. Change is great! Let's change our boring routine!

Short Man   Let the routine, repetition, and stagnation fall!

Tall Man   Long live the army, the shield of the nation!

Old Man   No one mentioned the army, disperse now and resume your normal lives.

Café Waiter   But we agreed just a little while ago not to return to our normal lives.

Veiled Woman   Does this mean we'll stay gathered here?

Man in Hat   No, no . . . but honestly, I don't know how to change my life yet, even though I genuinely desire the change.

Short Man   Adjust to the new rhythm of the clock.

Tall Man   Yes . . . let's all conform to the new movement. I love conformity.

Shoe Mender   I still don't understand how this new movement will work. Will an hour only be ten minutes? Will the day only be six hours long?

Man in Hat   We'll embark on exciting adventures as we discover these things.

Old Man   Disperse now and let's gather here tomorrow. Let each of us share our new adventures with the new time.

Tall Man   Alright, alright . . . let's meet tomorrow. But when will we meet? At what time?

Short Man At . . . three and a quarter . . . the clock is still showing three and a quarter. Photographer, capture these moments. Folks, remember these moments. The clock has stopped working.

Café Waiter We're back to where we started.

Tall Man We haven't even celebrated yet the change we've dreamt of for so long.

Man in Hat And we won't live new adventures and experiences with the new time.

Veiled Woman And we won't break the routine.

Shoe Mender Now you confirmed that we are facing a real problem?

Veiled Woman The ruler must take full responsibility for this situation.

Unveiled Woman One of us must inform him about this matter.

Old Man Is it possible he hasn't heard about what happened? He can hear an ant's footsteps.

Short Man His silence up to this point is suspicious.

Man in Hat The matter might be more serious than we imagined.

Short Man Isn't it logical that the ruler himself is the one who ordered the clock to stop?

Tall Man It's possible, likely, perhaps. Why not?

Short Man In that case, we must . . .

Man in Hat (*taking off his hat*) We must go home.

The crowd disperses in silence.

Scene Three

The curtain opens to the same scene. The market is crowded with people in their various attires, women wearing traditional or vibrant clothes. An ordinary yet chaotic life. The **Café Waiter** *enters, looking confused. He stands in front of the clock for a while, then addresses the others.*

Café Waiter It's still showing three and a quarter.

Short Man It's stopped working. The photos and documents prove it.

Veiled Woman And the ruler hasn't done anything.

Unveiled Woman I saw him yesterday looking out the window with a huge telescope.

Old Man Maybe he was observing a flock of birds.

Tall Man Or perhaps he was looking at the clock.

Old Man I don't think he cares much about such matters. Maybe he was watching a girl hanging her laundry on the roof.

Short Man (*annoyed*) Things are starting to take a tragic turn. I couldn't adapt my life to this new pattern.

Man in Hat Maybe you need more time. I'm in the same boat . . . but I haven't given up yet.

Café Waiter How can we all agree in the middle of this maze?

Veiled Woman Everyone interprets time for their own benefit.

Short Man Now my wife only cooks for me when she pleases.

Tall Man My wife hasn't cooked anything at all . . . ever.

Old Man Children go to school to find their teachers leaving. Some government offices and departments are open at night.

Veiled Woman No one can make anyone else to do anything.

Shoe Mender The sun rises and sets. Days follow one another. We need to find a suitable timing for ourselves.

Man in Dishdasha Who said that one day following another is normal? A polar night might surprise us.

Tall Man Yes, a polar bear might surprise us. What will we do then?

Shoe Mender Rare occurrences happen.

Short Man Rare occurrences are happening a lot these days.

Veiled Woman Why doesn't one of us call someone in the neighboring state and ask them about the time there?

Short Man Communicating with a foreign state is a grave betrayal. And despite the ruler's silence, he's not asleep.

Tall Man Yes, yes . . . the ruler sleeps standing up. I mean, he's not asleep.

Shoe Mender So, we need to fix the clock.

Short Man You're just a shoe mender. You might be able to skillfully mend an old shoe. You might change a sandal . . . glue a slipper. But repairing the clock is beyond your capabilities.

Man in Hat Let's create a huge hourglass and place it in the square.

Shoe Mender It would need someone to flip it every hour to maintain its accuracy.

Old Man And someone to count the daylight hours based on it.

Café Waiter Let's come together as a team to solve this matter

Short Man A disciplined team means an assembly.

Tall Man   Regular gatherings are prohibited without prior permission.

Old Man   What gathering and what team? If we'd been able to put together a taskforce, we wouldn't have reached this state.

Short Man   I have a remarkable idea. Let's make an hourglass filled with chickpeas.

Tall Man   Bravo! An innovative idea!

Shoe Mender   The problem is not in the chickpeas or the sand. The problem is who will supervise the clock.

Tall Man   I have another idea. Let's fill the clock with . . .

Old Man   Keep your ideas to yourself. Let's find a way out.

Man in Dishdasha   Our ancestors invented a water clock a long time ago.

Old Man   We all know that, but we don't know how they invented it or how it works.

Tall Man   Why don't we create a wooden statue of a clock and rotate it ourselves every moment?

Shoe Mender   That might be a successful solution, but it still won't give us the accurate time.

Café Waiter   So, what's the plan?

Everyone   What's the plan? What's the plan . . . ?

Intellectual *wearing a suit enters. His hair is white, and he wears elegant glasses. Everyone makes way for him. He calmly steps forward and stands on a small platform. He addresses everyone with an authoritative tone and a loud voice.*

Intellectual   O people. O citizens . . . Truth, truth I say unto you . . . To fix the clock, you need . . . a clockmaker.

Blackout, chaos, uproar, and a rush on the stage. Screams, wails, the sound of gunfire mixed with the sound of sirens and police cars.

Scene Four

The **Police Officer** *is still standing in his place. The* **Intellectual** *is tied to an inverted torture rack, blindfolded, and enduring brutal beatings without uttering a sound. The* **Interrogator** *is seated at a large table in the middle of the stage. After minutes of torture, the* **Interrogator** *clears his throat and addresses the* **Police Officer***.*

Interrogator   That's enough for now. Pour a jug of water on him, and let's begin the interrogation.

The **Police Officer** *pours a bucket of water onto the* **Intellectual***. He ties him by his feet to a pulley hanging from the ceiling and lifts him, hanging him upside down.*

Interrogator Answer all the questions accurately.

Police Officer *kicks the Intellectual in his face.*

Police Officer Answer, answer, answer. (*Pause.*) He's very tough. Like a professional criminal.

Interrogator I wish he were a criminal. It would save us all this trouble. He's much more dangerous than you think.

Police Officer (*kicks the* **Intellectual**) Speak!

Intellectual I won't speak unless . . .

Interrogator . . . unless what?

Intellectual I won't speak unless you lift the tie from my face and secure it with the golden pin to my shirt.

The **Police Officer** *rushes. He lifts the intellectual's inverted tie and secures it with the golden pin on the shirt.*

Intellectual I always wear this pin in anticipation of situations like this.

Police Officer Now speak quickly and tell us everything.

Intellectual (*calmly*) I won't speak quickly, and I'll only say what I want to say.

The **Police Officer** *kicks the* **Intellectual** *in the face.*

Intellectual Van Heusen size eight . . . You arrogant officer, you're wearing mismatched shoes.

Interrogator *looks at the police officer. The* **Police Officer** *feels embarrassed.*

Police Officer He's right. I might have rushed while putting on my uniform. But how did you recognize my shoes? You are incredible! I must get back at you!

Police Officer *picks up a taser stick and strikes the* **Intellectual***. The* **Intellectual** *stirs without screaming. Then he speaks calmly.*

Intellectual Barbara 89. Made in the US, an old stun baton, no longer used.

Police Officer *strikes the* **Intellectual** *with another taser stick.*

Intellectual Hilary 98 . . . It's a special, luxurious type, but it drains batteries quickly. Don't you have a chargeable stick? It's more economical than battery-operated ones.

Interrogator *checks the stick, verifying* **Intellectual***'s claims, while the* **Police Officer** *fetches another one connected by a cord. He strikes the* **Intellectual** *with it.*

Intellectual You should have used that one from the start. It is Nancy 86, correct?

Police Officer Yes, indeed, you know the types of shoes and batons as soon as you are slapped with them.

Intellectual   I also know the shackle tying my wrist; it is 84 cm, UK-made. The British are skilled in these industries.

Interrogator *whispers to the* **Police Officer**. *The* **Police Officer** *opens the shackle from his hands and keeps it in an inverted position.*

Interrogator   Correct. This shackle is manufactured in the UK. You seem to be an expert in torture devices. Have you been arrested before?

Intellectual   Oh, yes. I've been arrested multiple times with Communists and leftists, then with nationalists and advocates of Arabism, then with the Muslim Brotherhood and Islamists. I've participated in both successful and failed coups with officers, and I've joined students in their sit-ins and protests. I've suffered a long time to gain this experience.

Interrogator   Our suspicion was justified. You've come to stir up trouble.

Intellectual   It's your foolishness that stirs up trouble for everyone.

Police Officer *beats the* **Intellectual**'s *back with the stick.*

Interrogator   Speak. Speak about everything clearly. Every word you've said is recorded. We have dozens of witnesses.

Intellectual   Fools. You're still fools. Why all this? Have you learned nothing about societies? You're strong but foolish. You still lack understanding. You still urgently need . . . an intellectual . . . an intellectual like me.

Police Officer   You're inciting revolution. Did you deny saying that fixing the clock requires a clockmaker?

Intellectual   Yes. And I will repeat this as long as I'm alive.

Interrogator   You're inciting revolution. Your words only mean one thing: that the right man should be in the right place. Do you deny this meaning implied by your words?

Intellectual   Why deny it? I came precisely to say these words to the people.

Interrogator   So, you openly incite revolution and insist on it.

Intellectual   I'm not inciting revolution. I'm urging you to think. How long will your stupidity persist? You will ruin things with your misconduct.

Police Officer   You're exposing yourself to the death penalty.

Intellectual   You won't dare to kill me. Your orders prevent you. You must not turn me into a martyr. Do you deny that these orders were issued to you?

Police Officer *and* **Interrogator** *are surprised and uncomfortable before the restrained* **Intellectual**.

Police Officer   Even if our orders prevent us from killing you, we can do anything else.

Police Officer *advances toward the* **Intellectual**, *striking him harshly, then stops.*

Police Officer (*frustrated*)   Torturing him is pointless. I don't even find pleasure in it. He doesn't scream. He doesn't try to avoid the blows. It's like . . . it's like he's enjoying the torture.

Interrogator   I told you he's not an ordinary criminal. He'll cause us a lot of trouble.

Police Officer   We need to arrest all the members of his network. We need to make him confess.

Interrogator   Leave him to me. I'll try a softer approach.

Interrogator *approaches the* **Intellectual***, lights a cigarette, and places it between the* **Intellectual***'s lips.*

Interrogator   Tell me again. Who are you?

Intellectual   I'm an intellectual.

Interrogator   Good. So, you're an intellectual. What kind of an intellectual are you?

Intellectual   I used to be a leftist, then rightist, then radical, but now, I'm cosmopolitan.

The **Interrogator** *and the officer look at each other in astonishment and confusion. The* **Interrogator** *remembers something and points to the small bookshelf behind the desk. The officer brings an old dictionary from among the books and starts flipping through it.*

Intellectual   An old dictionary. You won't find the meaning of this word in it.

Interrogator (*frustrated*)   You know everything and you're not telling me anything. Should I beat you again?

Intellectual   I would love it if you did.

Interrogator   Let's not resort to violence. I have enough to convict you. You won't be able to deny saying that fixing the clock requires a clockmaker.

Intellectual   And by saying this, I meant that the right person should be in the right place.

The **Interrogator** *and the* **Police Officer** *approach each other, getting closer with fear.*

Interrogator   Please don't say that sentence again in front of me.

Police Officer   If this were applied, we would be put in the trash.

Intellectual   That is where you belong. Even though you're an officer, you haven't washed your socks or your feet for a long time. Civilized officers clean their clothes every day. The stench of moldy socks is reserved for soldiers and young police officers. You don't deserve the rank on your shoulders.

Police Officer I'll wash my feet. And I'll wash my socks. I promise you that. I'll definitely do it before I kick you again.

Intellectual (*to the Interrogator*) You've made a grave mistake, sir. You arrested me without a warrant. And you brutally interrogated me . . . and you'll pay the price dearly. I'll put you in your rightful place.

Interrogator Who are you to do all this!?

Intellectual You'll know who I am soon. Your bad luck led you to collide with me. You collided with a person who possesses power and authority.

Interrogator You're a stranger to this town. What power and authority do you have?

Intellectual I possess the power of knowledge . . . and the authority of discourse. I am much more important than you think.

The **Interrogator** *and the* **Police Officer** *show fear. They speak to each other in hushed voices, and the* **Intellectual** *appears calm, confident in his victory despite his upside-down position. The phone rings. The* **Interrogator** *answers, standing up while looking flustered.*

Interrogator Yes. Yes, of course. We will definitely do that. Yes. Yes, sir.

He hangs up. He gestures to the **Police Officer** *in a confused manner. The* **Police Officer** *and the* **Interrogator** *rush toward the* **Intellectual**. *They gently help him down, then remove his shackles.*

Interrogator I'm sorry. I'm so sorry, Mr. Intellectual.

Police Officer You should have asked us to use the phone at least, dear guest. You would have spared yourself and us all this torture.

Intellectual You are fools . . . ignorant people. You and your likes are the cause of all these disasters.

Interrogator Indeed, indeed, Mr. Intellectual. We are two great fools. How did we not recognize you from the beginning? We and the city's police would have come out to welcome you. The police choir would have sung for you.

Intellectual Don't be a kiss-ass. The city's police and its choir . . . don't you know that I hate formalities?

Police Officer Of course. Of course, Mr. Intellectual. You undoubtedly hate formalities and only care about substance. All intellectuals are like that, I believe. Please, come with us and wash your hands and face from these bruises. I will send a request to have them covered up. To fix the damage done to you.

Intellectual Remove these bruises? They're the best thing that has happened to me this year!

Police Officer Please, Intellectual. Let's remove these bloodstains from your wrists at least.

Intellectual I don't accept compromises. I refuse, I refuse, I refuse. The people need to know the truth. The whole truth. This is my role. This is my message as an intellectual.

Interrogator But we can't let you leave and meet the people in this condition.

Intellectual That's what I want. And that's what the people want from me. Don't interfere in my affairs again. Your role is over now.

Intellectual *walks toward the* **Interrogator***'s desk. He picks up the phone and dials a number. After a while, his* **Secretary** *enters carrying the* **Intellectual***'s suitcase.* **Intellectual** *sits behind the* **Interrogator***'s desk, opens his suitcase, and starts sorting his papers and his* **Secretary** *helps him. He uses the phone that the* **Secretary** *took out of the suitcase to make several calls, speaking in different languages. The* **Interrogator** *and the* **Police Officer** *do not interrupt him. He puts a large cigar in his mouth as the* **Interrogator** *and the* **Police Officer** *rush toward him, trying to light the cigar for him.* **Intellectual** *scolds them.*

Intellectual Hypocrites . . . there's no reconciliation between intellectuals like me and those like you, who suppress freedom.

He turns toward the **Secretary***, who elegantly lights the cigar. He ends his conversation on the mobile phone and turns to the* **Secretary***.*

Intellectual Did you bring the bag of masks?

Secretary Of course.

She brings the bag and places it on the desk. **Intellectual** *seems indecisive. He turns to the* **Secretary***, addressing her.*

Intellectual Should I wear the mask of optimism? Or the mask of anger?

Secretary Perhaps it would be better to wear the mask of the wise man.

Intellectual No, no. That's not useful in such circumstances.

Secretary What about the mask of the rebellious man?

Intellectual It's not appropriate now. I fear it might have the contrary effect.

Secretary Then try the mask of the sad man.

Intellectual The sad man. The sad man. I'm not entirely sure.

Secretary Why not . . . why not try . . .

Intellectual Exactly. Why use a mask at all? I don't need any of them. I'll stick with my face. Isn't that what you wanted to say?

Secretary Exactly. You'll be more successful that way.

Intellectual *looks at the* **Interrogator** *and the* **Police** *Officer with disdain, then points to the* **Secretary** *as she grabs her two large bags.*

Intellectual Let's get to work. (*Addressing the* **Police Officer** *and the* **Interrogator**.) Carry the bags instead of standing here like statues.

*The **Interrogator** and the **Police Officer** hurry to assist the **Secretary**, carrying the bags, while the **Intellectual** talks on the cellphone in a foreign language and smokes a cigar.*

Scene Five

*Wild chaos engulfs the square. Papers are strewn everywhere, people in miscellaneous attire move about fervently and agitated. A perpetual movement sweeps across the stage, excluding the stationary policeman and the trumpet player. A man lost in shisha fumes is steeped in stupor, and the **Shoe Mender** remains frozen as he gazes at the clock.*

Old Man Didn't I tell you that even in his isolation, the ruler sees and hears everything?

Short Man Absolutely. He still senses everything.

Tall Man And he moves with tremendous speed.

Café Waiter And with even greater cruelty.

Shoe Mender Who knows where that intellectual is now? Our salvation from this crisis was in his hands.

Veiled Woman May Allah have mercy on him.

Man in Dishdasha I won't forget his eloquent words. Do you remember his illuminating words? To mend the clock, you need a clockmaker.

Man in Hat Shh, lower your voice. Haven't you learned from what happened to that poor soul?

Unveiled Woman We should have acted when they arrested him.

Old Man We should have done many things. We face myriad predicaments. The clock, the intellectual, and our daily livelihood. Where should we turn? What can we do?

Shoe Mender I don't know, but I feel guilty.

Old Man We all feel guilty, but what should we do? We live in exceptional circumstances and we must endure.

Man in Hat Indeed. These extraordinary circumstances will pass quickly, and everything will revert to its state. These circumstances have only lasted a hundred years.

Short Man Or a bit more.

Tall Man Indeed. No need to hasten. Let things settle. Then, we might regain the freedom to move.

*The **Intellectual** enters the stage, with an undone tie, tousled hair, and shattered glasses. Bloodstains mar his shirt sleeves and chest. A commotion pervades the stage.*

The crowd hoists the **Intellectual** *onto their shoulders, cheers resound, and everyone twirls around the stage.*

Crowd   Long live freedom!
Down with tyranny!
Down with ignorance and darkness!
Long live the clock. Long live the rightful man.

Short Man   Long live our ruler.

Tall Man   Long live justice. Long live justice.

The **Intellectual** *stands on the platform once more, modestly magnifying his gestures as he greets the enthusiastic crowd. He raises both blood-streaked hands aloft, forming the victory sign with his fingers.*

Intellectual   The will of a vibrant people like you must triumph. Thank you, thank you. You've saved my life.

Café Waiter   It is you, you're the one who will save our lives.

Shoe Mender   Everything we did and will do is nothing compared to your sacrifices.

Unveiled Woman   Long live the Intellectual! Long live education! Death to ignorance!

Short Man   Long live the ruler. Long live the ruler, the man of justice and education!

Intellectual   Words fail me. Where are you, oh words? Gather, oh letters, and form new words so that I may express the greatness of these moments and their awe. I cannot say anything in the face of this great situation. I am on the verge of tears. (*He puts his head between his hands in a dramatic gesture*).

Old Man   Death to the enemies of education!

Shoe Mender   Death to the enemies of the intellectual!

Café Waiter   We won't let you down for a second.

Unveiled Woman   Never let you down!

Intellectual   Even crying eludes me. I want to cry with tears of a new kind. I wish I could shed tears that are solid, so I can keep them to remind me of these immortal moments . . . moments of direct connection with you. Remember I am among you, with you and for you! Help me, oh language. Form, oh letters!

Man in Dishdasha (*enthusiastically*)   God is great! God is great!

Intellectual   Words desert me. What do I warn you about? Do you need a warning? Oh, you who craft your magnificence moment by moment, shaping your history and the world's history second by second. Oh, you who reshape the universe with a novel mold. Oh, you the simple ones, no, oh you the great ones! No, the simple yet great ones. You've elevated culture and intellectuals. Be sure of it. Be sure that now you're creating something that all nations have failed to create.

A group of people dressed in uniform work clothes enter, bearing a colorful stall with Coca-Cola logos. They position the stall on the far right of the stage. The appealing colors of the stall clash with the rest of the worn set. The people are absorbed in the **Intellectual***'s speech. Some glance backward and murmur words, but the* **Intellectual***'s voice ascends.*

Intellectual   You have fallen victim to a conspiracy. Yes. I say it with all conviction. You have fallen victim to a conspiracy that almost jeopardized your unity. But the deep accumulated wisdom within the subconscious of this blessed people prevented the catastrophe from happening. It nullified the plot of the conspirators. Look at all of you, observe the traces of this conspiracy. Its remnants are still visible here. Isn't this the clock?

The crowd looks on in surprise at the unexpected question.

Crowd   Yes, it is the clock.

Intellectual   Excellent. Well done. I anticipated that from the very beginning. Everyone knows that it's the clock. But who among you can tell me what is it?

Shoe Mender   It's a clock. Just a clock.

Intellectual   No. It's not enough to just say it's a clock. It's the means by which we measure time. Isn't that so?

The crowd excitedly applauds and cheers.

Crowd   Correct . . . correct . . . God is great. How did we miss that?

Intellectual   Your confusion won't surprise me. You should be confused, and I should find the right answer. Isn't that my role? And from here, from this place, in this historical moment, I declare to all of you that if the clock is the means by which we measure time, then time is the thing we measure with the clock.

Complete silence falls. Then the stage erupts with a storm of cheers and applause.

Intellectual (*exalted*)   We must accurately comprehend everything around us. It's not reasonable for us to live in absolute chaos in a world governed by a precise system. To achieve this understanding, we must scientifically analyze everything meticulously. We must dissect reality precisely. And to reach this stage, we need a revolution. A comprehensive revolution to reassemble the reality we've dismantled.

Café Waiter   Long live the revolution! Long live the revolutionaries! Rise, people, rise!

Intellectual (*shouting*)   Yes, we need a revolution. A complete revolution on the ontological, epistemological, and existential levels. Without this, we won't be able to change our reality at all.

Old Man (*disappointed*)   I thought he would talk about a revolution against the ruler. Did you understand any of what he said?

Man in Hat Who can change the ruler? Look at that anvil. Only the State has a towering crane that can move it, and the State is in the ruler's hands.

Old Man True. I missed that. And how will we achieve the ontological revolution, as the Intellectual said? Let's listen now.

Intellectual They're trying to make us doubt everything. We must find a solid truth to start from. A truth so firmly established that no one doubts it. Otherwise, we'll be forced back into the cogito de Descartes. Should we return to the cogito de Descartes?

Café Waiter I won't leave my homeland!

Man in Dishdasha Cogito? No way! I'll never go back.

Short Man Long live the soil of the homeland!

Tall Man Long live the homeland. Long live the homeland.

Intellectual Let's look at the clock. And remember for a moment what Emmanuel Kant said about the deception of the senses. It's there. It's there . . . Isn't the clock there? Can't we see it and touch it? Isn't that a truth?

Everyone (*with anticipation*) Yes, it's there.

Intellectual This is a positive point of agreement. Let's move forward once more from this simple truth.

Another group of people in work uniforms enters, setting up more colorful booths, and another group of men and women leaves the **Intellectual** *and heads to the café to smoke shisha, near the silent man.*

Intellectual Let the clock be a firmly established truth in our lives. Let's move forward from it, attempting to unravel the mystery of this matter. Pragmatists say the clock ceases to be a clock when it stops working. This is equivalent to saying that a mother ceases to be a mother if she loses her ability to give birth. Now, answer me, all of you, can we abandon our mothers?

Man in Hat I seek refuge in God. Paradise lies at the feet of mothers. I seek refuge in God.

Intellectual Therefore, this is another truth we add to the first one: the clock is present. And we don't want to part with it.

Short Man Things are clearer now.

Tall Man Yes, much clearer.

Veiled Woman With the help of this Intellectual, we might reach a solution.

A massive crane enters, and some look at it.

Man in Hat This is a foreign crane. Will anything change? Will the crane move the anvil?

Old Man It might be a despicable foreign conspiracy, and tomorrow might be worse than today.

*The **Ruler** appears in military attire with his insignias, wearing a sleeping cap, on the tower's balcony. He gazes calmly at the crane, which places a second anvil on the tower's surface.*

Veiled Woman   We couldn't move one anvil, so how about two?

Man in Hat   Let's hear the rest of the Intellectual's speech.

Another group of listeners leaves the circle and heads to the café, while men in Western attire carrying mobile phones and smoking cigars fill the background. Workers in matching uniforms paint sections of the stage with bright colors, and they move toward the palace.

Intellectual   Don't let appearances distract you. Return . . . return to yourselves, to the deepest point within you, and reflect. Reflect on everything, and you'll find that the truth is as clear as the sun, untouched by clouds. Reflect . . . reflect.

Veiled Woman   He starts making sense.

Unveiled Woman   But it's an exhausting talk.

Short Man   Let's try reflection. What have we got to lose?

Tall Man   Indeed, let's reflect. We have nothing left to lose. But what do we reflect on?

*The workers arrive at the palace tower. One of them places a long ladder, and the policeman doesn't object. The worker climbs the ladder and starts affixing a long advertisement for a fizzy drink. The **Ruler** appears on the balcony, holding the edge of the ad, while the worker secures it with screws.*

Intellectual   Let's move on now to a third step, and you'll find that we've reached a decisive solution to our problem. No one but us can solve our problems. When the top converges with the base . . . when the proletariat melds with the elite . . . when . . .

*Another group of listeners departs, leaving only the **Shoe Mender**, the **Police Officer**, and the **Interrogator** facing the **Intellectual**.*

Police Officer   Does anyone understand any of this? I still don't understand . . . What has this Intellectual done? It seems like nothing will happen.

Interrogator   And that in itself is significant. Maybe I begin to understand.

Intellectual   And the merging of the proletariat with the elite has led us to solve this puzzle. The clock is present, and we're holding onto it. But its hands aren't moving. Who among you can prove that the clock has stopped working? No one. The fact that the hands aren't moving doesn't mean the clock isn't there, nor does it necessarily mean it's broken. We must adjust ourselves to the new clock, a working clock with stationary hands.

*The **Police Officer** and the **Interrogator** leave. **Shoe Mender** stands alone in front of the **Intellectual**.*

Shoe Mender   What's the use of it then? How will we determine time?

Intellectual (*calmly*) A trivial question from a trivial person. Who are you to ask me questions? (*Raising his voice as if addressing a large crowd.*) So, let's leave this problem, whose dimensions have become entirely clear, and let's all move on to work. Time is passing, and we must make the most of every moment. Let's catch up to the others. Shall we catch them? No, let's surpass them. Let's move forward swiftly and surpass everyone. Head toward the vanguard . . . onward . . . onward.

Intellectual *leaves the small stage and heads toward the café, where the waiter prepares a large shisha for him. The* **Intellectual** *starts blowing smoke.* **Shoe Mender** *stands alone in front of the clock. The* **Café Waiter** *replaces a "Free Smoke" sign with a larger sign that reads: "Free Smoke Only for* **Intellectuals***." Everyone starts exhaling shisha smoke. The stage becomes engulfed in a cloud of smoke and the lights from the advertisements.*

Notes

1 In Iraq, shoe mending is often considered one of the lowliest occupations, looked down upon or pitied.
2 A dishdasha is a traditional Iraqi men's garment that covers the entire body except the hands, feet, and head and doesn't have pantlegs.
3 A customary Iraqi woman's garment that is long, loose-fitting and covers the entire body except the head and hands.
4 The Fajr is one of the five daily Islamic prayers and is offered before sunrise; Dhuhr (or Zuhr) prayer is performed at noon.

Introduction to *The Curse of Chopin*
Atyaf Rashid

Iraqi society is constrained by prohibitions that suppress emotions and restrict human freedom, particularly for women. Patriarchal authorities marginalize women, restricting their movement, freedoms, and intellectual and emotional choices. Additionally, the volatile politics in my country, along with pervasive and rampant corruption, make it possible for the few to control the resources of the community, and women specifically bear the brunt of this entrenched corruption throughout official, public, and private life.

Hence, the appearance of an individual in the life of an oppressed woman, bearing love and sincerity, becomes a kind of savior. This savior, or dream, has the potential to quench the thirst of the dry land, the human spirit, especially that of women, and the harsh conditions they face. This idea of a savior comes in a completely different form in *The Curse of Chopin*. The main character discards the influence of the ideal family, diverging from the sharp boundaries drawn for her future, and sees what others do not see, settling within the music school. In my opinion, the writer should find a unique approach for their story drawn from everyday experiences, adding their own perspective and viewpoint to the subject or idea. The savior has a religious or transcendental purpose for peoples and societies, but I wanted to show that everyone has the right to dream of their own savior, whether intellectual or emotional, amidst various sufferings such as loneliness, neglect, a lack of care, and a yearning for love and emotional support.

These are themes where human values manifest in their purest form, and this is the fundamental motivation for all my writings—humanity. However, as in many of my plays, I do not provide a traditional ending to the story; instead, I leave the ending open to the reader's imagination, allowing them to fill in this space with their thoughts. In this way, real participation is achieved between the author/text and the reader.

The Curse of Chopin

Atyaf Rashid

Characters

Piano Teacher, *in her forties*
Student, *in his mid-twenties*

Evening in September. A room in the teacher's house, elegantly furnished with a piano, a small bookshelf, a wardrobe, and a comfortable bed. The room is well-lit with a stylish lamp and has a window with white and red curtains. The walls are covered with wood wallpaper, and there's a red carpet in the center of the room. The atmosphere reflects refined taste. The lighting is initially dim and gradually brightens after the teacher exits the bathroom.

The sound of the teacher's voice is heard from behind the bathroom door. She's muttering to herself. Exiting the bathroom, she has a graceful figure with short black hair, wearing a black knee-length skirt and a white blouse. She quietly closes the bathroom door behind her, sits on the bed, and adjusts her earrings and hair.

Teacher Why did I say yes? Why did I say yes? I should have refused. I should have said no. How did I allow myself to be in this situation? This "yes" exposed me completely in front of him. (*Putting on the shoes.*) In the institute, when I'm in the lecture hall, my eyes freeze on the spot where he sits. (*She stands up and, holding the shoes, stares in the direction of the student.*) I stare at him as if he's the only student in the room. I hear my heart beating when I talk about Chopin and write notes on the chalkboard, as if I'm sending him a private message. I tell all the students, "Do you understand the idea?" What idea? I don't even know if I wrote the notes correctly. (*She sits back on the bed to put on the second shoe.*) The lecture ends, and I'm completely distracted and anxious, my mind scattered. Students leave, and I turn my face towards the chalkboard. I wish I could bury my head in the written lines. I don't want to see him when he approaches. But I can't hear anyone's footsteps except his. Only his footsteps ring in my ears. (*She takes a deep breath.*) I turn around, and he's standing behind me, looking at me with confidence, a probing gaze piercing my soul. I ask him, "Why didn't you leave with the other students?" He doesn't answer, just stares at me. Stares with those brown eyes full of pure love. The only time he spoke was on the last day of the music course at the institute, the very last day. He stood before me, smiling, put his hands on my desk, leaned closer to me. I was sitting there like a statue, unable to breathe. His scent invaded every pore of my skin, his gaze fixed on my bewildered eyes, and the waves of his voice crashed into my face and heart, shattering my lips. I asked him, "Can I help you?" He said, "I want piano lessons. Teach me more. I want private piano lessons." And without hesitation, without thinking, like a captive bird, I replied with "Yes, yes." What have I done? What will he think of me? Why do I feel so weak? Then, how do I meet him? I am sure my fingers will stiffen, and I won't be able to play in front of him, or with him. Do you think he understands any of what's in your heart? What will he make of this hasty "yes" that flew out like a trapped dove? Did I say something that prompted him to ask for piano lessons in my home? (*She stands in the middle of the room, observing herself.*) Do I look okay? It's important to know how he sees me, how I appear in his eyes. What will he think of me, a woman who recently turned forty, single and alone? (*She looks at her watch and then at the wall clock.*) There's still time before he arrives.

She runs her fingers over the piano keys, playing a quiet Chopin piece #20. The teacher becomes isolated from her surroundings, engrossed in her playing. The student enters the spotlight, quietly standing beside the piano, then enters the room. He is tall and confident, wearing a black shirt with the top two buttons undone, revealing part of his chest, and black trousers. A few minutes pass as she plays before she notices his presence.

Student   Dreamy music . . . memories of the past.[1]

Teacher   How did you get in? I didn't hear the bell, or even the sound of the door. (*She stops playing and stands up.*) Was the door open? (*She wants to check the door.*)

Student   Forget about the door for now. The important thing is that I'm here, right?

Teacher (*still concerned about the door*)   But . . .

Student   Leave the door for now. What piece are we playing today?

Teacher (*uncertain*)   What piece? I don't know . . . What's piqued your interest in music?

Student   Something hidden, a desire or obsession. The important thing is I want to play . . . with you.

Teacher   That's what music does. It's a gift from heaven.

Student   Especially when it's Chopin's music.

Teacher   Indeed, you're lucky to have discovered its greatness. It's a profound gift that only pure souls can grasp. So, you've decided to learn it?

Student   Yes.

Teacher   But you already play well in class at the institute.

Student   I've trained myself well.

Teacher   Well, it seems you don't need a teacher then.

Student   Who says someone who plays well doesn't need a wonderful teacher like you?

The lighting in the room suddenly brightens.

Student   So, this is your home?

Teacher   Do you like it? (*Thinking to herself.*) What a silly question.

Student   I like it very much. (*As he moves around the room, he runs his fingers over the wardrobe, the bed, the bookshelf, and the nightstand, all while speaking.*) During our lessons at the institute, you stand in front of me, talking about notes and mentioning Chopin a lot.

Teacher   Really?

Student   Yes, and your lecture feels like a smooth melody.

Teacher   Chopin is an excellent example for music enthusiasts and piano players.

Student Many world-class musicians share that sentiment.

Teacher Except there's something different about him. Did you know he asked for his musical compositions to be burned after his death? He was a delicate soul, fearing others might play his music without the proper spirit, maybe he was anxious it would be performed mechanically, devoid of emotion.

Student You view it from a romantic angle.

Teacher Indeed, how so?

Student I don't know; it's like you know him or lived with him, like you are him.

Teacher Yes, I know him well, to the extent that he caused the separation between me and my beloved.

Student I'm sorry.

Teacher It's nothing.

Student But I had heard . . .

Teacher Then why have you been pretending you didn't know?

Student Because I love hearing from you, I love hearing you speak, just as I love hearing you play. (**Teacher** *goes to close the open window.*) The cold September winds penetrate the skin and reach the soul, just like you.

Teacher I think you're pushing the boundaries of the student and teacher relationship.

Student I think you're pushing all boundaries, being here. (*Pointing to his heart. Holding her hand.*) Come, let's play together.

The teacher goes to the piano; they sit side by side and play a part of Chopin's "Memories of the Past."

His sister was absolutely right to hide this divine piece.

Teacher Chopin composed the piece when he was in his twenties and dedicated it to . . .

Student To his sister as a birthday gift. That's why she hid it. It's truly a unique piece. Maybe he asked her to do so.

Silence.

Teacher There was no love between us. If you want to know what really happened between him and me, he felt trapped with me. I could see it in his eyes as they drifted away. He wanted to be free, so I set him free. He was suffocating. I understood this from his eyes, turning them away from mine when he said, "I love you." I didn't know that his connection to me was just . . . . a sense of responsibility for a woman he had loved earlier in life. He couldn't bear the idea of always staying in the same place, so he began to use my busyness with music as an excuse. The music, the same music that brought us together, especially Chopin's music that I loved, became the pretext for our separation. I understood him then; he wanted to soar, he wanted to fly away, so I let him go.

Student   You set him free?

Teacher   I released him from our connection. We separated, and he left.

Student   Just like that?

Teacher   It wasn't simple at all. It was a surgical extraction from the soul, so severe that the anxiety ate away at me for nights. Painful and distressing, but it passed.

Student   He never contacted you or asked after you?

Teacher   He sent a message or two, saying how he wished we could be together while he roamed the world and enjoyed walking in old alleys, affectionately through rain-soaked streets, deserted train stations, buzzing bars filled with the scent of drinks, music, and women. But I understood it was just temporary guilt, a fleeting sense that quickly dissipated in the new life he had built for himself. Love for me no longer existed in his heart because it felt like a prison.

Student   And what about you?

Teacher   I told him that he shouldn't come back only to leave again. His departure should be permanent. I couldn't bear to wait, waiting is a slow death. So, since then, when I felt his new life beginning, I started a new beginning as well. Here I am, living with music. Music is the only thing that feeds my senses and stokes the passion in my soul.

Student   Those are beautiful words, but I didn't ask you "How are you living?"; what I want to know is "how is your soul?"

Teacher   I told you, and maybe I also felt some freedom in his departure. His pitiful looks filled me with sadness. It's sad to turn your entire life into constant anxiety, to pretend you're happy for the happiness of others and, in the end, discover that it's all in vain. That the real source of unhappiness is staying together. Now you know everything. Does it quench your curiosity?

Student   No, it's not curiosity, it's interest. I felt something while you were playing, something like confession or complaint . . . even a prayer.

Teacher   Really, all that? Well, you didn't tell me about yourself.

Student   Ah.

Teacher   You've been at the institute for two years. Every time a course ends, you enroll in the next. Even when there are no lectures, I see you in the institute's library.

Student   I don't know how to explain it to you. It's . . . will you understand the state I'm in? Will you believe me if I told you that I, one day . . . I suddenly changed.

Teacher   No one changes suddenly.

Student   You're judging me without hearing me.

Teacher   You're right. Okay, I won't interrupt. Go on.

Student   I . . . I used to be an obedient son and a diligent student. I didn't allow myself to get anything less than excellent grades. My focus was on studying; I didn't know anything beyond textbooks. I Even spent my free time talking with my teachers about their lessons. So, I fulfilled my family's dream of getting into engineering college. My family believed that the future belonged to engineers. (*Imitating his father's rough voice*:) "Engineers are the builders of the future." They thought I would have an important role in rebuilding the country, especially in these troubled times.

Teacher   Everyone dreams of important roles. The important thing is to have faith in yourself.

Student   With our country in such turmoil, dreaming is the bare minimum we must do. Aren't these dreams merely idealistic hopes for the country's uncertain future. The point is that I listened to them and joined engineering, architectural engineering, and things went well for me.

Teacher   But?

Student   (*sits at the piano and plays the keys while speaking*)   Yes, and of course, but . . . but the magical moment, the mysterious moment came and resembling all the madness and chaos surrounding us, that sudden moment that swept through my mind and soul, like an epiphany for an inventor or scientist. (*Presses and holds a key, then stops playing the piano.*) Just like that, suddenly, as I sat in my seat in the lecture hall at the college, the great engineering college, and the days of studying were almost over, when I leaned my head on my shoulder, looking at the 3D models of buildings and skyscrapers being displayed on the screen . . . but I didn't see buildings or architectural shapes, instead, there were black lines with dark round heads. I looked carefully, wanting to make sure. I didn't initially know what these lines were. It didn't cross my mind what they could be, but the situation repeated itself the next day and the next and the next, compelling me to search for their meaning. Am I nothing more than that obsessive seeker and studier?

Teacher   So?

Student   I finally realized that they were musical notations, and at that moment, precisely at that moment when I recognized them, strange voices echoed in my head: bustling voices, human voices, and musical instruments playing.

Teacher   Do things like that happen in real life? I thought they only happened in the movies.

Student   After what happened to me, I became convinced that everything impossible is just a path we lack the vision to see. One day, when a professor was showing us models of buildings on the screen, a woman's shadow crossed over the designs and played hide-and-seek with me. She moved between the designs as if she were moving through their alleys, floors, and rooms, or as if she were part of a hidden life inside the screen. I shouted in the hall, "Do you see her? Do you see her?" The students looked at me in surprise; one of them tried to calm me down. I said to him, "Don't you see the woman's shadow on the screen?" (*The student stands in front of the teacher and opens his arms to both sides, taking the teacher's hands and pulling her in the opposite direction of his movement, pulling her to the left at times, then to the right at times.*) When I followed her to the left, she would hide to the right, and when I went to the right, she would glimmer from the left like a gem. I went left again, and her smile echoed from the right like a song. She smiled enchantingly and beguilingly.

Teacher (*pulls her hand away from him and moves away*)   There is no place in this world for fantasies.

Student   Fantasies are glimpses of the world beyond adventure.

Teacher   Fantasies and dreams are dark tunnels, deep and desolate abysses.

Student   The abyss is a mirror, reflecting exactly the importance of life above.

Teacher   Why, as we dive deeper into ourselves, do we hear this sound?

Student   What sound?

Teacher   This, this sound, don't you hear it? (*Hits a piano key once.*) After the melody, after the sound's resonance, this, don't you hear it?

Student   I hear it well. Maybe because I'm with you?

Teacher   The sound of pain, of solitude.

Student   I'm with you.

Teacher   This conversation tires me.

Student   I'm exhausted by the shadow of a woman who taunts me.

Teacher   What woman?

Student   The shadow of the woman who kept appearing before me when the music resonated in my head, and I followed it every time it appeared. It would take me to "green fields among palm trees, olive trees, oranges, lemons, and pomegranates."[2] It would spin in the field like a butterfly, taking me to places bathed in the sun's warmth, and high in the sky it would fly like a seagull. I followed her and listened to the music that accompanied whenever she appeared. Everyone thought I was crazy because I was walking without direction, like a lost person. Even my family thought I was crazy, my parents, and they thought it was because of their continuous pressure and insistence on studying. But no one understood what I was experiencing.

Teacher   Sometimes the people closest can't understand you.

Student   Yes, but what's strange is that at the time when everyone was worried about me, I felt a surge of life flowing in my veins, like my blood was moving for the first time, as if doors to a hidden strange world suddenly opened before my eyes.

Teacher (*looks in his eyes*)   The point is just to change the angle of your vision.

Student Yes, when we do that, we can reach the highest levels of understanding, or consciousness. I don't know, perhaps truth and perfection. A bit of all that. I felt like I saw people more clearly, deeply within the individuals around me. I saw their souls, heard their breaths and sighs. At first, my new discoveries intrigued me, but the matter ceased to be as amazing as when it started. It became disturbing and strange to see the beauty and ugliness together beneath the skin. It became extremely difficult. I couldn't keep up with my insight and vision, and the music that was echoing inside me started to overflow like a sea of fire. So, I decided to be alone. I left the university, left my family, but the shadow of that woman never left me. So, my life became a quest where I searched as feverish music followed me. Until one day, I saw an advertisement for your music institute.

Teacher Don't say it's me.

Student And how did you know?

Teacher That's how it looks. Is that right?

Student It's right, and the sounds calmed down a little when I saw you. The melodies began to take shape bit by bit in my head, becoming clear music, pieces I had never heard before, ringing in my skull.

Teacher (*to herself*) The only thing missing now is . . .

Student Say it, this madman.

Teacher No, I was going to say, the only thing missing now is someone who worries me and disrupts my life.

Student Great emotions uplift us if we are able to hold these emotions in our hearts feeling heavenly love and the bliss of tranquility

Teacher Love and tranquility? Do you really believe in their existence?

Student Believe? No, I have faith in them, I live them.

Teacher (*looks at him intently*) Listen, please . . . This institute is an attempt for me to stay alive. You surely won't understand. (*She looks at his face with intensity and desire.*) You are still young, but you must understand. I'm trying to start anew, to have something I do and something I love to do. Please, don't disrupt my life now, especially not now. I created this institute to feel like I can breathe. Secondly, to secure a source of income for myself after leaving the music school.

You probably don't know, and how could you? (*He moves closer to her confidently.*) Anyway, I don't have a stable job right now, and I want to take care of my affairs on my own, quietly. I don't want to be the woman who looks at things with idealism and naivety anymore. That phase of my life is over. I want to start anew, to be strong and resilient. It might not seem logical to start over at this age, but I've realized, albeit late, that there's no point in living with others. They bring me misery. I've also realized that language isn't a means of communication as much as it is a language of conflict. So, here I am, building my own world, shaping its facets to suit me, and setting the boundaries I want. I'm furnishing it with what sustains and strengthens my soul. It's the most beautiful way to live. I just have to keep going.

He stands in front of her and runs his fingers through her hair.

Student   Why did you leave the music school?

She steps back, looking puzzled.

Teacher   Because of Chopin again.

Student   What do you mean "because of Chopin again"?

Teacher   Because a student applied for an audition to join the school. He arrogantly claimed to be a piano master. So, I asked him to play Chopin.

Student   Was his performance any good?

Teacher (*sarcastically*)   If Chopin were alive, he would have poured oil on his head and set himself on fire because of that terrible, deadly performance.

Student smiles.

Teacher   Is there something to smile about?

Student   Sorry, you look beautiful when you're angry. Well, how did it end?

He stands at the piano, takes the leather-bound notebook, flips through its pages, and hands it back to her.

Teacher   I failed him for the audition and didn't allow him to join the school, of course. But the spoiled brat got accepted into the school anyway. I went to the director for an explanation, and he said that the student had connections to someone important in the government, and ours was the only school that would take him.

Student   What did you say to him? (*He moves closer to her.*)

Teacher   I refused to teach him, of course. But I was shocked to find him in my class. I again went to the principal, and he told me there were bigger things at work than me. I tried to make the best of it, to see if this boy could improve or adapt to the school's environment, but nothing worked. He was a ridiculous brat who had no respect for any instrument and lacked any musical sense. I found him hitting the piano keys with the heels of his shoes.

Student   That's criminal. What did you do?

Teacher   I gave him a failing grade in piano.

Student   Well done.

Teacher   Immediately, I received a dismissal letter, offering as a justification incompetence and disrespect towards the students. Can you imagine anything worse? I'm not competent? I don't respect the students? What do you call someone who disrespects music? But later, the colleague of mine who took my place told me that the dismissal letter was meant to protect me. I learned that it was a grubby conspiracy to keep these kinds of students in the music school.

Student   And what did you do? It's a clear threat.

Teacher   They're like multiplying insects. Lately, I've been seeing a lot of these students.

Student   There must be a solution.

Teacher   What can I do? Complain to the ministry, which is already corrupted, or write in the newspapers for public opinion? People don't care about the country, so will they care about music?

Student   So?

Teacher   They fired me. What else can I do?

Student   You should have resisted, stood up to them, fought against the corruption.

Teacher   Corruption . . . I don't want to hear that word. It's like black smoke invading my lungs and suffocating me. How can I resist when they've taken away my beloved place in this world?

Student   It's absurd for these stupid students to dominate in this place of beauty. You should have resisted for your own sake.

Teacher   Yes, I tried. I tried so hard, but they took over and spread, so I stopped. I stopped resisting.

Student (*staring at her intently*)   You really stopped?

Teacher   Yes, I stopped. Do you know why I stopped?

Student   Why?

Teacher   I felt it was better to create a private space for myself, where I could embrace my artistic and spiritual beliefs, away from all these deformations. Here, at the institute, at home, I live with the beauty and serenity that enriches me.

Student   Chopin seems to be the cause of all the changes in your life, but it's the school's loss. You are a treasure.

Teacher   A treasure? Even if I am, how many treasures are neglected?

Student   You won't be like that after today.

Teacher   What do you mean?

Student   Maybe what we're caught in is fate's design. Let me be by your side, and together we can make music like colorful balloons.

He takes both her hands and kisses them, but she pulls them away.

Teacher   You're intruding on my life, imposing yourself on everything, entering hidden parts. You wander into my room as if it's yours, touch my belongings, and I swear I can almost hear you sniff the walls of my room. What do you want from me?

Student (*pause*) That notebook, the leather-bound one, it's a special notebook.

Teacher And why do you ask?

Student It's a notebook for writing notes, but it's empty.

Teacher It's a gift, an old gift. But a very precious one.

Student Whoever bought it for you probably wanted you to use it so that he's always with you.

Teacher Maybe. I hope to write my own music in it.

Student By "him," you mean your father?

Teacher Yes, my father.

Student But you haven't written in it.

Teacher No, I haven't.

Student Yet you write your notes.

Teacher Of course, I have to write them down. (*She takes out some papers with notes from the bag.*) I'll write them here. This is my own music.

Student (*holding her hand*) Why not write in it?

Teacher You don't have the right to . . .

Student Does being alone make you feel powerful?

Teacher Please . . .

Student Does this surrender satisfy you?

Teacher Why are you doing this to me?

Student Free yourself from the past.

Teacher The past is an unending river.

Student Write your notes and let the river advance.

Teacher Only age and suffering advance.

Student "Your souls are imprisoned in your fingers; release them now." Aren't these your words to every student?

Teacher An eccentric student like you has no right to interfere in my private affairs. Who are you to dictate what I should do? You come in like the wind, filling my mind with your strange and imaginative stories, thinking I'll believe you. You even think you're responsible for changing my life.

Student (*raises her hands before his eyes*) These fingers that play with so much love must compose the most beautiful music.

Teacher Why are you doing this to me, why now? I might not be able to . . .

Chopin's music, Op. 28 No. 4 in E minor, known as the Prelude, starts softly. The music gradually gets louder as they continue their dialogue.

The next dialogue is prerecorded and played through the house:

Teacher's Inner Voice   Why did you come now? You're trespassing on my soul, and I have no strength to resist you. I can't help but think of you, of the desire to have you in my life, of the image of you with me, and more than that, of you holding me. But this is all wrong, wrong. I am still the teacher, and you are the student. Plus, there's a significant age difference, many years.

Student's Inner Voice   Why are you overthinking this? I understand you completely. I'm here simply for you. Don't burden yourself with questions and worries. There's nothing important except us being together. I hear your heartbeat, the pulse of blood in your veins, your thoughts, dreams, and memories. Listen to me or listen to the music of our union.

Teacher   Are you real?

Student   Very real.

Teacher   You've startled my soul.

Student   I understand everything. From the moment I entered the music class, my soul flew to you like a bird. Your fingers, as you played, captured my soul. Sometimes, I stood outside the window and watched you play Chopin, completely lost in it, like a dreamer or a lover. I imagined you all year long dancing with me.

He pulls her to dance with him, and they remain captivated by each other, with the music gradually getting louder.

Teacher   Do you know, then, which piece I love?

Student   Here, you are hearing it now.

Teacher   The fourth prelude.

Student   The introduction.

Teacher   Or above the tomb.

Student   Or suffocation.

Teacher   On the enchanting small-scale ladder of Mi.

Student   So, let us be the enchanted ones with no cure except being close to each other.

She wraps her arm around his shoulder, they spin, their gaze fixed on each other's eyes, while the music gradually intensifies.

Teacher   I don't want us to stop.

Student   We won't stop.

Teacher   But the age difference . . .

Student   Is there really a difference?

Teacher   What do we tell people around us?

Student   Tell them it's Chopin's curse.

They continue to spin, and the music rises, filling the entire space. They're inside a spotlight, spinning and dancing for a few minutes. They spin and spin, and during their rotations, she remains inside the spotlight while the student steps slightly outside the edge of the spotlight with each turn. They continue to dance in perfect harmony with the music, she inside the spotlight, and he outside it, until the student disappears into the darkness. She continues to spin on her own, dancing as if she's dancing with someone, and the music continues to crescendo . . . and it keeps rising for a few more minutes. The music stops suddenly, but the teacher continues to dance. Suddenly, she hears knocking on the door. She stops dancing. Blackout and then the music resumes softly.

Notes

1   Author's note: "The piece being referred to is 'Memories of the Past,' composed by the renowned Frederic Chopin. Chopin composed this piece when he was twenty years old, and it is considered one of his tranquil and dreamy compositions. He played it slowly, and it was not published until six years after his death. The piece was a gift to his sister, who kept it privately. After his demise, she decided to publish it, making it part of the valuable musical heritage."
2   Footnote provided by the author: "The words are from Chopin about the island of Palma de Mallorca, Spain, which he visited with his lover novelist George Sand for its sunny atmosphere, suitable for Chopin's tuberculosis. It is also where the "Raindrops" prelude was born."

Introduction to *Princes of Hell*
Abdul Razaq Al-Rubai

When director Farouk Sabri presented the first performance of *Princes of Hell* on Saturday, March 25, 2006, it was considered the first theatrical production in Arabic in Auckland, New Zealand. After its performance in Copenhagen, the director indicates that the significance of the play lies not only in being the first play in Arabic but also in addressing the most dangerous ideological disease facing Islam, one that no theatrical production in the Third World or European countries had dared to tackle. Hence, the play raises a thunderous cry against terrorist operations targeting the innocent, life, art, and beauty. In those years, suicide bombings were consuming Iraq, and this deeply saddened me. I even wrote a short poem titled "Hell" in response:

Recite the Shahada
Wrap around the waist of the earth
The black belt of death
And ascend.
The path is adorned with the feathers of God's angels.
He said to himself,
While wrapping around his lifeless body
The kingdom of the One,
Then made a concise statement:
"Our appointment is in Paradise,
When my parts shatter
To bid farewell to the night of the barren earth."
After seconds
His parts exploded.
In the street,
A passing man,
His parts also flew to paradise.
When both arrived there,
The killer and the killed,
Fought at the gates of paradise:
Who should enter before the other?
Who has done better in deed?
Who holds eternity in his hands?
The killer and the killed fought,
The killer and the killed fought,
And the Lord observed this cosmic chaos in astonishment!

I was deeply concerned about the terrorist attacks that my country, Iraq, was facing, and the operations that claimed the lives of civilians, the poor, laborers, and construction workers with the aim of disrupting the flow of life. At the peak of the terrorist attacks, I received an email from my friend, director Farouk Sabri, who wrote with a heart squeezed by the pain of what was happening in Iraq. He urged me to write a play that reflects our stance as theatre artists. It was necessary for me as a poet as well, to have a word about what was happening, as the poet Pablo Neruda says, "The poet must be a historian of his time, not necessarily that history be a selection, representation, but it must be a rough, spoiled, and muddy terrain, containing the miserable traces of the days that pass, carrying hardships and the sorrows of humanity."

Sabri proposed the idea of writing a play about a group of terrorists planning to blow up a major Iraqi symbol, the Freedom Monument by sculptor Jawad Saleem, located in the heart of Baghdad's Freedom Square (al-Tahrir Square). The operation would be carried out by five terrorists from neighboring countries. I liked the idea, and when I started writing, he requested that the play be a monodrama to perform himself since he resides in Auckland, New Zealand, where there was no Arab/Muslim actor that fits the character's description. Therefore, the play had to adapt to that atmosphere. Although the number of terrorists carrying out the operation was five, this technical problem was resolved by using masks. We agreed on that, and I began writing, sharing with him every scene once finished. As the director and actor simultaneously, he would jot down his notes, and we would discuss and work on utilizing them. Sabri suggested reaching out to a famous musician Naseer Shamma to write music for the play. When I approached Shamma, he welcomed the collaboration but hesitated about the theme of the play, fearing that this might bring the terrorists' attention to the Freedom Monument, and consequently, they might blow it up. However, we continued the work to the end without Shamma's involvement. I finished writing the play, and director Sabri began working on it with individual efforts, being the director, actor, and producer. His family supported him in his work. After completing it, the play was presented in Auckland, Erbil, the Netherlands, and Copenhagen and received invitations to be performed in Brussels and Berlin. However, he declined due to other commitments in Auckland. After the security situation improved and terrorist attacks diminished, life returned to its natural course, and the play fell into a deep slumber. Nevertheless, it came back to life through the hands of the translator Professor Amir Al-Azraki. Creative and artistic experiences that speak to the painful circumstances that humanity has gone through should not be sidelined or forgotten. They carry lessons for future generations. Historical events tend to repeat themselves.

Today, as I revisit the play, I recall those challenging moments that Iraq and the region endured, appreciating the blessing of security and peace.

Princes of Hell
a Monodrama

Abdul Razaq Al-Rubai

Characters

Ayad
Abu Dulama
Bahjat
Qutada
Wife
Hassan
Mansour
Bakri
Policeman
Construction workers
mourners

The curtain opens on an arid and desolate place. The stage is filled with debris from destroyed houses and the sporadic sound of moans. The morning call to prayer sounds from far away. **Ayad** *enters. He is a bearded young man in his mid-thirties wearing a short dishdasha. He walks on the stage cautiously, feeling his stomach and fastening an explosive belt. He carries a small piece of paper in his hand containing information about the location. After making sure that this is the place for the operation, he catches his breath, letting out a sigh of relief. Moments later, the sound of an explosion goes off, followed by sounds of gunfire, ambulance sirens, and a commotion, disturbing the serenity of the dawn. Sounds of crows.*[1]

Voices God is great, the terrorists blew up a mosque full of worshipers . . . bastards . . . bastards!

Ayad God is great . . . God is great . . . So, he struck the target, and he quickly ascended to Heaven to break his fasting with the Messenger of God (peace be upon him). He went after trouncing the infidels . . . He must have reaped dozens of heads. The rotten ones of them . . . won the honor of martyrdom. He's become ethereal now, like the breath of the righteous angels . . . and I will join him . . . I will join him without delay . . . The table is waiting for me with all its delight and delicious food. I will join him and Bahjat, the Turkish truckdriver, but not now . . . the roles are carefully assigned, and the plan is being executed precisely. I will be the last to join the table. I have time until the largest number of construction workers gather in this square, which I will paint with blood. I will blend their limbs together, so nobody can recognize their body parts. I will turn the world upside down. I will become ethereal, and my procession will be surrounded by angels . . . hahahaha. Qutada, may God have mercy on you. Away from the land of Egypt, after you left it twenty years ago to work and marry in Iraq. It was a good life for you. Your pain of homesickness and for your wife has ended . . . wait for me . . . take a short nap . . . Soon you will find me with you and with the rest of the group: Hani, Hassan Zada, Mansour and Bakri. After we make this morning hell for the infidels and the Crusaders, as our Sheikh, the Amir, Abu Dulama said in the meeting last night.

He puts on a mask with the face of **Abu Dulama** *. . . and the scene looks like a hypnotic ritual.*[2]

Abu Dulama We asked you to meet for an important matter. We lost one member . . . a martyr Bahjat. First of all, let's read Al-Fatiha[3] for his soul, may God rest his soul. He is the first and we are the next.

Ayad *takes off the mask.*

Ayad Bahjat was transporting goods from Turkey to Iraq, he was just an innocent truck driver who didn't know the goods he was carrying were expired.

Ayad *wears* **Bahjat's** *mask.*

Bahjat What do you want from me, my lord? I did everything that you ordered me to do. I do not deny the favors that your people have done for me. I cannot deny this. You helped me distribute my goods and protected me from the mujahideen on the highway, you bestowed money on me . . . I didn't forget your favors at all, especially after I was deceived by the Agha group[4] with those expired goods, that was what you revealed to me and you covered up for me, so I was able to sell the goods. My profits doubled . . . No, of course, I do not want to be imprisoned or die . . . If the matter is only to drive a truck of vegetables to the market, then I am ready . . . I am ready and willing to sell them too . . . we agreed then . . . God is with you.

Ayad   And the poor man walked to his inevitable fate . . . He did not know that Abu Dulama sent him to his martyrdom when he inserted explosives among the vegetables. And with one push of the control button, everything ended.

Sounds of explosion.

Abu Dulama   You know that we have come to this good country because it is in distress and it is our neighbor, the neighbor's obligation to his neighbor. The sacred duty calls us, and paradise awaits us, so we must do something for its land that has been defiled, as the occupier has disgraced it, and its people have forsaken religion and wallowed in sins. Everyone who stays silent about this is an infidel, and every infidel goes to Hell, and killing an infidel is Jihad. So, let's kill them. Have no compassion and no mercy. Blow them up and burn them to the ground. Do not have mercy on a child, or an old man, or a tree, or an oil pipeline!! Turn their light into darkness, terror and fear. Cut their throats like sheep without mercy, just like your prince does. (*He says it proudly, pointing to himself and performing it in an energetic movement.*) Spill their blood, destroy their land and slaughter them. Rape their women, as you saw your prince doing it. (*Demonstrating.*) Cut off their swollen breasts with stale milk, the milk of vice, so their children won't even get the milk.

Let the devastation prevail in this ruined land. Let the plague insert its teeth in their souls which are burdened with impurity, sins and every wrong thing that angers God. Let tuberculosis eat the bones and chests of those infidel men. Make death their wish for they are the heirs of Satan. (*Silence.*) Oh youth of Paradise, you came to this place to atone for your big mistakes. May God forgive you and let you enter Heaven without judgment. We are all sinners.

Your father Adam who started it
And separated you from Heaven.

I came to make Heaven want you. Yes, Heaven with its Companions and rivers of wine, so you will enjoy the pleasure of drinking, sex and eating fruits. You have come to us burdened with sins and transgressions.

Takes off the mask and speaks like a drunken person.

Ayad   Leave the mosques for the worshipers to inhabit,
And let's go to the tavern to quench our thirst.
Your Lord did not say, "Woe to those who are intoxicated,"
Rather, He said, "Woe to those who neglect prayers."[5]

I spent all my life on lost wars . . . I lost my youth . . . and I lost my older brother, Imad, who was killed in the war with Iran . . . but I escaped death in that war, which I joined as a boy when I proved my ability to repel an attack in Dezful,[6] so they gave me a medal . . . then they put me in with the firing squads who executed soldiers who deserted the war. (*As if addressing a group of soldiers on a battlefield with sounds of explosions.*) Stop! . . . Do not move . . . cowards . . . you do not deserve to live . . . victory is our destiny . . . there is no room for defeat . . . this is what the commander always repeats . . . then you must die . . . you are between two deaths . . . death by the enemy's bullets or death by our bullets, and you chose the latter because you are cowards . . . If you were brave, you would have chosen to die by the enemy's bullets. You should have fought to occupy the land as our commander wanted us to . . . not to be defeated like mice . . . and now you must be shot in the back so you can remember this shame on the Day of Judgment.

He shoots, pointing the gun toward the audience.

So, I received another medal, and then medals poured down on me . . . hahaha, money . . . and cars . . . and rank and plots of land . . . until America came with its damned army, so I ran away from my bosses and found myself lying on the sidewalk without a job and being pursued by the eyes of my victims and their families. I couldn't sleep . . . because I was condemned to death sooner or later, so I had to die by my own will . . . I put an end to my loss . . . and I found you . . . a shield that protects me from my enemies . . . but this shield brought me closer to death again. I do not know how. (*He looks hypnotized in his sleep, and* **Abu Dulama** *takes the form of a hypnotist.*) . . . death and nothing but death . . . to join my brother Imad . . . he is better than me . . . at least he left Salim . . . his only son . . . As for me, I will leave nothing . . . but losses . . .

He wears **Abu Dulama's** *mask.*

Abu Dulama   You will go to Heaven, oh, Ayad . . . (*Pause.*) Your brother Ayad has repented to God and knew that the path to Him will only be through jihad. And God accepts repentance, but repentance needs proof and the proof is clear. Kill an infidel and you will win Paradise without being judged !!! Right?

Ayad   Yes, my lord.

Abu Dulama   . . . and you too. (*Addressing* **Qutada**.) And you, Qutada, were not you from a destitute family? But your wife was the very beautiful neighbor who hated poverty and wanted to live in prosperity. She controlled you with her beauty and made you her servant.

Wife   Oh lazy man, it seems that I have sinned. That's why God punished me to be your wife.

Qutada   Perhaps you did well in my life, so God honored me with you.

Wife   You're nothing.

Qutada   And you are everything.

Wife   Yes, I am everything, that's why I am tormented.

Qutada   What do you want from me? Just order me and I will do anything.

Wife Go find a job.

Qutada I looked for a job everywhere.

Wife I have a relative who works in the intelligence service.

Qutada Intelligence?!

Wife Yes, it is an honorable and clean job. It pays tons of money.

Qutada But . . .

Wife But what? Are you still hesitant? Everyone is looking for such an opportunity, and I am handing it to you on a gold plate. Oh, my miserable luck!!! (*Pretending to cry.*)

Abu Dulama She kept pressing you until you agreed to please her, and there they removed your conscience, so you proved your competence and your wealth increased and your status improved and you won the approval of your wife, hahaha, and the trust of officials. So they assigned you to monitor our groups by going to the mosques, until you got to know one of our righteous followers, where you found guidance, and we revealed that your wife was cheating on you with her cousin, the senior officer who helped you get the intelligence job.

Qutada Oh, immoral woman . . . now I know you . . . you were but a lie walking on two legs . . . so I've sentenced you to death with shame.

Screams of a woman.

Abu Dulama We did you a favor . . . We guided you, and when you became a killer, we protected you from going to jail.

Qutada After discovering my wife's betrayal, my life became hell . . . unbearable . . . Then after the fall of the regime, I was chased by everyone whose sons were buried in the mass graves, especially after the security files were revealed. So it was imperative that I came to you.

Abu Dulama May God bless you, (*Heading to* **Hassan Zada**.) and you, Hassan Zada, weren't you experiencing a psychological crisis from your drug addiction and didn't you desperately need the substance and transport it during your frequent visits to Karbala? Until we caught you red-handed.

Hasan Zada (*kneels down*) Have mercy on me, don't kill me, I am willing to be your servant, take everything but keep me alive even for a day. Please, I beg you, take all my possessions, please, do not hand me over to the police.

Abu Dulama We had mercy on you, and you became a brother to us, so we saved you from your predicament when you were on the edge of a pit of the Fire.

And you, Mansour, weren't you desperate after failing your classes and the interruption of government aid that was coming from Kuwait, after you were expelled from the university, lost and homeless, until we took you in and provided you with a decent life and until God guided you and asked us to train you to become a martyr in the land of Iraq?

Mansour   Praise be to God for his guidance!

Abu Dulama   And you, Hani, weren't you sent to prison unjustly after being accused of murder, so we were able to smuggle you out of prison through one of our followers on the inside. We smuggled you from your home country, and you came here, so we took you in and fed you so you chose this path. (*Looking at* **Bakri**.) And you, Bakri . . . you asked us to accept you with us after you lost the ability to walk when a mine exploded and amputated your right foot in the Afghanistan war. We told you, "Jihad needs a strong man."

Bakri   There are things that do not need feet . . . there are things that only need will and determination. After my return to Turkey from the Afghanistan war, handicapped . . . I found a life that can only be on a volcano's crater . . . I told myself that I must continue walking . . . because I want to do work that makes me stand on my feet again, even in the other world . . . What is the value of life for a man like me who went out to liberate the world from disbelief and returned disappointed and lost everything even his foot . . .? Death is better for me . . . much better.

Abu Dulama (*heading to others*)   Very well. Death is wonderful. It is better than a life in a wheelchair . . . You all sit in wheelchairs . . . Do you know why? Because your feet are on the ground . . . full of dust . . . Why don't you go to glorified heaven with light? You came to our group by your choice . . . your belief demands this. You chose this path to get rid of your shabby life for what is better . . . for *hoor al-een* who are waiting for you.[7]

Ayad *lifts the mask.*

Ayad   We have planted explosive devices . . . kidnapped . . . and slaughtered. What is required of us today, my lord?

Abu Dulama   I know that you have done all these good deeds . . . and this is why I invited you to meet. I have chosen you carefully due to your courage . . . and the strength of your faith . . . What I want today is completely different . . . We no longer need to plant explosive devices, we have received a new group of young Mujahideen who will do those simple things. As for you, I chose for you what is better and greater . . .

Everyone seems confused.

Everyone   Martyrdom.[8]

Abu Dulama   Yes, we will assign you a great mission . . . martyrdom.

Everyone   Martyrdom.

Abu Dulama (*angry*)   What's the matter? It seems that you do not believe this good news!! You're right, it is such great news! We all wish to attain martyrdom . . . which is our goal . . . Oh, heroes, give your bodies as a sacrifice to Heaven, and we have brought you explosive belts whose flames will spare no one. (*He gives them explosive belts.*) Tighten them to your pure bodies. (*They are in a panic.*) What's the matter with you? . . . It is the lifeline from the Hell that surrounds you . . . tie it tightly . . . And there in Heaven when you fly like birds . . . (*Crows sounds.*) you will find what is delightful and pleasant. Tighten your belts . . . whose flames will spare none of the infidels and bawdy enemies . . . To rise up to the heights of Heaven and be next to the righteous saints . . . tie it up . . . do not hesitate . . . (*Silence.*) It seems that you are exhausted . . . Take a sip of this holy liquid . . .

He passes them a drug. After a little while they feel relaxed and obey his orders as if they are hypnotized. He continues encouraging them to tie the belts, and his voice gradually diminishes until they wear the belts with full obedience.

Abu Dulama   And now it is time to assign the tasks . . . (*Silence.*) Qutada . . . We have assigned you the task of blowing up a mosque of infidels.

Sound of explosion.

Everyone (*in unison*)   Congratulations on your martyrdom! God is Great!

Abu Dulama   And you, Mansour, you will blow up an elementary school for girls . . . As for you, Hani, you will blow up the Maryam Church in Karrada with your belt. We want to unleash the storms of chaos, destroy love, smother the Sunday candles under the pieces of church bells that will fall silent.

The sound of people in prayer in a church.

We will wage a war against the Crusade. Hahaha.

The sound of church bells ringing and then gradually fading.

As for you, Hassan Zada, you will blow up a bus station full of vehicles heading south.[9]

The sound of an explosion.

Everyone (*in one voice*)   Congratulations to both for martyrdom! (*Exchange hugs and congratulations.*) God is great!

Bakri (*dragging himself in his wheelchair*)   What about me?

Abu Dulama   You and I will carry out a complex operation . . . in a very vital square . . . and close to the Iraqis' heart . . . It is Tahrir Square . . . specifically under the monument of idols . . . the imitation of God's creation . . . the Freedom Monument.

Bakri   Yes, yes, a great mission. It is a great honor to be with you in the operation. But how?

Abu Dulama   Let me explain the details of the operation. You know how Iraqis need gas these days after our groups blew up the gas pipelines in Dora . . . I will pretend to be a street vendor and offer cans of gas at discounted prices in the market.

The lights are dimmed. **Abu Dalama** *changes his appearance and is shouting.*

Gas . . . gas . . . a thousand dinars for the cylinder, only a thousand dinars . . . . . . Come on . . . Come . . . (*As if he addresses people in a crowd.*) come around, gather around . . . gas . . . gas . . . gas . . .

Policeman   What is this chaos? Oh, old man . . . what are you doing in this place?

Abu Dulama   Don't you see that I'm selling gas . . .? Have mercy on those poor people who can't buy it in the black market.

Everyone   Your ID please? (*He checks it.*) We have to search you. There are lots of infiltrator . . . I have to search everything in the vehicle.

He inspects it carefully. He doesn't find anything. He opens the back door of the cart, he searches in several cylinders, and then he leaves. **Abu Dulama** *closes the door.* **Bakri** *enters the stage in a wheelchair.*

Abu Dulama   Good people, make way for this wheelchair-bound man . . . He has a family like you . . . Make room . . . Let this crippled man be the first to buy gas. It is a blessing. I am hopeful for him . . . Make room for him and God will make room for you in paradise. (*He tries to open the back door of the cart in order to drop the gas cylinder. He pretends that he has lost the key.*) Where is the key? The key, folks. The key . . . the key . . . It seems that I lost it after the policeman searched the car . . . allow me a few minutes . . . I will get a copy of it . . . don't move . . . and you good man, (*Addressing* **Bakri**.) the first cylinder of gas will be yours . . .

He exits.

Crowd   He is late . . . Wait for him . . . He is a good man . . . God is with the patient . . . Wait . . . It is an opportunity that won't come again, getting a gas cylinder for only a thousand dinars. It is the blessings of the Freedom Monument . . . the monument of beauty . . . the blessings of Jawad Salim . . . the whole monument is full of blessings.[10]

Bakri   Look at the monument, look at it, its glory . . . the hand of time has not touched it . . . look at it . . . look . . .

He detonates the explosive belt. The sound of a loud explosion, a horse's neighing, bereaved women's cries, the Iraqi national anthem: my country . . . my country . . .

Abu Dulama *returns.*

Abu Dulama   And that's how we will direct a devastating blow to the infidels . . . the idol worshipers . . . and to the idol in the middle of Baghdad city center . . . Tahrir Square . . . and be sure that gas cylinders will contribute to the killing of hundreds and to the demolishing of the infidels' monument.

Everyone   A great mission, worthwhile for the great Mujahideen.

Abu Dulama   Thank you, thank you . . . May Allah reward you with goodness . . . As for you, Ayad, you will blow up a gathering of construction workers.

Everyone (*in one voice*)   Congratulations! Congratulations to you for martyrdom! God is greatest!

Abu Dulama   And now I have prepared for you small bottles of this holy water . . . It helps you to perform your mission . . . because it is sacred and I blew into it and read many prayers over it for a whole night.

Everyone   May Allah reward you!

Abu Dulama   Now . . . let us celebrate this occasion.

*Everyone is practicing a strange ritual. They circle around incense and smoke. Each one takes a sip from **Abu Dulama**'s small bottle that contains a drug. Unconsciously, they shout, scream, and say words that are incomprehensible amid the beating of tambourines and drums. They continue.*

Ayad *wakes up from his slumber and finds construction workers arriving in the square. He sees his nephew, Salim, and is shocked.*

Ayad   Who is this? It's Salim, my nephew!!! Who threw him into the path of death? Who put him in my way? Who brought this boy now? Where would I hide my face from my brother Imad? (*He talks to himself as if he is speaking to Salim.*) Go home to your mother, who you'll find praying for your safe return. I can see her blaming me. Go back quickly for God's sake. Don't burden me with the memory of your body soon to be scattered in pieces. Go home. Your mother's prayers are echoing in my ears. You are too young to die . . . Go home and sleep in your mother's arms. You are too young and have not lived a full life. It is ill fated for you to die.

*He remembers the voice of **Abu Dulama**.*

Abu Dulama   Attack them . . . Have no mercy on them. Blow them up! Don't spare anyone. Do not have mercy on a child, an old man, a tree, or an oil pipeline!! Turn their days into fearful and horrifying nights, slaughter them like sheep without mercy!

Voices   It is a new explosion . . . damn you terrorists!

Ambulance sounds, followed by another explosion.

Ayad   To heaven for eternity, oh, Qutada and, oh, Hani!

Voices   They blew up a church!

The killers blew up the bus stop.

Blew out the smiles . . . and the joy on the lips . . . They blew up the past and the present.

Tomorrow is ours.

Ayad (*making a sarcastic voice*)   If there is a tomorrow.

Voices   Where is the government? Where are the Americans? Where is Heaven? Don't they see what is happening?

Passerby   Heaven? Heh. Heaven is on vacation.

Ayad   What are you saying? You are such an unbeliever!

Construction Worker   Doesn't what's happening today make you doubt your faith? Where is mercy? Where is the conscience? Conscience is on vacation.

Ayad   That is enough. (*He looks at Salim and talks to himself.*) Salim is still in his place. Fortunately, he does not recognize me. This veil is useful.

Construction Worker Does no one have a conscience? Let me tell you this painful story . . . Let it be our breakfast for this bloody morning. A month ago, terrorists kidnapped . . .

Ayad (*to himself*) There is no power or strength save in Allah. Salim go away, let me do my job.

Construction Worker . . . my cousins . . . they were two young men. They completed their university studies in the translation department at Al-Mustansiriya University. They were working in the Ministry of Information, but after the fall of Saddam, they found themselves without work, so they worked as journalists for a foreign news agency. Both of whom were married, one with a first child and the second waiting to have one. A month ago they were kidnapped while they were working, and the kidnappers demanded a large ransom, $50,000 after negotiations. The family didn't have it. Their tribe met and decided to free them at any cost, so they started collecting donations, and indeed they succeeded in collecting the whole amount . . . they handed it over to the kidnappers . . . and they waited but in vain . . . and one day a policeman was martyred when an explosive device that was planted in the road went off next to his car. We carried his limbs, part by part . . . We put them in a wooden coffin, and, without washing, we carried him to the new cemetery we've made because we can't bury our dead in the Al-Salam Cemetery in Najaf because all of the terrorists block the road . . . death happens because of your identity on that road . . .[11] Before we got to the cemetery, we saw a group of dogs gathered around some prey . . .

Mourners carrying the coffin.

Mourners There is no god but God . . . there is no god but God.

A Mourner Our dogs have become wild . . . they shout wild cries . . . There is no god but God . . . no god but God . . . What is this? Look! One of them is carrying a human hand . . . There is no god but God . . . no god but God . . . and the other carries a thigh . . . They eat people . . . There is no god but God . . . There is no god but God . . . Shoot the dogs. There is no god but God . . . No god but God . . . (*sounds of bullets*) There is no god but God . . . There is no god but God.

Construction Worker And when the dogs dispersed after hearing the sounds of bullets . . . we saw the ugliest sight . . . There is no god but God . . . No god but God . . . The dogs had been devouring my cousins' bodies after the kidnappers dumped them in the cemetery. There is no god but God . . . There is no god but God . . . No god but God . . . There is no god but God . . . There is no god but God. We belong to Allah and to Him we shall return.

An explosion is heard.

Workers What is that? It's a fourth explosion . . .

Sounds of ambulances.

Ayad God is great. God is great.

Workers   God is greater than murderers.

Ayad   Heaven will receive the fourth body. Salim, move away from this place.

Worker   Heaven is on vacation.

Ayad   I seek refuge in God . . . Are you still in this place? I have warned you, so don't blame me when we meet in Heaven.

Voices   The terrorists have bombed an elementary school for girls . . . What do they want from us? What did those innocent children do to deserve this? Criminals, killers!

Ayad   To the mercy of God, Mansour, to the vast Heaven. Where the beautiful Companions and all that is good and delightful await. As for me, my turn will come . . . I will join you after there are enough construction workers to satisfy Abu Dulama. Soon I will turn them into stairs to Heaven where the Paradise of eternity is, to escape from the hell of the body . . . and its suppressed desires and rottenness . . . rottenness . . . (*Dogs barking.*) human rottenness, which I will kick with my feet as I kicked pleasures.

Leave the mosques for the worshipers to inhabit,
And let's go to the tavern to quench our thirst.
Your Lord did not say, "Woe to those who are intoxicated,"
Rather, He said, "Woe to those who neglect prayers."

Soon, the righteous angels will accompany me. After this body scatters, hahah.

He spins around and runs into a construction worker who feels his explosive belt beneath his clothes.

Worker   Why is your body so stiff?

Ayad   Pardon . . . nothing . . . I am wearing a bandage from an operation.

Worker   Operation? Oh, poor man!!

Ayad *is terrified when he hears the word "operation."*

Ayad   I had surgery, my brother!

Worker   You had surgery and came here to find work?

Ayad   I had to. What are we going to eat if we starve? Democracy?!

Worker   You reminded me to eat. Would you like to have breakfast with me? I have fresh bread. My wife baked it. It's fresh . . . See . . . bread with red cardamom tea . . . a good meal that you will not find in the Sheraton Hotel. (*Laughing.*) The truth is I come every day from Hilla looking for work here . . . I often have my breakfast here. Then when the time for the noon prayer comes, I return home and subsistence is provided by God . . . Do you think that we will work today?

Ayad   Subsistence is provided by God . . .

The sound of a distant explosion followed by the sound of an ambulance. Crows' cawing, the sound of a horse's neighing, a mother crying, and a child screaming.

Workers Criminals . . . murderers!

Worker We knew that they wouldn't let the country live in peace.

Another They want us to leave the country.

Another How could we leave our beautiful skies for their exploding crows to frolic in?

Another They want us to stay home so they are free to do whatever they want.

Another But we won't return to our homes . . . We will not leave the sky to these exploding crows.

Another Hey, guys, have you noticed that today's massive bombings have kept the contractors from getting to us?

Another Of course, the streets are full of barriers and checkpoints. We've got no hope of a job today . . . Why don't we go home?

Ayad (*confused*) No . . . they will certainly come. (*To himself.*) I must carry out my mission now . . . My people are now waiting to hear the explosion . . . I must do it now before the crowd disperses . . . But what should I do about Salim? (*As if he is addressing Salim.*) Salim, move away . . . go away . . . The explosive devices are merciless. They have no heart.

Workers It looks like a new explosion . . . traitors . . . terrorists . . . killers . . . Where is the government?

Worker My head aches from all the explosions today.

Another Do you need an aspirin?

Worker No, I need a safety pill.

Another This pill is not found in Iraqi pharmacies.

Another If found, it is sold only with a prescription.

Worker I have a terrorist recipe. (*Laughs.*) The worst misfortunes are the ones that make you laugh.

Ayad (*to himself*) I think the time has come now . . . I have to push myself into the midst of the workers in order to reap the largest number of them. But what about Salim, who is standing in the middle? Go away, Salim . . . the time is running out . . . move away so your mother's blaming eyes will leave my sight . . . I don't want your body to be torn apart like mine . . . or for the fragments to injure you . . . If only you moved a little to the side . . . Move, Salim. Move . . . forewarned is forearmed. I want to do my job . . . My job will not be completed until I am in your place, Salim. It is a strategic place to die, indeed . . . You know well where to stand. Your mother's prayers were answered as my lord did not send anyone but me . . . otherwise your body would have been scattered by now . . . So, I beg you to move away a little from here . . . The operation should have been done 15 minutes ago . . . Because of you, I am still here, not in Heaven . . . Move away . . . I do not want to hurt you . . . I do not want . . . I do not want . . . Move away . . . Salim, you've distracted me from drinking the holy water. (*He drinks a sip.*) Praise be to Allah . . . Salim, why are you still here? Salim . . . Salim

A speeding car drives towards the crowd. Sounds of a large explosion shaking the stage . . . blackout . . . Crows' caws rise, then gradually fade away.

Notes

1 In Arab culture, crows often symbolize death and bad omens.
2 Throughout the play the single actor switches characters by putting on masks representing all characters except Ayad who is performed without a mask.
3 The first verse of the Quran.
4 A group that imports goods to Iraq.
5 From a poem by Abu Nuwas, a classical poet from the Abbasid Caliphate famous for his poetry about wine.
6 A city in Iran and the site of a significant victory for the Iraqi military in 1980 during its war with Iran.
7 Female companions with beautiful, big and lustrous eyes who await martyrs in the afterlife.
8 Martyrdom.
9 The designation "South" pertains to the southern provinces inhabited by a majority of Shia Muslims.
10 Designed by Jawad Salim in 1961, the Freedom Monument (*Naṣb al-Ḥurrīyya*) is located in Tahrir Square in Baghdad. It is an iconic symbol of freedom for Iraqis, depicting significant events in Iraqi history and commemorates the Revolution of July 14, 1959, which was led by Abdul Karim Qasim and marked the end of Hashemite Monarchy and beginning of the Iraqi Republic.
11 *Wadi-us-Salaam* (The Valley of Peace) is the largest cemetery in the world, located in the southern city of Najaf. Because of the cemetery's association with the first Imam of Shia Islam, it is revered by Shia Muslims, and the reference to identity in this passage refers to Shia Muslims being killed by terrorist groups, such as Al-Qaida and ISIS.

Introduction to *Counterfeit*
Ali Abdel-Nabi Al-Zaidi

The themes of the post-war periods have deeply preoccupied me as a playwright born and raised in Iraq, especially during the First and Second Gulf Wars, which significantly impacted the structure of Iraqi society. Hundreds of thousands of soldiers and civilians fell victim to these wars, and the economy was devastated after the country endured a crippling economic blockade in the 1990s. I have written many plays rejecting war, death, and hunger and dramatizing the importance of peace and love.

Following the political change in Iraq in 2003, new topics emerged that were entirely different from what came before. Iraqi writers became engrossed in writing about the issue of terrorism, which catastrophically ravaged the people of Iraq, transforming the external war front of the 1980s into an internal front in cities and the streets. The nightmare of terrorism haunted everyone without exception. While we had produced numerous plays addressing terrorism, I perceived most of them as straightforward, lacking a fresh and shocking perspective. We needed to write in a different and unprecedented direction.

Therefore, *Counterfeit* was conceived to address the horror of terrorism and its profound impact on the structure of society and the family, but through comedy. This means ridiculing or mocking extremists and highlighting the alienation of a person's body and soul from the family and society within which they live. I argue that this type of comedy speaks more clearly to the audience, as it addresses pain, injustice, terrorism, and torment but does so through laughter at what has transpired.

Counterfeit[1]

Ali Abdel-Nabi Al-Zaidi

Characters

Wife
Husband
Father
Neighbor
Surgeon

A living room. Sofas are distributed in an orderly manner in the space. Doors on the right and left lead to different rooms. Candles on a dining table. **Wife** *enters pushing* **Husband** *in a wheelchair.*

Wife   Finally . . .

Husband   Finally . . .

Wife   O my husband, finally.

Husband   O my wife, finally.

Wife   You are back home safe.

Husband (*surprised*)   Safe?!

Wife   You are back with me so we can live out our dreams.

Husband   I hope so.

Wife (*lighting candles*)   I know you came back for your dear wife, your love, your . . . (*Tries to remember.*)

Husband   Your what!?

Wife   What's the matter? O my soul, you are back with me.

Husband   Incapacitated!

Wife   Don't worry. I will never let you out of our bedroom again.

Husband (*confused*)   Bedroom?!!

Wife   I mean our house.

Husband (*madly*)   I was at the café when . . .

Wife   I know you were at the café when . . .

Husband   I don't remember anything except that a man entered the cafe and shouted "God is great!" and exploded in our faces.

Wife (*laughing*)   And you, what did you shout?

Husband   The man did not give me a single moment to even say "Ouch!"

Wife (*longer laugh*)   What did the people in the café shout?

Husband   The explosion did not give them a single moment to even say "Ouch!"

Wife (*longer and louder laugh*)   And what did the café owner shout?

Husband   The explosion did not give him a moment to deliver the tea to his customers or shout "Ouch!"

Wife (*shouting*)   What did their mothers shout?!

Husband   The man did not give time to shout "*Yiboooeeee!*"[2]

Wife *Yiboooeeee*! O life! *Yiboooeeee*! O mothers who can do nothing but scream *yiboooeeee* for their dead children! (*Changing the subject.*) What's important is you are back with me.

Husband (*laughing*) They were torn into pieces, all of them. I'm the only one who survived after they fixed me.

Wife They fixed you. (*Laughs.*) Sorry. Everyone was asking about you. Our good neighbor was always asking about you.

Husband Oh, our good neighbor, and what were you saying to him?

Wife I told him you will be back home safe from the hospital.

Husband (*sarcastically*) Yes, safe just like the scattered limbs in that café.

Wife Don't worry. You're still alive.

Husband I came back a pathetic cripple.

Wife I don't care. You're here, and that's all that matters.

Husband I came back a shadow of a man.

Wife For six months, the house was gloomy without you.

Husband For six months, the hospital was dark without you.

Wife (*shy*) I missed you. I did not wear perfume for six months.

Husband I didn't smell anything but medicine.

Wife For six months, I was dead.

Husband For six months, I was dead. They recreated me in the hospital.

Wife Recreated you?

Husband I was remanufactured.

Wife You were remanufactured?

Husband They re-drew my face. My face was . . .

Wife Please stop.

Husband As for my soul . . .

Wife Stop, you are the same.

Husband I feel pain simultaneously with fear.

Wife Shall I call your surgeon? Your doctor?

Husband He was a skilled surgeon.

Wife Darling, I will be your doctor.

Husband You have a loyal heart.

Wife   And I will always be loyal to you my darling.

Husband   I love you forever

Wife   I love you forever.

Husband   I missed you.

Wife   I missed you too.

Husband (*shy*)   I miss our bedroom.

Wife   Really? Tonight, and in this bedroom, we will celebrate your homecoming. O knight, who came back from—

Husband (*interrupting*)   The hospital.

Wife   Shut up!

Husband   I'll shut up. Take me to the room of our love.

Wife   Let's go, my darling husband.

They enter the room. Off stage, the **Wife** *screams and then lets out a cry. She comes out of the room crying.*

Wife (*shocked*)   Oh God . . . what was that?!

Husband (*coming out of the room walking with difficulty*)   What!?!

Wife   Say something!

Husband   I can't.

Wife   I want to know.

Husband   I . . . I . . . I don't know.

Wife   You don't know what?

Husband (*ashamed*)   I don't know.

Wife   Why . . . ?

Husband   I was in the operationing room.

Wife   I know.

Husband   Anesthetized.

Wife   And when you woke up . . .

Husband   I didn't say anything. I was silent.

Wife   Did you know what they did to you?

Husband   I knew later.

Wife   But it is not the same one . . . It's different.

Husband Yes, it was amputated in the explosion.

Wife Amputated?! They installed a new one?!

Husband It wasn't me. The surgeon did it.

Wife The surgeon. Where did he get it?

Husband Not sure, maybe from the remains of the bodies that were scattered in the café explosion! Maybe it belongs to my friend, maybe they borrowed it . . .

Wife Oh my God!

Husband Try to understand what happened . . .

Wife Understand! How?

Husband (*embarrassed*) Please.

Wife IT IS NOT IT. DO YOU UNDERSTAND WHAT THAT MEANS?!!! How could I live with human remains attached to your body?

Husband Please lower your voice. The neighbors may hear.

Wife Let them hear.

Husband No, please. It is embarrassing.

Wife I know but you should have refused.

Husband How could I? I was sedated.

Wife After you woke up, you should have told them that it was not yours. It was someone else's. You should have filed a fraud case. But you didn't because you liked it.

Husband I swear to God I was ashamed. I didn't know what to say. I said nothing and neither did they.

Wife What should I do now? You've become two husbands.

Husband Please keep silent and keep it a secret.

Wife (*yelling*) How?! Yours is borrowed from someone else!

Husband Please lower your voice. They may hear. Don't make me the butt of their jokes.

Wife (*sarcastically*) To replace an amputated penis, a surgeon has transplanted a new penis to a husband while he was asleep! His original penis was lost among the scattered limbs, eyes, noses, fingers, and teeth. (*To her husband.*) Everything can change except for this!

Husband I am not responsible for what happened. He shouted, "God is great!" So, our limbs, our eyes, our souls, our hearts, and our dreams were blended. We thought he was calling us to pray together or maybe to drink tea together.

Wife Are you aware of this haram![3] It's *sinful*!

Husband   They transplanted haram to my body.

Wife   Whose is it?

Husband (*laughs*)   I don't know.

Wife   How could you not know?

Husband   And how should I know?

Wife   Oh God!

Husband   I told you that I had nothing to do with this.

Wife   I cannot grasp this change in your body.

Husband   What is important is that I am still a man.

Wife   A man . . . but with something that isn't yours.

Husband   That thing does not define manliness.

Wife (*yelling at him*)   This house doesn't need new slogans. In your absence, our home has turned into a cold bed. It's not enough to say that you were a victim or silencing me with nonsense.

Husband   Calm down. I told you the neighbor may hear you.

Wife   I don't care.

Husband   It will be a scandal.

Wife   Your scandal, not mine.

Husband   Please stop it!

Wife   Our homeland has shaped you in its own way. You are a *counterfeit*. Just like how they change the steering wheel in a car from the right side to the left side, then soon it becomes junk.

Husband   LOWER YOUR VOICE!

Wife   Who are you?

Husband   Your husband.

Wife   I mean now.

Husband   Still your husband.

Wife   You can't touch me or put your cold body against my warm body. I feel like I am sleeping with two different husbands with two different souls and hearts.

Husband   They've changed the features of this body, cut it according to their way, repaired it according to their plans, and made a strange mixture of it to fit their schemes . . . They made someone else's thing live in my body. I don't know it, and it doesn't know me. We are totally different.

Wife   Can you answer my questions?

Husband I have no answers but silence.

Wife So, we must consult an expert in this matter, someone must solve this mystery, my honorable husband. I will not live with you under one roof while you're carrying haram in your body.

Husband I am a good man, who has never done haram and you know it.

Wife Isn't it haram for you to try to sleep with me using someone else's . . . Aren't you ashamed?

Husband Enough! Show some respect!

Wife And you should show respect to our halal[4] marriage.

Husband I married you according to Allah's Sunna.[5]

Wife Yes, you did but with your old thing, not with this alien which came into being accidentally.

Husband We are all accidental.

Wife We need a third party.

Husband How would that person keep my secret?

Wife We would require the third party not to disclose it.

Husband I don't trust anyone.

Wife You are defiling this house with evil.

Husband You have been my wife for years.

Wife I was your wife before they replaced your penis; the situation has changed.

Husband Nothing has changed.

Wife Yes, your thing has changed.

Husband I don't want anyone to know about this, please.

Wife We should separate then. I'll ask for a divorce.

Husband Alight. In case I agree to have a third party, who would it be?

Wife You can suggest someone.

Husband I don't know anyone.

Wife We can consult our neighbor who is well-versed in religious matters.

Husband Our neighbor?!

Wife He seems like a good man.

Husband Yes, he looks so, but he may tell his wife, and his wife will tell others.

Wife Don't be pessimistic.

Husband I am not. How shall we ask him?

Wife Leave it to me.

Husband I'm anxious now.

Wife I told you he is a good man.

Husband I hope so.

Wife Trust me.

Husband You're the best wife in the whole universe.

Wife Stop with the BS! I'll be back soon. (*She leaves.*)

Husband (*looks at his penis*) It seems that you will be a major crisis in my life. If I had gone home without you, that would have been less of a scandal for me. (*Shouting.*) Who are you? Whose is it? Please say something! Do you belong to one of the café customers? What's wrong with you?! Can't you see I'm in big trouble because of you? (*Laughing.*) You look happy, for sure . . . Instead of being buried with severed limbs, you are grafted to my body. You are overjoyed because a new fate was written for you instead of being eaten by worms. As for me, as you saw, I will be a laughingstock in the neighborhood because of your thorny existence in my life. They will give me a new name . . . I think they will call me . . . (*Laughing hard.*) The whole country will stop talking about politics and start talking about my strange story. You too will laugh at me. They may tell me that there is corruption in my body and then accuse me of stealing public funds, and I will be charged with forgery of human organs. (*Yelling at his penis.*) Will you be happy with this chaos, O . . .? Be a real man and tell me who you are. Please don't be silent.

Wife *and* **Neighbor** *enter.*

Neighbor What do you mean?!

Husband What do I mean?! Who is this?

Wife This is our good neighbor.

Husband Oh, our neighbor, damn memory!

He extends his hand to **Neighbor***, who does not take it.*

Neighbor I can't believe it!

Husband What?!

Neighbor I always saw you as an exemplary religious man.

Husband Religious! What did you tell him?

Wife He didn't want to come; I had to tell him.

Husband (*to himself*) Let the scandal begin.

Neighbor He who is silent about a counterfeit body is a dumb devil.[6]

Wife (*to* **Neighbor**)   He wants me to be silent and live with the devil.

Husband   I'm the devil now!

Neighbor   You will burn us with your fire.

Husband   My good neighbor.

Neighbor   I can't be silent. Now, you are like an apostate.

Husband   An apostate?!

Wife   An apostate!! Yeeboooyeee!!!

Neighbor   Yes, an apostate. O husband who was virtuous? The religion and sect of this thing in your body is unknown, and you want me to be silent. I won't do that at the expense of my religion. It is one of the signs of the Hour of the Judgment Day, it is the trial of the end times, men change their creation according to fashion.

Husband   Do you mean what happened to me is a sign of the Hour?!

Neighbor   "I seek refuge in the Lord of Daybreak. From the evil of what He created."[7]

Husband   What's the charge?

Neighbor   Your charge is carrying this haram. I seek refuge in God.

Husband   The surgeon, he did that to me.

Wife   I can't live with a husband who carries a sign of the Hour.

Neighbor   This thing should be cut off.

Husband   What?! Cut off?! What did this poor thing do?!

Neighbor   Its existence in your body is what's forbidden. It is not permissible for a Muslim's blood to flow in a non-Muslim's organ or a Muslim from a different sect. Also, it doesn't belong to you; it belongs to another man as you know. This is very dangerous. Oh God, be kind to us and have mercy on us.

Wife   I am leaving the house . . . going to my parents. I can't live with you and your haram.

She tries to leave, but he stops her.

Husband   Please stop. Let's find a solution.

Wife   There is no solution but cutting it off.

Neighbor   Or divorce

Husband   Divorce!

Neighbor   This matter is nonnegotiable.

Wife   Our neighbor knows what's best for us. He is a good, devout man.

Husband   He will destroy my life and expose me to others.

Neighbor   Too late, people already know.

Husband   When?! How?! Who told them?

Neighbor   My wife was an eyewitness when your wife came and told me about your situation, and I know my wife very well. She is a very professional and reliable reporter.

Husband   Oh God! What should I do now?

Wife   Be ashamed of yourself. You shouldn't use that thing even to urinate. It's not yours.

Neighbor   The matter is clear, my neighbor. First of all, your Muslim blood runs through the veins of a non-Muslim's organ. This is forbidden, and because of that you will go to hell. Second, do you think the descendants of the man's penis will accept this, don't you think you need their consent?

Husband   I can't live without it.

Wife   What a predicament!

Neighbor   You have to amputate it and return it to the heirs, and they will dispose of it however they want.

Wife   They are the lawful heirs. What should I do my good neighbor?

Neighbor   Don't let him touch you. It is forbidden.

Wife   Isn't he my lawful husband?

Neighbor   Before the transplant, not now.

Husband   I won't cut it off! I can't live without my manhood.

Neighbor   It's not yours. You stole it. This is the devil's work.

Wife   Oh God what should we do?!

The **Surgeon** *enters.*

Surgeon   I've arrived on time.

Neighbor   Who is this?

Husband   He is the surgeon who performed the operation.

Neighbor   I seek refuge in Allah.

Surgeon   The science of surgery means you recreate things your own way.

Wife (*sarcastically*)   Especially if the surgeon's specialty is counterfeit alteration, amputation, implantation, installation.

Surgeon (*joyfully*)   Yes, it was such a unique, successful, and precise experiment, your good husband's operation.

Husband Doctor, would you please tell us where you got the organ, the penis?

Surgeon That's not important now. What's important is that the operation was a success.

Wife No doubt about that!

Surgeon (*whispering in* **Husband**'s *ear*) Is your penis working?

Husband (*shy*) Yes, it is.

Wife Please tell us where you got the organ.

Surgeon Okay, I'll tell you.

All Really! Thank you!

Surgeon According to the medical report, the implanted penis belonged to the terrorist who blew himself up in the café.

Wife (*screams*) Yuboooooeeee!!!!

Husband Oh God! NOOO!! Impossible!

Surgeon I had to do it.

Neighbor The world will be upended. Did I not tell you that it is a sign of the Hour? It is the great Trial! O Lord have mercy on us!

Husband Is it possible that what I am carrying now in my body belongs to the man who shouted "God is the greatest!" then blew himself up? This is insane!!!

Neighbor What made me enter this house steeped in the forbidden?!

Wife The terrorist!!

Husband I am carrying the terrorist's penis!

Surgeon It was one of the most successful operations that I've ever done.

Neighbor It should be amputated!

Husband It is the symbol of my manhood.

Wife It's the terrorist's manhood, not yours.

Surgeon I don't mind amputating it.

Husband Please try to understand where I am coming from. How could I live without it? (*To* **Neighbor**.) You, get out of my house!

Neighbor My religious duty requires me to warn the *ummah*[8] about you and those like you who live in two bodies . . . pure and profane. (*Leaving.*) O God, let the earth swallow him up, along with his home. O Lord, do not destroy us for the deeds of the fools among us!

Wife O God, I am a miserable wife who has no sin except for being the wife of this man who opposes your law.

Husband   I am a libertine now!?

Wife   Please agree to amputate it!

Husband   I won't. You (*To* **Surgeon**.) get out of my house!

Surgeon *goes to leave.*

Surgeon   I will be willing to do it anytime you want. (*Exits.*)

Wife   I will also get out of your house, because I cannot live with such a strange man.

Husband   This is your home, and you are my beloved wife

Wife   This penis will infect you with death, and you will scream "God is great!" and blow yourself up indoors, in a cafe or on a work site.

Husband   You know that I am a good husband, right?

Wife   I can't trust you anymore.

Someone is knocking at the door.

Husband   Scandals start knocking at my door.

Wife *opens the door.* **Father** *enters carrying his son's* Kafan.[9]

Father   This is its Kafan.

Wife   Whose?

Father   It is its!

Husband   What are you talking about?

Father   You don't know? You must be shy!

Wife   What do you want?

Father (*screams*)   WHERE IS MY SON? I smell my son's scent in this house. MY SON! COME OUT! YOUR MOM IS ASKING ABOUT YOU!

Husband   Who are you?

Father   I am the father who lost his only son.

Husband   Why are you here?

Father (*cries*)   My only son. The city is talking about the man who stole my son's penis, which is the only organ left after he shouted "God is great!"

Husband   Your son!!

Father   I am a father who has nothing but sadness and tears for his lonely son.

Husband   I reassure you that he is in Hell now.

Wife   What do you want from us?

Father   Are you the husband?

Husband Yes.

Father jumps toward Husband and places himself between his legs.

Father My son! (*Sniffing between* **Husband***'s legs.*) That's what remains from my son. It smells like my son.

Husband (*pushing him off*) Get off me, crazy man!

Father Let me embrace my only son. Oh, how much I miss him. He is a disobedient son, but he is dear to my heart and the heart of his mother, and he has the right to have a grave that we can visit and (*To* **Husband**.) I think the right place for what you're carrying in your body is in a grave and not in . . .

Husband But I am . . .

Father Not buts . . . you must return my son's penis so it can get a respectful burial.

Wife I totally agree with you. You must return it to the father.

Father You have no choice. The penis is not yours. It belongs to our family.

Husband But I have nothing to do with what happened. It was not my fault.

Father It wasn't ours either.

Wife It's not mine either.

Husband You are my wife and will continue so till the last moment of my life.

Wife We have only one solution, and that is divorce, strange man. I will leave this house to let you live alone with your uncircumcised thing that belongs to the wicked murderer . . . Bye.

She leaves quickly. We hear the door slam.

Father I have to file a case against you, charging you with theft.

Husband I did not steal from anyone.

Father You can't deny it. It is in your body.

Husband Do whatever you want. I will not give anything from my body.

Father We will see who will surrender in the end.

Father *leaves.*

Husband (*alone, addressing the penis*) You are the one who shouted, "God is the greatest." I feel your hatred towards me. What a joke when your assailant is attached to you, and you are nothing but a victim?! You are the remains of a murderer who blew himself up in our faces and wants to live in my body. (*Laughs loudly.*) My life comes to nothing but an ironic fate, carried on hopelessly by hope! Everything in this life provokes hysterical laughter. My wife left the house and went away, and my neighbor told everyone my story, and the surgeon only cares that the operation was a huge success, the father wants to cut off my penis, his son's penis, and I have nothing left to do but laugh at myself . . . (*Laughing.*)

Notes

1 The title of the play, *Tahweer*, refers to the process in which right-hand steering wheel cars are transformed into left-hand steering wheel. This was very popular in Iraq after the war in 2003, when Iraqis were buying cars from right-hand traffic countries and turning them into left-hand steering ones. Now, the word *tahweer* is notoriously used to describe anything that is not original, fake, or disreputable.
2 A wailing sound Iraqi woman make when hearing bad or sad news especially death.
3 Haram means forbidden or proscribed by Islamic law.
4 Halal refers to practices sanctioned by Islamic law, the opposite of haram.
5 The sunna refer to traditional practices in the Islamic faith based on the life and sayings (hadith) of the Prophet Mohammed and the Quran.
6 Based on Prophet's hadith, "He who remains silent about truth is a dumb devil."
7 The Quran (verse 1-2, The Daybreak).
8 *Ummah* refers to the entire global Islamic religious community.
9 A white shroud that wraps the corpse before burial.